MORE THAN A FRACTION

BASED ON A TRUE STORY

KERRI MOSELEY-HOBBS

CONTENTS

Dedicated to my son, Anthony Michael Hobbs. Thank you for coming on these adventures to find our history and our roots. I hope you are enjoying it as much as I am. Thank you for the idea to put all the notes and documents about this part of our history into a story for all to enjoy. Also, thank you for editing a few chapters. You are brilliant.

CHAPTER 1
FIRST GENERATION

Virginia, 1805

Virginia was a beautiful state of expanding green fields, mountains, and hills that seemed to go on forever. Eleven-year-old John Fraction stood in the middle of a clearing, turning around in circles as he looked up to the sky and took in the scene around him. He stretched out his long arms and placed his callous hands palms up to the sky. The warm sun felt loving as it caressed his face. He closed his eyes and took in the heat, imagining that he was somewhere else. He thought that if Virginia can be so large, he could only imagine the rest of the world; the Carolinas, Kentucky, Tennessee...Africa. Yoruba is what he wanted to see.

Most days in Virginia were hard, but something about the hills made John happy. He hoped to one day climb the hills, and go over the mountains to see what was beyond them. He already worked real hard. He had a quick wit, strong muscles, and fast feet just like his father. He also had the charisma to talk anyone into anything like his mother. He was sure he could make it over all those Virginia hills and to Yoruba.

John's father was also named John[1], but the House called him Jack[2]. Jack had come from Africa, and John always thought that he was *really* African. Many of the people that worked on the plantation, or who visited occasionally called themselves African. Heck, even White men had come and said that they had lived in Africa before, but there really was no mistaking his father Jack for anyone but an African man. That's why some of the White men that came to visit or do business with Mr. Preston would stare at his father like they were afraid of him. Jack was the type of man that they would only see if they went to Africa themselves. He was tall and had lots of muscles. His hair was course, high, and curly, and his skin was decorated with scars that Jack told John were tribal. The scars were straight and curved lines on his cheeks and around his mouth. John liked them because he thought they looked like tiger stripes. Mr. Ballard, Mr. Preston's son, once asked John if Jack turned into a tiger at night. John had lied and told Mr. Ballard that his father Jack *did*, in fact, turn into a tiger at night. He thought Mr. Ballard would be impressed, but instead, now Mr. Ballard was a little afraid of Jack. John's mother, Fanny, who was standing behind Mr. Ballard at the time, had looked at John that day and did that thing she did when she gave him a look, let out a breath of air from her nose like a dragon, and John knew exactly what that meant. It was a warning, and the game was over.

When Jack walked around without a shirt, you could see all the scars on his body. He looked like something from another world. Sometimes John thought Mr. Preston asked his father to come around just to shock everyone, to show his father off like a special prize. His father always took it as an opportunity to watch the White men and learned their customs and their ways. They thought Jack was quiet because he was either afraid of them or did not understand them, but he was quiet because he watched them.

"They say that he was a nobleman[3] where he's from," Mr. Preston once told a colleague. "Though I suspect that nobleman there isn't the same as the nobleman that we speak of- like the royal nobleman of Ireland," he said with still a small hint of his own Irish roots in his speech. "He's smarter than the average nigger, but I doubt he's a Socrates or could read Shakespeare."

The White men that Jack had come across did not understand that where he was from, he spoke many languages, including, though a bit more limited, some English. Many African countries, after all, had been trading with English speakers for centuries. Not only did Jack know Shakespeare, but he had seen White men perform it for themselves when they had created settlements in the area. So Jack watched them and left them squandering in their own ignorance of his intelligence.

John's father did always tell him that he was African. "You may be in this place," he would say. "But your spirit will return there."

There being Africa. Jack's real name was Oyewole, and that is what they called him sometimes when Mr. Preston and others weren't around.

John wasn't quite sure why his spirit would return to a place he had never been to, but he supposed that if his father loved it so much, it must be better than Virginia. He was looking forward to returning to the Yoruba. He guessed going in spirit was fine, as long as he gets to learn his father's tongue. Here in Virginia, his father spoke English because he had to. Either that, or he didn't speak at all because he wasn't allowed to speak any other language. The House would get mad if he did that. But even when speaking English, his father's accent made every word sound like power.

John took one last moment to take in the warm sun rays on his face before looking down and at the scene around him. The thought of Africa and tribes reminded John of his task. Mr. Preston sent him to deliver a letter to the Shawnee tribe. His father told him that Mr. Preston was always trying to build an alliance with the natives[4], but it wouldn't work because Mr.

Preston's father, William, had soiled their family name with the native tribes. "They told me the story of what they called Drapers Meadow," Jack had explained once. "The Shawnee's legend is very different from what Mr. Preston has told. In the Shawnee's story, the Prestons did not honor their word, so a war occurred, and the Prestons lost."[5]

John lifted the letter from between his trousers and his waist, which is where he put it when he decided to soak up some sun. He looked down at the letter held tightly in his hand and then looked back up at the sky to gauge the time. He needed to get to the Shawnee and then back to Smithfield before merriment at the Merry Tree. The merriment at the Merry Tree is something that they all looked forward to. John's favorite part of merriment is when Mr. Preston would come down to the tree at the end of the gathering, completely at his wits in with the loud sounds of the celebration. That's usually when the songs were sung a bit louder for just a few minutes. John would always watch Mr. Preston listening to the songs, waiting for him to realize what that meant, waiting for his reaction because sometimes the songs were making fun of them. When his father sang, he was reminding them of his name. He was not John or Jack, he was Oyewole, meaning "honor has come."

Smiling, John began running towards the Shawnee tribe. He ran as fast as he could until he heard the sound of the native drums. Soon the air was filled with the sounds of the drums and the chants of the Shawnee voices.

"It reminds me of home," his father once said, speaking of the Shawnee drums.

"Is it exactly the same?" John asked.

"No, not exactly," Jack said. "I think, in the Oyo tribe, we did more with the drums. It was not the same sound over and over. It was more of a song and dance."

"A song like when they dance at the House? Like what Mr. Preston and Misses do?" John asked.

"No," Jack said. "The way they dance at the House is strange. I will never get used to that," Jack said, smiling down at his son. "The slaves that play the fiddle and the banjo for them try to do more with the music, but I do not think that they like it too much."

"Are there banjos and fiddles in Africa?" John asked.

"The fiddle is the White man. The banjo is from Africa," Jack answered. "But we did have the fiddle in Africa. I think because the White man brought it with him."

"There are White men in Africa?" John asked.

"Yes," Jack answered. "That *is* how I got here," Jack said, looking down at his son again.

John smiled, thinking about that conversation with his father. He liked to ask his father a lot of questions.

John's thoughts were interrupted when he thought he saw something in the bush. Or was it behind that tree? Suddenly the drumming stopped. Behind him, John could hear a whooping sound that definitely did not come from an animal. John stood very still.

"Watch those Indians," John remembered Mr. Preston warning his father once when he had sent Jack on an errand. When his father returned from the errand, John couldn't wait to ask him if he had seen the Indians.

"Shawnee," Jack had corrected him.

"Shawnee?" John asked.

"Yes," Jack said, sitting down in the chair next to the fireplace. "They are not Indians," he continued, closing his eyes. "If you were home, you would call yourself Oyo or Yoruba[6]. You would not call yourself African because that would not be your tribe. They are a tribe. They are Shawnee."

"But Mr. Preston calls 'em Indian," John said.

"I know. When you are with Mr. Preston, you can call them Indian. White men are lazy about names," Jack said, smiling slightly and opening one eye to look at John.

Another yell from the Shawnee snapped John back to his present situation. He decided that although he was brave, he wouldn't be as brave as his father was until he was as big as he was. He turned around to run, only to slam into a solid figure that knocked him down.

John hit the ground hard, landing on his stomach with a *humph* as the wind was knocked out of him. Not to be knocked down and undone, John quickly rolled onto his back. Looking at his hand, he made sure he was still clutching the letter to the Shawnee from Mr. Preston. He looked up atto the man towering above him. His face was stoic, his arms were strong, his body covered with clothes made from cloth, animal fur, and hide, and his hair hung over his shoulders in two separate braids wrapped in leather strips. John's eyes widen as he saw the man clearly. With his brown skin and wide nose, the man looked like some of the people on Smithfield.

"I once heard talk in the House," John remembered his father telling him. "'dat before the White man came and took us, they took the Shawnee and the other tribes. They made them slaves, but when they grew sick, they needed other slaves. Slaves that would not get sick. They came to Africa and began to take our tribes.[7]"

"Then why don't the slaves and the Shawnee get together to stop slavery?" John asked.

Jack stopped what he was doing. He stroked his chin in thought. "I think," he began. "I think it is because we all think that we are different tribes. But the White man thinks he is one tribe.[8]"

The Shawnee man cocked his head to the side and raised his eyebrows in question. All John had done was stare back at the man because he was lost in thought again.

"I am like you!" John proclaimed, lifting his hand with the letter to the face of the Shawnee man. Two more Shawnee approached, flanking the Shawnee man at his sides. "I am like you!" John proclaimed again. "but I am *still* a slave!" The word slave seemed to get a reaction out of one of the Shawnee that had just approached them. The man clutched the weapon at his hip, but the first Shawnee man, who John had bumped into, placed up his arm to hold the man back.

"Ack," he said in warning. He looked at the other Shawnee men. "Wah-kohn'-tohn-kah(good spirit)." He said, "Wah-kohn'-tohn-kah." The man turned his attention back to John, "Ni-yah'-hohn-goo (Do you understand me)?"

John looked at the man with confusion. He had been told that the Shawnee had their own language and wished he, too, had his own. He almost did because Jack had his own language of the Yoruba. He had taught John a few words, but John did not know enough to have a conversation. Besides, he thought to himself, he doubted the Shawnee would know it.

Trying to find common ground, John said the first word he knew in his father's language. "Oyewole!" he said, screaming out his father's name. It was the closest he would get to his own language. It was Yoruba, and he knew it meant "honor has come." John was honor, and he had come. It was the right word. "Oyewole!" he screamed it again. The Shawnee man's face fell back to its stoic expression as he looked at John. Then he smiled.

"That is not the White man's English," the Shawnee man said.

"No," said John. "It's Yoruba."

"Yoruba?" The Shawnee man asked.

"Yes, it's in Africa where *my* tribe is," John answered.

"Ah," the Shawnee man said in approval. "The language of your ancestors."

"It is my father's name. But he can't use it here," John said.

"Wah-see'-chon (White man)," the Shawnee man spit out in disgust. "These White men steal land from our oh-yah'-ta (nation), dishonor us and our ancestors, and take your name." The Shawnee man shook his head. "Ack," he says again in disgust.

"You sound like my father," John said, feeling a bit at ease at the connection he was developing with the Shawnee men.

"T'i'-nah koo'-ah (come here)," the Shawnee man said, waving his hand, indicating to John to stand up and come forward. "Come, stand up." He offered his hand to John. John accepted the Shawnee man's hand and stood to meet his gaze.

"What is your father's tribe?" The Shawnee man asked.

"Um," John hesitated. "We are not Indians."

"We are also not Indians," the Shawnee man said with a smile. "We are Shawnee, the original people."

John smiled. "My father is of Yoruba. Oyo tribe," John paused. "At least that is what I think he said."

The Shawnee man looked at John with sympathy. "I hope you find your people."

John looked around to look at each of the Shawnee men. He noticed their unit and their tribe. He wondered if coming here reminded his father of his home, of his people. John could not miss what he never had, but he bet that his father Jack thought about it every day. John could only imagine how deeply he missed home when he heard the native drum or how much Jack missed his mother and father. John's eyes went wide as he realized that he did not know much about his grandparents and did not ask many questions about them. He had to fix that when he got home. The Shawnee man whistled to get John's attention, making John realize that his thoughts had drifted again.

"I have this message for you," John said, lifting the letter in his hand up again to the Shawnee. Without moving his head, the man shifted his eyes to look at the letter, as if he were avoiding any real acknowledgement of it.

"Is that from a wah-see'-chon (White man)?" the Shawnee man asked.

"I don't know," John said. "What does wah-see'-chon mean?" John asked, trying his best to pronounce the word.

"It has many meanings," the Shawnee man said, his mood further sobered by the business of the letter. "White people, stranger, foreigner. Someone who does not belong here."

"Am I wah-see'-chon?" John asked. "You don't seem to like them very much."

"No," the Shawnee man said. "You are wah-kohn'-tohn-kah."

"What does wah-kohn'-tohn-kah mean?" John asked.

The Shawnee man stared at John for a long minute. "You ask many questions, little one. What is your name?" he asked John.

"John," he said.

"Do you have a name of your father's people?"

"No," John said a little disappointedly.

"Ack. A wah-see'-chon name," the Shawnee man said.

"It's all I got," John answered with a shrug of his shoulders.

"I think if you were Shawnee, you would be... Night Owl," the Shawnee man said with thought. "For all the questions you asked. You must seek wisdom."

John shrugged as if undecided. "I like to know things".

The Shawnee man nodded in appreciation. "Be careful," he began. "From what has been said, a slave is not to know things."

John looked the Shawnee man in the eyes and then looked away to a tree in the distance. He didn't like being called a slave. There was a pregnant pause of silence before John took a deep breath to come back to the business at hand.

"So," John began. "What does wah-kohn'-tohn-kah mean?"

"Good spirit," the Shawnee man answered.

John smiled. He liked that. "I like being a good person," he said. "I once heard someone say that I'm not a person at all. So I like being a good person."

The Shawnee man nodded in agreement. "You are," the Shawnee man said. "But I will not take the letter. Go back to wah-see'-chon and tell him 'his word has no honor'".

John looked surprised. He was unsure what to do next. He looked at the faces of each of the men standing around him.

"Ok," John said. "You sure?"

The Shawnee man nodded.

"Mr. Preston might not think that I came if I still have the letter," John said.

"I could burn it," the Shawnee man said as a genuine offer to John.

"Nah, it's ok," John said with a deep breath. "I'll deliver your message."

The Shawnee man nodded. "Be safe, Night Owl."

John began walking away from the Shawnee men. He looked up at the sky and smiled. He had plenty of time to get back for merriment. This time, his father was going to tell a story.

Mr. Preston - James Patton Preston (June 21, 1774 – May 4, 1843)[9]

CHAPTER 2
PATRIARCH

Virginia, 1805

J ack threw his last tool into his old wooden toolbox. Smithfield was full of the sound of urgency and short deadlines. Much like everyone else, he rushed to get things completed as quickly as possible so that he could wash his hands and get ready for merriment. He was supposed to tell a story today. It wouldn't be the first time he took to the bonfire to tell a story to the others, but this would be the day he finally told *his* story. The others had asked him many times about his story of how he ended up here at Smithfield, but Jack would always just shake his head and tell them that maybe he would tell the story later. This time, Jack thought, his son John was old enough to really hear the story that he wanted to tell. The story of who he was. He was able to save some skins and some animal fur from the meat prepared for the House, and he planned to use them to show the others a bit of culture from where he had come from; from Yoruba.

Jack closed his eyes so tightly that he began to see stars behind his eyelids. He was slightly obsessed with holding on to the ways of the Yoruba people, of teaching it to his son, and of holding on to the best parts of himself. *Oyewole*, he thought his name to himself. He missed hearing his name on his family's tongue. He missed hearing it ring with the Yoruba people. He smiled, thinking about Fanny. She always knew the right moments to comfort him. When he was his most down and almost defeated, she would hug him and whisper his name, "Oyewole," as if to say, "Hold on. You're not gone."

Jack's story was John's story, and it was important for John to know his story so that he could tell his children, and *his* children would tell their children the story of why they were meant for so much more than this. That their story doesn't start here. In Yoruba, Jack had learned as a child and continued to believe that your ancestors follow you and protect you from evil spirits, helping to lead you to all good things. He believed that there were many gods too, but it was the ancestors assigned by the gods to help you access all the wisdom that they have accumulated through their countless lives. Jack thought that his children should know that those spirits are here and who those spirits are.

"Emi ni lati Oyo ẹya (I am of the Oyo tribe)," Jack said to himself in a whisper. "Mo bu ọla fun mi ile ati awọn enia mi (I honor my home and my people).".

"Jack!"

Jack's thoughts were interrupted by a voice quite obviously annoyed with him.

"Jack, are you listening to me?"

Jack looked over his shoulder to see Fanny. Attached to her leg was William Ballard, Mr. Preston's oldest son. The House just called him Ballard. He was about five years old but hung on to Fanny's leg so tightly Jack was sure the boy thought that if he let her go, he'd fall off the earth.

When he saw Fanny, Jack immediately thought of his son since he was not by her side. In the back of his mind, Jack was always anxious when Mr. Preston sent John out on a task without him, so

Jack had to take comfort in knowing that he had trained his son to be a man even though he was only about eleven years old. Jack knew that his son was wise and strong. He had trained him for the work expected of him here at Smithfield, but he had also prepared him in the ways of a nobleman of the Yoruba. His son knew pride, strength, and strategy. Jack was anxious about was the way of the people here in this land they call America. He had cut enough hanging bodies from trees to know that any feeling of safety was a risky illusion that they could not afford to believe. But if something were wrong with John, Fanny would know. Fanny was John's inna, his mother, and she worked in the House. She is also what the White men would call Jack's wife. From what he has seen, the title of wife meant very little here. In Yoruba, she would be so much more to him.

"Yes," Jack said, acknowledging Fanny. "Yes, I hear you," he continued. "Is there something wrong?"

"No," Fanny began. "There's nothing wrong. Me and Mr. Ballard here," she said, nodding down at Ballard clutched to her leg, "came down to ask if you can help Mae gut that bore for the House dinner tomorrow. She wants to gut it now so it can soak until tomorrow".

Jack nodded in agreement. "Yes," he said, clapping his hands together to knock off the dust that was there. He looked at the young boy clutched to Fanny's leg. "Mr. Ballard," he said, nodding to the five–year-old boy as he bent down to pick up his toolbox. He touched his hand to his chest in acknowledgement to Fanny of love and honor and began to walk towards the Smithfield house.

"Jack?" Ballard said, stopping Jack from leaving. Jack stopped and turned back to Ballard. Ballard ducked back behind Fanny's leg.

"He's scared of the way you talk," Fanny explained, referring to his West African accent. "I think he thinks that you are bbiiggg and ssccaarryy, and mmmeeannn." Fanny smiled as if telling a story.

"Mean!?" Jack exclaimed in fake shock. He made an effort to lighten the bass in his voice. "Now, why would you think that I was mean?"

Ballard peeped around Fanny's leg. His eyes ran across Jack's face and arms as he looked at the tiger stripe-like scars that were there. Jack watched Ballard look him over.

"Fanny, do you think that I am mean?" he said to Fanny as he bent down to place the toolbox on the ground before standing up straight, towering over Ballard.

"No," Fanny said with a smile. She looked down at Ballard. "Well, except when he hits his finger with that there hammer," she said, nodding her head to point to the hammer in Jack's toolbox.

"I was mean once when I hit my knee on the stairs," Ballard exclaimed, seemingly happy to find something in common with Jack. "You know that part at the top that sticks out?"

"Yes," Jack said, nodding in agreement. "That makes me mean sometimes, too. But, it doesn't last long."

Ballard nodded in agreement. "Jack?" he asked again. "What happened to your face? Do you turn into a tiger at night? And why do you talk like that?"

"Like what?" Jack asked.

"I don't know?" Ballard began. "It's kind of like there is water in your throat. Like when you put your head back and make bubbles."

"This is how people where I am from sound," Jack answered.

"My father said we once had White men that were like you," Ballard said, referring to Jack's slavery and the Smithfield history of also having indentured servants up until about twenty years earlier[1]. "But my father says that they were from where my grandfather was from. My father said my grandfather is from Ireland and that Ireland is a great place full of castles and kings. He said they got to work for a while, to pay their debts for the passage to America, but then they left to make their own way." Ballard stopped his explanation. It was clear that he was trying to understand something that didn't make sense to him.

"But," Ballard continued. "I think you've been here for a while. When will you go home?"

Jack didn't answer for a while as he just watched Ballard trying to understand this world that he would grow up to rule. "I will not," Jack finally answered.

"Why?" Ballard continued. "Why did they get to go home?"

"I do not know why I am different. Where I am from, a slave was very different. Our slaves could work for freedom too," Jack explained. He bent down to Ballard's level to meet his eyes. He reached his hand to the ground beneath him and brought up a handful of soil to Ballard's face. "In this land," he continued. "I am told that I am different. I am different from your father. I am different from you. I am told that I am not a man." Jack let the soil run through his fingers.

"You look like a man to me," Ballard said as a matter of fact.

"Because I am," Jack answered him. "But me and Fanny, we will always be…"

"Well," Ballard said, interrupting Jack. "when I grow up. I'll let you go home. I'll let Fanny go too, but she has to come back and visit me allllll the time."

"None of that talk now," Fanny interrupted, a little fearful of how the conversation turned. "Your father's not going to like that kind of talk." Fanny rubbed her hands together nervously. "Let's get moving, Mr. Ballard. Jack has to go and help with the boar for your dinner tomorrow, and I have to get you in the house and get you settled."

"You going to merriment tonight?" Ballard asked Fanny. His eyes lit up as if he's heard about a prize.

"Yes, sir Mr. Ballard," Fanny answered, beginning to walk back to the house. She looked over her shoulder back at Jack. "I'll see you later, Jack?" she smiled a little flirtatiously. "Let me get back up to this house and help Mrs. Anne with that baby," she said, turning back around to watch her path as she walked back to the house. "Robert's going to be trouble as soon as he can walk, and Lord knows Mrs. Anne don't know what she doing."

Jack smiled back at Fanny. He knew his ancestors sent Fanny to him. She was a beautiful spirit to give him light.

Fanny suddenly stopped in her tracks and looked back over her shoulder to Jack in shocked pity. In front of her stood Mr. Preston, another man, and a short and skinny twelve-year-old boy who looked down at the ground. The boy's clothes were too large for him and hung on him like they were out to dry, rather than as something he should be wearing for labor. His feet were bare, his face was dirty, and his hair was matted into a knotted glob of mess.

"There he is," James Preston said, leading the other man over to where Jack was. "Jack! Here now!" he said with a wag of his finger.

"Yes, sir," Jack said, slowly moving towards Mr. Preston.

At the sound of Jack's voice, the young boy jerked his head up. When he saw Jack, his eyes immediately went to the markings on Jack's face. The boy ran forward, grabbed Jack's hand, and fell to his knees.

"Iyìn si awọn ẹmí (praise to the spirits)!" the boy said in his native tongue. "O ti wa ni ọlá mi (it is my honor)."

Jack looked up at Fanny, who was wide-eyed. "What's wrong?" she asked, looking around nervously, worried that Mr. Preston and the others would be upset with the boy for running forward to Jack.

"I brought the boy to you to see if you understood him," James explained. "So that you could tell him his work here. He's Mr. Blackman's boy. Fresh off the ship."

Fanny shifted her stance, uncomfortable with the facts.

"Mr. Blackman needs you to explain to him that he's a slave now," James said.

The boy, now kneeling down, still grasping Jack's hand, was now in tears. He mumbled in Yoruba. He was begging and pleading to Jack and to the spirits to help him. The boy was so afraid.

"Now! Here we go. See Mr. Blackman. I told you Jack here would help the boy," James announced to the other man waving his hand to indicate the boy's recognition of Jack. "Jack. You know the boy? You know his talk? His language?"

Jack looked down at the boy again in shock. *Of course he didn't know the boy* Jack thought to himself, growing angrier by the second. *He'd been here too long himself to know this young boy. What kind of stupid question was that?!* Jack took a deep breath and worked to keep the horror off his face.

"O gbọdọ jẹ ki wọn ri o lori rẹ ẽkun (you must not let them see you on your knees)," he said to the boy. The boy looked up at Jack, his face streaked with tears. "Emi ni Oyewole (I am Oyewole)," he said to the boy. "Kunrin ti Oyo ti Oyo Mesi (Nobleman of Oyo of Oyo Mesi). Jagunjagun to ọba Esigie (Warrior to King Esigie). Ti o ba wa a ondè ti ogun (You are a prisoner of war). Duro pẹlu ọlá (Stand with honor)."

The boy immediately stood up, looking at Jack.

"Now, would you look at that!" James said, letting out a mighty laugh and slapping Mr. Blackman on the back.

Jack peered over at Mr. Preston like he was death preparing to hand out his mark. If he were paying attention, he would see that Jack was holding on to his composure with a thin thread. "Kini o ti ṣẹlẹ (what happened)?" Jack asked the boy, looking back down at him. "Bawo ni o nibi (how are you here)?"

The boy looked over to Mr. Preston and Mr. Blackman.

"Ti won ko le ni oye (they cannot understand)," Jack said to the boy. "A sọ ọpọlọpọ awọn ede (We speak many languages), awon eniyan nikan sọ ọkan ede (these people only speak one language). Nwọn o si fẹ lati ko eko won ede (they will want you to learn their language). Ki o si sọ nikan wọn ede (And speak only their language). Maa yi lati gbe (Do this to live). Bayi, ohun to sele. (Now what happened)?"

"Nwọn si ilee o si mu ọpọlọpọ awọn ti wa (They raided and took many of us)," the boy said.

"Ṣe o ranti awọn gun ajo (Do you remember the long journey)?" Jack asked the boy. The boy nodded in agreement. "A ni o wa ju jina fun elomiran lati wa lati ja (We are too far for others to come to fight). Ki o gbọdọ jẹ lagbara lati ran mi dabobo awọn enia nibi (So you must be strong to help me protect the people here)," the boy nodded in agreement again. "Lọ si ọkunrin (Go to that man)," Jack said pointing to Mr. Blackman.

"Awọn funfun Bìlísì (The White devil)?" the boy asked, the expression on his face skeptical.

Jack gave a short laugh, void of humor. "Bẹẹni, ṣugbọn ko ba so pe ninu rẹ èdè (Yes. But do not say that in his language)," Jack said. The boy looked back at him. "Kí ni orúkọ rẹ (What is your name?)" Jack asked the boy.

"Babawale," the boy answered.

"Ah, Babawale," Jack said, pounding his fist once against his chest. "Babawale, Pe eniyan yoo gba ọ si ibi kan (That man will take you to a place)," Jack said, pointing at Mr. Blackman again. The boy's gaze followed the direction of Jack's finger. "Ibi ti nibẹ ni o wa miran ti o wo bi o (where there are others that look like you). Wọn iya ati baba wà elewon nibi (Their mothers and fathers were prisoners here). Wọn ko ba ko ranti Africa (they do not remember Africa or their tribes), tabi wọn ede (or their language). Nwọn o si kọ ọ (They will teach you). Ati awọn ti o yoo kọ wọn (and you will teach them). Lọ si awọn ọkunrin ati ki o sọ (Go to the man and say) 'Hello. My name is Babawale'," Jack instructed the boy.

The boy repeated Jack, "Ello. Mya name iz Babawale."

"Ti o dara (good)," Jack said, still not smiling. He wanted the boy to know that he was sending him on a warrior's journey, not anything to smile about. "Ti o kan wi (You just said) 'Ẹ kí orukọ mi ni Babawale (Hello my name is Babawale)'."

The boy nodded, now serious with his new mission from his missing nobleman, and repeated it, "Ello. Mya name iz Babawale."

"Mr. Blackman named him Timothy!" James yelled across the space between him and Jack before turning to Mr. Blackman and nodding to him with a proud smile. Jack lifted his eyes to look at Mr. Preston without changing his posture from standing in front of the boy. He did not move his face or his body in James's direction. He took a deep breath and turned his attention back to the boy.

"Nwọn fẹ lati pe o Timothy (They want to call you Timothy)," Jack told the boy. "Wọn ti wa ni ju karachi lati sọ wa awọn orukọ (They are too stupid to say our names)." The boy looked back to Mr. Preston and Mr. Blackman. "O si le pe ti o Timothy, ṣugbọn ti o ba wa Babawale (He can call you Timothy, but you are Babawale)."

The boy nodded in agreement. "Ello. Mya name iz Timo-tea."

"Ti o dara (good)," Jack said. "Sango o wà pẹlu nyin (Sango be with you)," Jack said, blessing the boy with the Yoruba god of warriors. He touched the boy's cheek and led him back to James.

"Ello. Mya name iz Timo-tea," the boy said to Mr. Blackman. Mr. Blackman looked at James with a smile. "That's a mighty fine negro you got there. I hope this one grows up real nice just like him."

Jack's nose flared in anger. He turned around and walked back towards where he had just been working. He walked past Fanny without a word. He then grabbed the box of tools so aggressively that the tools jangled together, causing Fanny to jump slightly from surprise. Ballard hid behind her skirts again. Jack stood up straight and stood still while he stared at the wall of the building in front of him. He took a deep breath before he walked away.

"Fanny?" Ballard whispered to her, still clutching on to her skirt.

"Yes, Mr. Ballard?" she said, keeping her gaze on Jack's back as he walked away, her hand still resting on her chest from feeling startled.

"I think Jack might have been a king, not a tiger."

Fanny's eyes swelled with unshed tears.

———

Fanny walked around the outside of the Smithfield house, her skirt rustling the dust across her path. As usual, Ballard was still holding tight to her hand. "Why can't I go to the merriment tonight, Fanny?" he asked her, already pouting about not getting what he wanted.

Fanny didn't answer. She wasn't quite sure how to answer Ballard in a way that he would understand. Honestly, she thought this was a conversation for Mr. Preston. He was better to explain to his son why he could not go to merriment. Why he should not go to merriment. Ballard was to grow up and run this plantation, and Fanny doubted Mr. Preston would be keen on Ballard getting too close to the enslaved. Little did Ballard know of the trajectory for power that Mr. Preston was preparing him to take on.

"We on our way to the house, Mr. Ballard. It's best if you ask your father questions like these. I'm sure he'll have some answers,"

Fanny said.

Ballard clucked his tongue in frustration. Fanny was right, his father would give him answers, but not answers that Ballard wanted or even understood. Before Ballard could drag Fanny to move faster into the house, back from his errand to the Shawnee, John ran up to his mother and Ballard, surprisingly, only slightly out of breath.

"I'm back, Mama," John announced to Fanny. "Just in time for merriment." He turned his attention to Ballard. "Hey, Mr. Ballard!" John said, happy to see his friend. Ballard's face lit up.

"Hey, John!" Ballard said, finally releasing Fanny's hand.

John and Ballard were friends, as much as friends could be under these circumstances. Fanny gave a slight smile that was more sad than happy. At this age, the innocence still triumphed over the society, but Fanny did not look forward to the day when John would be heartbroken when Ballard learned that John was his own property. Most Master's children were kind, tolerant, and forgiving at this stage. Fanny had warned John on several occasions, but he was convinced that Ballard would be different.

"He'll always be my friend," John would say. Jack didn't help the situation much during those talks.

"If he is a man of honor, you will be right," Jack would tell John. "He will always be your friend." Jack hadn't quite let go of his Yoruba traditions and ways of thinking.

Ballard approached John and came so close to him that John stiffened, unsure of what to do. "I'd like to play with you," Ballard announced. It wasn't a question.

John glanced at Fanny. He knew the expression on her face, the "see?" look. He knew his mother thought that what Ballard said was a command, like one that someone would give to a dog. John thought it was a request. Ballard wanted to play, and so did he, but he couldn't right now, he had to get ready for merriment.

"Mr. Ballard," John began. "I need to go see Mr. Preston."

"Well, I'm going to see my father too," Ballard announced. "You can come with me. I'm going to ask if I can come to merriment."

John looked at Fanny again as if asking for direction of what he should do.

"Go on," Fanny answered. "I'll be right behind you."

Ballard led the way towards the front of the house. He quickly ascended the stairs, opened the front door, and entered into the house's vestibule.

"Papa!" he yelled, running through the master bedroom and the dining room to find his father in the office. "Papa!" Ballard proclaimed once he saw his father standing at the desk reading a document.

"Yes, Ballard, my boy," James said, greeting his son.

"Papa," Ballard began. "John is..." Ballard turns around to point to John, but he was not with him. "Wait," Ballard said, gesturing to his father to wait a second.

Ballard turned around and ran back through the house to the front door. He exited the house and landed on the front porch with heavy footsteps. Fanny was there with her hands clutched together as if waiting for Ballard to return.

"Fanny, where is John? Why didn't he come with me?"

"John can't come in this way, Mr. Ballard. He has to come in through the back. Go to your father and John will meet you there."

Ballard gave a heavy sigh. "Ok," he said as he retraced his path back through the house to his father in the office. "Is John here yet!?" Ballard asked James.

"John is back?" James questioned. "Why hasn't he come to report to me about the Indians?"

"I don't know," Ballard shrugged. "I wanted John to come so I can ask about merriment."

"Not this again. Ballard, I have told you before, we do not go to merriment. We do not celebrate with the ne---"

"Wait," Ballard cut off James' speech before he could really get into the details about how "they" don't celebrate with "them," and about how "their" place isn't with "us," but that Ballard could play "with" John because it was John's job, amongst other things, to play "with" Ballard. None of it made sense to Ballard because John was his friend, and a friend doesn't have the job of being a friend. That's something that two friends just *are*. Ballard ran to the side door of the office that lead to the outside. He was sure that John would be there waiting to come inside. Ballard's little hands struggle with the door until eventually, he was able to open it.

"There you are!" he announced when he saw John standing at the bottom of the three stairs that lead to the ground.

"Yes, sir," John answered, overwhelmingly aware of the presence of Mr. Preston there towering behind Ballard.

"Come in," Ballard gestured to John. "I was just about to ask my father about merriment. I hope you have some good news to give to him so that he will be in a good mood."

James approached the doorway, pulled out his pocket watch, and checked the time.

"It appears you made good time," James said to John, one of his hairy eyebrows raised. "Are you sure you ran the errand?" James questioned John.

"Yes, sir," John answered. "I just ran the whole way to make sure I was back in time for…" John cuts himself off and quickly glances to Ballard before looking back to Mr. Preston. He knew from his own experience that Mr. Preston didn't like Mr. Ballard always wanting to come to the slave quarters, or go to merriment. John didn't go on with his statement in fear that Mr. Preston will think that Ballard wanted to go to merriment because John urged him to want to come.

After an awkward pause of silence, James continued. "Well, yes, I suppose if you ran the length, it would be possible to return this quickly."

John grabbed his trousers and balled up a large patch of the material in his hand. He looked around, not sure what to do next. Mr. Preston hadn't told him to come into the house, so he wasn't sure if he was supposed to give him his report out here in the open or wait and go inside.

"So what is the Indian's response?" James said, moving closer to the doorway to continue to fill it with his presence.

"Well, sir," John began, "the Shaw...I mean, the Indians um," John stopped talking as he tried to think of a way to deliver the Shawnee man's message in a way that made it clear that he had delivered Mr. Preston's message even though he still had the letter.

"Come out with it, boy!" James said to John, taking another step forward.

He pushed Ballard to the side so that he could fill the entire doorway at the top of the stairs. John lifted his hand that still held James' note to the Shawnee tribe. He turned his hand palm up to show Mr. Preston that he still had the letter. At this moment, John braced for an explosive reaction from this peculiar situation. Mr. Preston had already questioned whether or not he ran the errand at all, so to return to the house with the original letter was further evidence that he did not, though he, in fact, did actually run the errand. James raised a hairy eyebrow again. He looked at the letter in John's hand and then looked at John.

"You still have the letter?" James questioned.

At the corner of his eye, John could see Ballard rest his head on the door frame and then look down at the floor in defeat. Ballard had realized, just as John had, that this wasn't going well at all.

"Yes, sir," John said. "I ran over to the Shawnee...I mean the Indians. They were out for the hunt, so I didn't have to go too far to find 'em. They scared me at first," John continued hoping to gain points for bravery. "But I was brave and just kept going even through the yellin' they were doing."

"But you didn't deliver the letter," James stated as a matter of fact.

"Yes, sir, I did," John said. "They just gave it back to me."

"So it appears," James stated, showing no emotion or reaction. John couldn't read Mr. Preston. He didn't know what he was feeling. He didn't know what he should be saying. John looked behind him, hoping his mother was nearby to help him, even his father. He squinted from the sun as he looked around, wishing for anyone to approach and maybe change the subject and distract Mr. Preston. John turned his attention back to the matter at hand and chanced a short glance at Ballard, who was looking at John shaking his head. John wasn't sure if that meant that Ballard was disappointed in him, or that Ballard was telling him not to say another word. James cocked his head to the side. It reminded John of a dog when he was confused about a weird sound he had heard.

"So," James said. "What did the Indian say?"

A little late to the rescue, Fanny came around the house with Ballard's little brother, Robert, on her waist. She stopped a few steps behind John and put herself in the view of James so that he could see that she was there, but still focus on John.

"He said...," John began. Then he stopped as he gained a boost of bravery with his mother now there. He went on with his explanation. "He said that your word had no honor and that I asked too many questions."

Ballard lifted his head from the door frame and slapped his forehead in disbelief. Fanny's eyes widened. James stared at John for a second. His shoulders began to shake, and then he exploded into laughter. James held on to the waist of his pants as he tried to gain his composure. Ballard looked up at his father with surprise and hope. Here is the good mood he was hoping for!

"Well, boy," James said, calming himself down. "With that, I am sure you, in fact, delivered my message to the Indian. How many times have I told you that you ask too many questions? How many times do I have to send you on labor for asking too many questions? I can't have you around here with the business if you keep asking all those questions. You ask questions to your mammy so she can teach you all the jobs around here that you'll do the older you get. You ask questions of your Pa. He's one of the best slaves around here. You'd be valuable if you learned what he knows, but the other questions that you ask; it's not your place to ask them." James shook his head in disbelief.

Ballard interrupted his father's lecture to John. "At the notion of questions," he announced.

James looks down at his son. "Merriment?" he asked before Ballard can ask it.

"Yes!" Ballard exclaimed. "Can I go to merriment? Just this one time, Papa? Please!? I won't even join the circle!"

"How do you know there's a circle?" James asked Ballard, a clear attempt to make Ballard too uncomfortable to move the conversation forward.

"Circle? Did I say circle?" Ballard said with convincing confusion, as if James had heard things.

"Lord almighty," Fanny whispers to herself, pressing her fingertips to the bridge of her nose. James looked over to Fanny.

"Mr. Preston," Fanny began to explain. "We was talking about the circle, trying to prepare for merriment tonight. Jack has somethin' planned and we..".

James held his hand up in an obvious signal for Fanny to stop.

Fanny gave a quick glance to Ballard. She could feel him staring at her, clearly afraid that he had gotten her in trouble. Fanny gave him a short *no* with a nod of her head. *I'm sorry*, Ballard mouthed to her.

"Fanny," James began,. "You're a good mammy, but Ballard has to be prepared to take over Smithfield, and there are a lot of things he needs to learn. Keep him focused on that. Ballard should always be raised as if he could take over at any time. Negro spirituals and stories and merriment should not be on his mind. If you're going to talk about anything with him, explain to him how the different jobs and tasks of the slaves are managed. Point out the troublemakers and explain to him why you, Jack, and John here know better."

"Yes, sir," Fanny agreed. She shifted Robert on her hip, part nervous tick, part for comfort.

"Go on now, John," James said, turning his attention back to John. John took a few steps backwards before turning around. He looked at his mother before fully retreating.

"Go on now," Fanny said under her breath.

John took a few steps to leave. "I'll be right over there, Mama, waitin'," John said to Fanny under his breath when he passed her. Like any son, he was going to protect his mother. John left as he was told but waited under a tree for his mother's workday to so that they could go to merriment together.

Fanny continued to stand at the same spot with Robert on her hip. She stared down at the ground. A silence filled the air. "I don't want Fanny in any trouble, Papa," Ballard proclaimed.

He felt bad about everything that just happened. Fanny had told him days ago not to ask about merriment. She said if he were quiet, he would probably hear merriment from his window. Ballard already figured out that he would see the Merry Tree from the window at the top of the stairs. If he was quiet enough, he could watch without anyone knowing. He might have ruined any chance he had now in watching merriment through the window by bringing it up at all. Now, his father would make sure he didn't see *any* of it.

James bent down to look Ballard in his eyes. Fanny took a step back as if to leave. "Fanny, stay," James demanded, not looking in Fanny's direction. Fanny stopped retreating. "Ballard," John continued, "you have to learn and know when something should matter to you, and when things, even when they matter to you, don't matter. Fanny is your mammy, but when she's finished here, she goes, and she lives a separate life. Ok? You play with John, but when you're finished with him, he goes and lives a separate life. You focus on education. You learn how all this works-both Smithfield and Virginia. You hear me, son?"

Ballard shook his head in confirmation. "But, Papa," he began. "How do I learn Smithfield if I don't learn what the slaves do?"

James smiled at Ballard, proud of his realization. "Maybe I can go to merriment on another day? Merriment can just be something else I learn?"

James nodded in agreement. "Surely," he agreed. "Now go on with Fanny so she can get you and Robert ready for supper."

"Yes, Papa," Ballard agreed, happy that he was a step closer to going to merriment.

With a huge smile, Ballard turned around to walk back through the house. Fanny walked around to enter through the back entrance of the house to meet him on the other side. When Ballard made his way through the house and met Fanny at the back door where she entered, he met Fanny's eyes. The smile disappeared from his face as he approached her and saw that she was not sharing his joy and excitement. She wasn't frowning at him, but he could tell that she was still hurt and, as far as Ballard was concerned, it was because of him.

———

John sat under a tree waiting for Fanny to come out of the Smith-field house. He didn't want to go back to the slave quarters without his mother, so he'd wait for her to finish with the Preston children so that she could come and take care of him. This is the time of day that he hated. Ballard was his friend, but he had to admit that he was annoyed that Ballard always got *his* mother first. Fanny was *his* mother. He should be first. Ballard has his own mother. His mother should take care of him when it was time for Fanny to take care of John. Sure, Fanny could take care of Ballard and Robert when John was off working, but after that, Fanny should be his. John grabbed a handful of grass, ripped it out of the ground, and threw it into the wind.

"Ha!" John said to himself. "Take that, Mr. Preston. I'm destroying Smithfield. Now send Fanny out here to fix it." Fanny didn't come. "Uuughhh!" John whined out loud. "Come on!"

A large figure sat down next to John.

"Are we waiting for Fanny again?" Jack asked, sitting next to his son.

"Yes!" John exclaimed. "He's keeping her longer this time. I bet it's because Ballard made him mad about merriment."

Jack scooted himself back so that his back rested against the trunk of the maple tree that they were sitting under. He and John had a clear view of Smithfield.

"Well," Jack started. "I guess merriment will have to wait for Fanny and then go *all* night." Jack said, closing his eyes and linking his arms behind his head as if to make a pillow.

Jack and John sat there silent for a minute; John intently watched the house, waiting for Fanny to come out.

Suddenly John stood up. "I'm going in to get her!"

"No, you can't go in to get her," Jack answered John with his eyes still closed.

"Then *you* go in and get her!" John said, turning to his father.

"No, I can't go in and get her either," Jack said.

"Well! What if he's doing something to her?!" John yelled.

Jack opened his eyes and looked at his son. He was silent for so long that John thought that he had done or said something wrong. John had ventured into some delicate territory. Jack brought down his arms and placed them between his thighs as if his hands were now cold.

"He won't damage her. He needs her," Jack answered John.

"Why won't you protect her?" John asked in a whisper that was as much of a plea as it was a question.

"Because I love her," Jack stated simply. "Because I love you. I do nothing to keep us all safe."

John did not understand what Jack meant. Before Jack could try to explain, Fanny came out of the back of the house, her skirt brushing the dirt on the path that she was walking. She was wiping her hands with her apron. John ran to meet her on the path, embracing her heartedly as he met her, almost knocking them both down.

"Ah, John," Fanny said, hugging her son. "What's all of this! As if you haven't seen me all day!" Fanny said with a giggle.

"Did Mr. Preston hurt you, Mama? When I left you, he looked kinda angry." John asked.

"Ah. Don't pay Mr. Preston no mind most days. I let him yell, but then he gets back to his business and forgets all about me…and his children," Fanny said, smiling down at John.

"Good," John said in relief. Fanny hugged John again and made eye contact with Jack. Her smile disappeared for a second as she and Jack spoke to each other without words. Jack bit his bottom lip, and Fanny's smile returned when she looked down at John.

"You ready for merriment!?" Fanny asked John.

"Yes!" John answered. "Let's go!"

Fanny let John take the lead towards the Merry Tree and walked over to Jack. He fell to the ground, laying on his stomach, before jumping back up to stand on his feet in greeting to her in the traditional way of the Yoruba people.

"Oyewole," she whispered to him, stretching out her hand to urge him to her.

He took her hand, brought it up to his mouth, and placed a gentlemen's kiss before holding her hand to his cheek and looking her in her eyes.

"I am sorry," Jack whispered to her. Fanny placed her hand on Jack's chest and kissed him on the lips.

Smithfield, Blacksburg, Virginia 2016[2]

CHAPTER 3

MERRIMENT

Virginia, 1805

The sun had set in the great Appalachia mountains, but unlike other nights, John wasn't afraid of the dark. He sat cross-legged on the ground under the Merry Tree,[1] staring at the orange blaze of the fire that was set a few feet away from both him and the tree. The fire was so bright that the rising smoke could be seen even in the dark. It looked like a ghost of soot rising in celebration. It wanted to see Jack's story just as much as John did. He shifted his position, propped up his knees, and laid his chin on the hard callous skin that had already formed there. He continued to watch the smoke dance up to the sky until it disappeared in the dark beyond. Around him, other people sat anticipating the arrival of Jack. Fanny was off helping him prepare. Apparently, Jack had spent weeks collecting scraps of animal skins, furs, fabric, and other supplies to make whatever he needed for his story. John had asked repeatedly to see what Jack was making, but his father always waived John away.

"Wait like all the others. I do not want you to see it until it is ready," Jack would say. Now, it was finally time for merriment, and John was very "ready."

Jack sat in the center of a group of trees a bit of a way back from the bonfire so that the group could not see him before he was ready to be seen. He looked down at himself, spread his arms out like they were wings, and then looked up at Fanny, who had just finished tying two straps behind his back to keep the hide on his waist and wrapped around his body from falling. Once she finished tying the straps, she continued to walk backwards in front of Jack, intending to get a good look at him. When she looked him over, she raised her hand and placed her fingers over her mouth.

"Is it good?" Jack asked, looking down at himself before looking back at Fanny.

Again, she just stood there with her fingers over a mouth.

"No?" Jack asked her again. She didn't move. She just stared at him. "Yes?" he asked again with a slight laugh in his voice.

Fanny slid her fingers down so that they only touched her bottom lip. "Can you..?" she began to ask, then she paused. "Let me know if this ain't proper, but can you do the Yoruba greeting for me dressed like that?"

A sly smile covered Jack's face. He went down to the ground, landing in a face-down position, never touching his whole body on the ground, holding himself up with his toes and his hands before jumping back up to a standing position with the agility of a cat. Fanny watched him, her head turning to the side like an inquisitive puppy as she watched every muscle in his body flex as he performed the greeting in the fur, skins, and straps.

"Lord Jesus," she said when he stood straight and looked at her. "Oh, Oyewole."

"It's good then," he said to her. It wasn't a question.

"Yeah, it's real good." She nodded in agreement.

"Emi ni ohunkohun lai ti o (I am nothing without you)," Jack said, marching quickly over to Fanny to kiss her.

———

Jack's story would be the last event of the celebration tonight. They had already sung and danced, and Philip had already given a sermon on hope, strength, and faith. Now, Philip walked around the circle of the Merry Tree, making sure everyone had a piece of the bread that was being served.

Caroline followed behind him, passing out a spread. "This here is special tonight," Caroline said adding, a little of the spread to John's bread. "It ain't much, but we mixed it with a little of that boar fat your father gutted for us. Gives it a nice little flavor."

John smiled up at Caroline. "Yes, Ma'am," he said, showing all his teeth. "Thank you!"

He went straight to work eating the bread. Caroline was right— the spread was delicious. He continued to watch the smoke dance up to the sky.

"Gah!" Philip exclaimed for all to hear. "If I didn't know better, I'd say that smoke was alive. Must be the ancestors," Philip said, turning to smile down at John. "I bet they done come all the way from Africa to hear their story told."

John smiled at Philip. He liked that idea, and if his father's stories were right, it could very well be true. John looked around, feeling motivated to perform some type of ritual. He wanted to do something so that the smoke could see he was of Yoruba. When John's eyes saw a stone, he almost lunged to grab it, but he stopped himself. A little embarrassed, he didn't want an audience when he performed his ritual. Quietly, John reached for the stone and quickly gripped it tightly in his palm so that no one would see what he had picked up. Adjusting the stone in his hand, he felt the texture of the stone in his palm. John tightened his body in his seated position to make it tighter and smaller so that no one could see his ritual. He rolled the stone around in his hand, looking for the sharpest edge. *There, there it was.*

"Alright," John whispered to himself.

John placed the sharp edge of the stone against the side of his shin on his leg. Immediately, the sharp stone made a white mark against his skin. John smiled, happy to learn that his ritual would leave a mark like his father's, even if it were temporary. He planned on giving himself one tiger mark that looked like the marks on his father.

"I am of the earth," John whispered, slowly running the sharp edge of the stone down his leg, continuing the white line. "I am of Yoruba, of the Oyo. I am my own home," he continued. "I am a warrior for Sango."

John stopped the trace of the stone at the bone that pops out to make the bump at his ankle. A light breeze blew, and the smoke from the bonfire circled him. He balanced the stone on his knee, wrapped his arms around his legs, and smiled into the crook of his elbows. The ancestors approved.

"What you so happy about?" Fanny asked, sitting next to John.

"Nothing," he said nonchalantly, purposely keeping the secret of his new agreement with the ancestors and with Sango.

"*Mhm,*" Fanny moaned like a mother who knows better. "I suppose you can't get in no trouble just sittin' here, right?"

"Right," John agreed.

Fanny looked up to the crowd. "Alright now, everybody!" Fanny announced to the group. "Jack's ready. If ya'll can just go 'head and settle down now, we can get started."

Philip clapped his hands in an attempt to get the group to settle. Everyone moved around as they took a seat in front of the bonfire.

"It's going to be a sure good time," Fanny said, smiling wide and excited. "He out there in the trees looking good."

John smiled up at Fanny. Suddenly, a drumbeat interrupted the conversations around them. Unlike the Shawnee drum circles that John had heard, this was one lonely drum only a few steps behind the trees. Just like Jack had said, the drumming was different from what John heard with the Shawnee. It was like his father had described, the same but different. The Shawnee drum and song were like a prayer; this song and drum were like a declaration. Jack was making a statement. What the statement was, John didn't know. The drumming became stronger and louder until Jack stepped out of the trees. His arms and legs covered in animal skins and fur, and his lower body in fabric. The straps were also wrapped around the top of his arms, making his muscles, which John had already thought were huge, appear even bigger. The clothing accented the tribal scars on his body. John squinted harder to see across the distance to his father with only the bonfire for light.

His father walked like a duck around the fire, playing the drum which sat between his legs. John recognized some of the pieces of the drum. Carved on the side were an owl and a moon. That made John think of the Shawnee man calling him Night Owl. Realizing that his father must have gotten the drum from the Shawnee, John's eyes went wide as he met his father's gaze in question, as if to ask him, *They KNEW I was your son?* Jack nodded in agreement, a father and son's bond without words.

Jack continued to drum his song. The beat became more intense, stronger, louder, and faster. The statement, John realized, was a challenge. The song was challenging whoever heard it to come forward. John watched his father, wondering if Jack was challenging Mr. Preston to come out of Smithfield and stop the merriment. Suddenly the song stopped, which made John look around. Had Mr. Preston arrived? Did his father see him approaching already?

"Africa!" Jack broke the silence of the dark. "I am from a place they call Yoruba; Tribe of Oyo. Our kingdom lay in the forest." Jack beat the drum again, ending in a light continuous rhyme that he played as he spoke. "In Yoruba we have obas. The Oba was our king. The last Oba I knew was Esigie. Esigie was the son of Ozolua. I served Esigie as one of his noblemen, as one of his warriors. I fought with him. I fought for him. We were known all over the land. White men and brown men came from the world to see our art, our oils, and our skills. Our elders of Oyo told the children stories of our ancestors-great kings and warriors. Even the low of us were seen by the White man as a sight to behold! But then Oyo began to struggle. The family of our Oba began to fight themselves," Jack started to drum feverously again.

The song was now urgent, like someone bad was coming, until suddenly the drumming stopped.

"Esigie tried to please everyone," Jack continued. "He gave titles, he gave power, he tried to stop the war, but the fighting continued. Oyo was being weakened. Our enemies were watching, so Esigie prayed to our ancestors. He prayed to the gods. Until one day, Esigie asked for me to come to him." Jack began the light drumming again and went back in time.

———

Oyewole, about twenty-years-old, jogged into the royal court where Oba Esigie sat waiting for him. At his arrival to the Oba, Oyewole threw his body to the ground face down, holding himself up by his hands and toes in traditional greeting, before quickly standing back up. He stood in front of Oba Esigie's bare chest, his neck flanked with a thick halo of iron, his head also covered with an iron headpiece. An assortment of knives and swords hung from his waist, and a long spear sat in his hand. In a battle, he might also be carrying a large shield, but under the circumstances, he did not find it necessary.

Esigie was flanked by his servants and other members of his Oyo Mesi. Oyewole was the last to arrive, but that was to be expected since he was coming from the furthest distance. In his role, he was warrior and advisor, but he also oversaw a village at the border of the land of the Oyo. Border villages, like where Oyewole was, were often the first to be attacked or visited when people came from the outside. Oyewole was also often the one to deal with the White men that would wander into their land looking for resources, and as Oyewole's experience had taught him, power.

"Oyewole," Oba Esigie said in Yoruba. "Oyewole, we need our men. I fear that war is coming. We sent many of our men with the brown men, the Portuguese, as slaves, but they have not returned. I do not understand how slaves of so long have not earned their way to leave and return to Oyo or Benin. Go to them and offer a trade, a return of our people for double the oils and spice."

"Yes, Oba Esigie," Oyewole answered.

"You may take men with you. Your father should stay in your village to protect the people," Oba Esigie said.

"Yes, Oba Esigie," Oyewole answered again. "Should I pick my men?"

Oba Esigie nodded in agreement. Oyewole looked around at the warrior men standing around him. He pointed to five men, nodded in appreciation to Oba Esigie, and proceeded to leave immediately for his task.

———

Back in the present, Jack continued to drum.

"When I found the Portuguese," he said to the group. "I told them that my Oba had sent me for our men. I told them, 'Esigie will give you twice the oil and spices for their return as payment of their remaining debt.' And the Portuguese said, 'Your men? Tell your Oba that your men were sent to America. He'd have to go there to get them.' And they laughed, but little did I know why they laughed."

Jack stopped drumming, his gaze lost in the fire.

"I did not know why they laughed," Jack said to no one in particular.

The silence seemed to last a long time with Jack's gaze intent on the fire, lost in thought. Fanny grabbed John's hand and squeezed it. John looked up at his mother. She wanted to go to Jack and hold him; tell him that it was ok; that he didn't know.

"Everything," Jack continued, still not drumming. "Everything is different there. The people, the land, the laws, the god. This is not what a slave is in Yoruba. What we are here! This is not a slave. If you were there, you could still be free with time. You were a part of the kingdom and of of the village. You were human." Jack fell silent again before he continued. "We sent people here. We sent people to die." He looked up at each of the faces of the people around the fire. "We did not know, and we are sorry," he said. It was clear that Jack still considered himself part of the people that he had lost. He was taking on the responsibility of an entire nation of people.

Philip stood up and placed his hand on Jack's back. He squeezed Jack's shoulder in reassurance. "It's ok, Ja...Oyewole. Tell us about Africa, 'bout Yoruba. Tell us about how you came here. Did you find your men?"

Jack rubbed the skin that made the top of the drum with his hands. He caressed the drum with a circular motion. He closed his eyes for a moment, calming himself down. Philip was right—the group came together tonight to hear about Africa, a place that they had never seen and likely would never see. Jack began to lightly beat the drum again.

"I asked the Portuguese, how do I get to this America because I thought it was a new place that they had created. They had already conquered so much. I asked them where in Africa is America. One of the men said to me," Jack paused and swallowed hard. "He said, 'It's not. For your people, you must travel by boat for many nights and weeks to the new world.' I asked them if there was a boat that I could take. They told me that if I could get to their town of Angola in 28 days, that I could board a ship to go there. So, I returned to Oba Esigie and told him that I must board a ship to a place called America to get our men. I told him that I would return when I could. Oba Esigie gave me his blessing, my men to come with me, and I said goodbye to my mother and father, and we made our way south to Angola."

Jack began to drum faster and with a more complicated rhythm. John could imagine the day in his head, his father on a quest to find his people to save them.

————

Oyewole stood at the Port of Angola,[2] taking in the scenery. He had arrived on horseback after many hours and thought that he would first seek rest before finding the ship to board to America. When he arrived and saw the conditions, all the people chained and shackled, some of them naked and starving. He was horrified. He looked at one of his men, who nodded for Oyewole to look behind him. There, they watched two Portuguese men throwing unmoving African bodies into the sea.

Oyewole looked around, trying to identify a leader. He spotted a man holding a paper and pointing, giving direction and instructions to others.

"Do you speak their language?" one of the warriors asked Oyewole in Yoruba.

Oyewole shook his head. "No, but I will see if they speak the White man's language," he answered back in Yoruba.

Oyewole marched towards the man, sure to place his spear point towards the ground and to not place his hands on his waist near his weapons to show that they were not approaching to fight. He had learned that even though these countries were made up of men that looked like him, these foreigners were still afraid and still saw the smallest gesture as a threat. Oyewole had fought enough to know that he could defend himself, but he was here for a purpose, to find his people and bring them home.

As Oyewole approached, the Portuguese man looked him over, from his feet to his face.

"Se você tem escravos para vender eles vão ali," the Portuguese man said, nodding to his right and proceeding to review his papers instead of looking at Oyewole while he spoke.

Oyewole did not move or remove his eyes from the man's face.

"We can speak English," he said to the man.

The man gave an impatient huff, as if he'd been dealing with them all day. "If you have slaves to sell, they go over there," he said again, pointing to a station away from the port at the water.

"We have no slaves to sell," Oyewole began. "I want to know where to board the ship to America?"

The Portuguese man raised one eyebrow.

"You want to just...get on the ship?" the Portuguese man questioned with skepticism.

"Yes, Oyewole said. One of your men said that is what I must do to go and get my people and bring them home."

The Portuguese man looked at one of his other men as if this was a joke. He looked back at Oyewole. "If you want to get on a ship to America, go to that one over there. The one that says *True Blue* on the side."

Oyewole looked around the port to identify the ship. This brought his attention back to the conditions of the people.

"What...is...this!?" Oyewole said. "You treat these people like cattle!? Like goats!? These are children of the Ogun! These are women and children! Where is the honor in this?!"

The Portuguese man looked at Oyewole like he was a child that just learned that his fantasies weren't real. "There is no honor in slavery. You people are just too stupid to see that."

"These people are coming with us," Oyewole said as a matter of fact.

The Portuguese men looked at each other again. "Your English sounds good. But you may not be using the words you think you are using because you're making no sense," he said.

"I know what I am saying," Oyewole said.

"Oh," the Portuguese man said. It wasn't really a question, it was more like a statement of interest.

Suddenly Oyewole and his men were attacked. Oyewole kicked the man back and quickly turned his spear weapon side up. He stabbed one of the men attacking them through the neck, and with his other hand, grabbed one of the larger knives from his waist and dived into the fray of the fighting.

Badly outnumbered, it did not take long for the Portuguese men to have Oyewole pinned down to the ground. He looked around and could see that two of his warriors were dead, and the others were pinned down like him. One of his men had already been chained around his neck. Three of the Portuguese men were dead, and one sat on the ground screaming, holding his arm, which was now missing its hand. Oyewole laughed at the sight.

With blood trickling from out of his mouth, he screamed, "PRAISE Sango!!" honoring the god of lightning, fire, and warriors.

One of the Portuguese men kneeled down to the ground. "I'll send you to your men. In America, they pay good for noblemen. They will like your strength, your mind, and the challenge of breaking your will. They'll pay good money for it," he said.

"Should it be the will of Sango," Oyewole said in Yoruba. "Should it be the wisdom of Ogun," he continued. "Ashe," he whispered with a hint of tears in his voice. "Ashe!" he screamed again.

The Portuguese man spit on the ground where Oyewole was and kicked him in the stomach once before he stood straight.

"Bring me one of those chains!" he screamed to one of the other men.

They put the chain around Oyewole's neck and dragged him in front of the line of people already chained and being led to the ships. They wanted to show that even the best warriors were weak against them. They wanted to break any last hope that the people may have felt that they would be rescued. One of the Portuguese men grabbed Oyewole's chain and wrapped it around his hand, dragging him up and down the line like a dog.

"You see this dog!" he yelled. "Even your best is not my equal. You are savages! Blessed by God to be saved by Spain! You will help build our nations for God. We will drag you to salvation, against your will if needed because it is God's will!"[3]

———

Jack stopped drumming and went quiet, staring into the fire again.

"What did you do!?" John yelled, bringing his father's attention back to the story.

With his head bent to the ground, and without moving his head in John's direction, Jack moved his eyes to look at John. The corner of Jack's lip raised in a half-smile. The decorative scars on his face shined with the light from the fire, further expressing his mood.

"I laughed," Jack said as a matter of fact. "I laughed because I thought that these people were crazy. Countries from the east had come to the west for trade for hundreds of years," Jack began to explain about African history. "And hundreds of years ago they were speaking of the god that this man was talking about. These Portuguese and these White men had recreated this god in their own image, for their own purpose. It is true that their god was not my god, but no god takes being used for a lie very kindly. We were a great continent of mighty countries. So do not listen to them when they tell you that in Africa, you are savages living in huts. If that were true, they would not want to conquer it. We were mighty and rich countries with spices, gold, routes for trade, diamonds, art, beauty, great schools of education; and they had come there to take it all."

"Why do they let them take Africa?" John asked, referring to the conquering of the countries of Africa.

Jack thought for a minute. "I think we did not understand a people who have no desire to honor their word and have no punishment for it. In our tribe, if we cannot believe what you say, what value do you have? You would be told to leave or be sentenced and used for sacrifice to the gods. The White men, the brown men, the Portuguese, they lie and then blame you for believing them. I still do not understand it," Jack said, shaking his head. "I think that is why they travel the world, to conquer it. They are all running from each other. They cannot trust each other. Soon, they will run out of places to go. Then what will they do?"

"They go to war with each other," Philip said, explaining what the White men would do. "But you're an African warrior," he continued, bringing the subject back to Jack, Yoruba, and other African countries. "If they needed you, then that means that we went to war in Africa too, right?"

"Yes," Jack said. "For larger territory and control over trade routes or resources like rivers, fields, farms, and mines. Often, an Oba from another country would send a message to another country or tribe asking for surrender, telling the Oba that he wanted his kingdom. If the other Oba did not agree, they would war to see which Oba would win to take over the other country, and the Oba's would join in the fight. What you wanted was clear. White men and Portuguese came and said to us that they wanted to trade, when we agreed, they attacked." Jack thought about the young boy that he had to speak to earlier that day. "They still attack."

"So what happened after you laughed?" John asked, trying to get back to the story.

Jack beat the drum a bit and then said, "He hit me in the face. But when I did not fall, he hit me with the end of a gun. By this time, they had begun to march the people in chains on the boat. One of the men at the end of the chain fell. He was older. He was weak and tired. 'Get up,' one of the Portuguese men screamed as he kicked at the man. The man that hit me with the gun walked over, still dragging my chain and said, 'If he can't even make it on the boat, he won't make it to America. Shoot him.' I jerked the chain out of his hands, and he lifted his pistol to my face. I did not take my eyes off his eyes, but I walked over to the man on the ground. I lifted him to my shoulders and carried him to the boat."

Jack stopped drumming and stopped his story. The song and story were obviously over, but no one around the fire said anything. Suddenly the silence was broken by Philip, who suddenly stood up. He brushed the dust off his pants and announced.

"Well! That explains so much!" he said.

Jack looked up at Philip. "What explains what?" Jack asked.

"How you handle Mr. Preston so well. We got ourselves an African nobleman here!" Philip exclaimed, patting Jack on the back again.

"Lord knows Mr. Preston thinks he's some type of king!" a voice from around the fire commented.

Everyone laughed. Jack half-smiled at Philip, appreciative of his efforts to better the mood that he just created.

"Let's not leave it at a sad story," Jack began. "I will now show you the dance that honors Shango."

Jack removed the drum strap from around his shoulder and neck.

"I have been teaching Philip a song. He will play, and I will dance."

Jack set the drum around Philip's torso and returned to the center of the circle near the bonfire.

"Shango," Jack continued, "is the god of thunder and lightning. The god of warriors. Are you ready!?"

The crowd around the fire clapped.

"Ah, you are not ready," Jack joked. "We must summon Shango to come with our song. Now! Are you ready!?"

The children around the fire shouted in affirmation.

"Ah," Jack said. "There we go. Philip?"

Jack gave Philip a queue to begin the drumming song.

Philip began to drum, and Jack began by taking small steps. "Now," he said loudly over the drumming. "In Yoruba, there would be many people here to help with this song, woman and men. I will do this for you first in English and then in Yoruba." Jack clapped two times towards John. "Are you ready?" he said to his son with a smile on his face.

John nodded, in a trance by his father's performance so far. Jack clapped his callous hands together again. He raised his hand above his head and bent his arm at the elbow to create an "L" shape. He shook his hand as if holding something in his fist that would create a sound if shaken. He walked in dramatic steps, his whole body wavering up and down as if he is walking on the waves. He does this while walking around in a circle. When he finishes his circle, Jack does a two-step in place and then swings in a circle on one foot like a ballerina. Jack then repeats the dance in the circle. After the second two step in place, and the circles like a ballerina, Jack moves his shoulders up and down while two stepping and turning in a circle. He then widens his poster as if riding an invisible horse. He jumps one foot to the other as if urging the invisible horse forward and dances with his shoulders again. He repeats this three or four times. John gets a knack for it and follows his father's shoulder dance. Jack makes a dramatic finish, and the crowd around the fire roars in applause.

John stood up excitedly. "That looks like how we dance now!" he yelled.

"Yes!" Jack agreed, happy that the connection had been made. "I was very happy to see that when I came here, that there was so much of home that was not forgotten!" Jack rushed over to John in joy. "Come everyone," Jack said to the others around the fire. "Dance with me. Let us celebrate that you had not forgotten and know that back home, we had not forgotten you!" Everyone stood up to dance.

CHAPTER 4
LEGACY

Virginia, 1839

Forty-year-old John bounced his new son in his arms while he stood by his wife's bed. They were in what looked like a tight attic that was a part of the cabin they had in the slave quarters. The attic-like space was large enough for them to sleep in, but John had to bend his head for the low ceiling when he was standing. A few years ago, his father Jack had passed on, joining the African ancestors he always talked about. John always smiled thinking about how Jack was back home now. John was now a grown man himself, and here he was standing next to his amazing wife, Ester, holding his eighth child. John thought she was just as beautiful as his mother, Fanny, who had also passed away a few years earlier.

Ester stared at the ceiling above her, exhausted and drenched in sweat from childbirth. She closed her eyes and took deep breaths as she took a moment to calm down from the efforts of giving birth.

"How do you know that's your baby?" John's oldest son, George, asked while leaning against the wall. George was already 20-years-old and convinced he was just as much the man of this house as John was.

"Hush up, George," John's seventeen-year-old daughter, Chloe, said with a dismissive wave.

"I'm just saying. You know how they talk on those fields. Some of *our* babies ain't *our* babies, and there's plenty of stories on those other fields. There's already seven of us, and we all ain't the same color," George said, raising his hands in surrender.

"It might be true," John's ten-year-old daughter Virginia said. "You're probably the son of a wolf or something."

"Hush up now," John said to George while still staring at his new son. "You done seen this baby come out your Mama. That makes him mines." John began to walk back to Ester at the head of the small bed. "Look at him," John said, holding their newborn son in his arms. "Ester..." he said, urging her while walking towards her bedside. "You did a good job. He has the grip of a hundred men. He's stronger than an ox." John motioned to pass the baby to Ester's breast. "Here, Ester," John urged her again.

With her breathing labored and hands hard with callous from a lifetime of work, Ester tore her eyes away from the ceiling of the old cabin and reached for her son. She gave John a smile before looking down at her new baby.

"What name you going to give him?" John asked her, following his tradition of honoring her labor by letting her name the child.

"Oyeloki!" Virginia said excitedly.

"Lord..." George began. "It's Oyewole. And Mr. or Miss. Preston ain't gonna let Mama give that baby no African name. That's why they renamed Oyewole, Jack. It's why I'm George, why you're Virginia, and why he," George said, pointing to the baby in Ester's arms, "will be named Preston or something White like that."

"Juda ain't no fully White name," Chloe said with a shrug, referring to their younger sixteen-year-old sibling.

"No, but it sounds an awful lot like that disciple that double-crossed Jesus. So, there's that."

"You got me there," Chloe shrugged again, accepting her defeat. She turned her attention back to her mother. "Just don't name that baby Preston."

"Thomas," Ester said, interrupting the conversation. "His name is Thomas."

"That's perfect," John said, sitting next to his wife. He placed his arms around them both.

"I'll take it," George said, pushing himself off the wall and walking towards the small and narrow steps down to the small cabin's main room. "Thomas is easy to remember. So that makes me, Chloe, Juda, Ellen, Virginia, Rebecca, Oscar, and Thomas there[1]." George wasn't angry about a new baby or even frustrated about the stress of having another mouth to feed and another little brother to watch over. He just felt like the excitement of a new sibling had worn off after baby number five or so. He walked over to his mother and kissed her on the forehead. He was thankful that she had lived through another childbirth. "I'll see you later, Mama," he said as he walked down the narrow stairs, leaving the attic space before going out of the cabin and closing the door behind him.

Ester was a nurse, and after managing her delivery on her own, she was exhausted. She stared down at the baby, who just as intently stared back up at her. The baby smiled at Ester and squeezed her finger. She thought about how this baby in her arms had just been born and did not know that he was enslaved. He was just an innocent babe, looking at the world new. Then again, Ester thought to herself, it's probably better that the enslaved don't remember when they learned that they were enslaved; as far as they knew, they just always were.

"He's just as beautiful as you are," John whispered as he sat next to Ester on the small bed. "Although I do believe his strength will come from me," John proclaimed with a smile.

The silence of the moment and the still of the occasion was rattled by a bang on the thin cabin door. A voice that seemed to yell and whisper all at once came from the other side.

"John! John, can I come in?" the voice said.

"I'll get it!" Virginia said from the corner of the room. She rushed down the narrow stairs to the front door. She always walked with a straight back and a tall, strong posture, like a woman beyond her years. Chloe and John followed her. "Who is it?" she asked.

"It's me," whispered the voice on the other side. Virginia opened the door to find Joshua, another enslaved of the plantation. "Mr. Preston's on his way," he warned them, looking as eager to leave the cabin as he was to get into it. "He knows the baby's been born." Joshua looked behind himself. He was obviously anxious. Realizing the silence coming from the cabin despite his announcement, Joshua turned back towards Virginia.

"Mr. Preston's on his way," he announced again. "He knows the baby's been born."

Virginia looked back at her father with a bit of apprehension. John slowly moved to the door.

"Thank you, Joshua," John smiled wearily. "We'll be sure to let him in."

Joshua nodded in agreement, turned around, and disappeared into the night. John closed the door and glanced back at Chloe. Unclear if his words were for him or his children, he said, "Don't worry about it. Don't worry."

Up in the attic space, Ester tightened her grip on the newborn, Thomas. The cabin grew quiet, and everyone waited.

———

Outside of the cabin, thirty-year-old Robert Preston was approaching. It was dark, and he was walking down the dirt path towards the cabin as if it hurt to walk, and a lantern raised in his hand so that he could see ahead of him. Robert was all grown up for the young baby that was always on Fanny's hips when John and Ballard were younger and circling around Fanny's legs. Fanny was very right when she said that Robert would grow up to be trouble. She hadn't known just how accurate she would be. While Ballard was fully trained in the workings of the plantation and the business of maintaining it, Robert spent his time terrorizing the enslaved regardless of Ballard's direction or wishes.

Ballard was now a lawyer and a legislator in the Virginia Senate, and he was convinced that he could get Virginia to follow the lead of the northern states and abolish slavery. He thought that there had to be a way to emancipate the slaves while ensuring the economy of the south, and he was determined to find that way. His first fight was convincing the other legislators that the constitutional right of property did not include the slaves. Ballard's argument was that since the forefathers were slave owners, if they meant for slaves to be property, they would have said so, but that they did not intend it that way because the forefathers do in fact mention slaves separately throughout the constitution and the law. If slaves were considered property, they would have used the word property throughout the constitution and the laws when referring to the slaves.[2] Besides, he was a Preston. He would know, his grandfather was part of the revolution and was even friends with George Washington himself[3]!

Robert, on the other hand, was limited to the shadow of his brother Ballard and all his rights and glory for being the firstborn. Robert had no status over Ballard, but he did have status over the enslaved, and he was sure to remind them of that every day.

"Ester!" Robert screamed, his voice booming through the night, more wanting to be heard than one of authority. "Ester!" he screamed again. "I hear that baby is here! My Lord, let me see!"

"I am sure our Lord can hear you personally and directly with his own ears as loud as you are," Ballard said, his voice reaching Robert before his presence does.

Not quite surprised that Ballard is there, Robert looked over to the shadow approaching from the dirt path. "Your esteemed presence is not needed here, brother. I assure you," Robert said.

"I beg to differ," Ballard said with a smile. He moved to remove a handkerchief from his pocket. "I thought that you might come here to see about your," he paused in thought for the right words. "Ever-growing assets?" he continued.

"Assets?" Robert said. "I am doing nothing but showing care for what is my property."

"Your property?" Ballard replied. "Father's promise to give something to you does not mean that that something was his to give."

"Are you still upset that your attempts to emancipate the slaves keep failing at congress, Ballard?" Robert says, attempting to strike a blow at Ballard. He waited for Ballard to react before the expression on his face softens with pity. "Jack and Fanny are gone. They aren't getting their trip back home to Africa," he said to his brother, pleading to his wishful childhood. "Besides, that baby in there is mines, like the law says."

Ballard wiped his nose with his handkerchief. "I am always amazed," he began, "when the God-given rights of some are dampened and deemed unnecessary just to uphold the man-made rights of others." Ballard walked intently towards Robert. "Slaves are property under statute, and they will remain property until that statute is repealed," Ballard continued. "But enslaved men and women were born with the rights of human beings, and the state WILL restore those rights."

Robert turned back towards the cabin. "You have a great speech, Ballard. But where is the drafted law? Where's the action?" Robert turned back to Ballard, ready to challenge him on his holier than thou attitude. "Free your slaves, Ballard. Or at least, have father free the Fractions. Free Jack and Fanny's children. Why haven't you done that? You can do that without a change to the law."

Ballard didn't answer.

"You haven't explained yourself to anyone, Ballard," Robert continued. "At least my position is clear. No slave will be freed until you can assure the economy of the state and the safety of all the citizens of Virginia."

Ballard rolled his eyes at Robert's use of the excuse that the enslaved could not be freed until the citizens felt safe. "I'll tell you the same as I told the senate," Ballard said to Robert. "If the slaves wanted to kill you, they would have done it already. You're better than the regurgitation of these excuses from the paper."

Robert did not turn back to Ballard but continued to stare at the cabin.

"I am sure you know father's decision to give you a handful of slaves was nothing but an attempt to keep you busy," Ballard said to Robert, feeling a little sorry for his brother's limits, misgives, and failings.

Robert paused, staring toward the cabin, seemingly deep in thought.

"You have your silver spoon and golden chariot, Ballard. You have your halo and your legacy. Let me have what is mine".

"And what *IS* yours, Robert?" Ballard asked, expressing "is" with vigor.

Robert looked at his brother with annoyance. While he may not be well known for his deep thoughts and wise choices, he hardly was the idiot that his older brother thought him to be.

"Master Ballard!" Ballard and Robert turn their attention to an enslaved man approaching from the darkness. "Excuse me, Master Ballard. I'm sorry," the man stated.

"Quite alright. What is it?" Ballard responded with distinguished poise.

"Your father, Master James, is calling on you. Two men just arrived from the congress."

"Ah!" Ballard acknowledged. "Yes, I will be right there."

In a hurry to leave the tension, the man rushed away. Ballard turned his attention back to Robert.

"Duty calls," he says with fake disdain.

"Yes," Robert acknowledged. "Duty," he said, trying not to show his relief.

"Well, I'll leave you to it then," Ballard said as he turned away. "You to your…'things'."

―――

Robert watched Ballard disappear into the night before he turned back towards the cabin. He stood for a long moment, holding up his lantern, staring at the house. He took a step forward before noticing John watching him from inside the cabin, out of the side window. John was staring at Robert, void of any expression. Robert only stumbled slightly as he moved forward, holding on to John's gaze. He caught himself before knocking on the cabin door. He didn't need to knock, he thought to himself, because this cabin and these Negroes were his. As far as Robert was concerned, he had a right to all of it. Robert opened the door, ducked his head to avoid the low beam, and walked into the room. Virginia took three steps back before proceeding to hold her ground. The cabin remained silent for a moment while Chloe, Virginia, and John all stared at Robert. Ester had come down from the attic space and was sitting in a chair in the corner. She was holding the baby Thomas.

"Evening, Mr. Preston," John said, breaking the silence.

"John," Robert said, acknowledging the greeting. "Chloe, Virginia," he said to the two sisters.

Robert took two steps deeper into the cabin. The cabin was not that large, and two steps took him halfway to the other side of the room. Ester clutched the baby Thomas closer to her chest.

"Mr. Preston," she began to say. "The baby's alive and well. We'll get him nice and strong, so he's ready to work for you soon."

"Name?" Robert said, showing no disdain or kindness.

"We call him Thomas," Ester answered.

Robert rubbed his chin. "Ah," he said, smiling in approval. "Good name. Good name." Robert looked around the cabin and noticed a young five-year-old boy hiding behind Chloe. He recognized him as the baby he had gotten from John and Ester before this one. "How's that one coming along?" Robert asked, nodding to the little boy.

"Oscar's coming along nice," Ester began to explain. "He'll be working in no time. Sure be ready to work the plantations by spring."

Robert nodded in approval. "Good. Good girl, Ester. You always do good."

John stared at Robert with cold eyes. He hated the way Robert talked about his children like they were cattle, pigs, and sheep. He hated the way Robert talked to his wife like a good dog. He hated that Robert seemed to have forgotten that it was *his* mother Fanny that cared for him and took care of *him*. Ester could feel the rage from her husband. She lightly touched his arm. When he looked down at her, she smiled at him.

"Mighty kind of you to come see the baby, Mr. Preston," John said, still looking into Ester's eyes. "I'm sure proud of my boy already."

Robert hesitated as he worked through multiply warring emotions and thoughts showing hints of psychological imbalance. He seemed to be triggered by John calling the baby *his*. "Well!" he exclaimed in unexpected joy. Virginia jumped, spilling a bit of water in a cup that she was drinking from. "Shall we celebrate!? Chloe, find me something to toast for here Thomas!"

Chloe looked around the bleak cabin, not sure what Mister thought that they had to give him. She looked over at Virginia in question and mouthed, *What am I supposed to give him?* Virginia shrugged her shoulders as if to say *I don't know* and proceeded to hold up the cup she was drinking from, offering to maybe give him some water. Chloe moved to fill an old tin cup with water. She looked back at Virginia and gestured, *Anything else?* Virginia placed her chin in her hands as if to think. She raised her finger with an idea. She pointed to the bread wrapped in the cloth in the basket. Chloe made an exaggerated sad face. She *really* wanted to eat that bread. Virginia shrugged her shoulders again as if to say, *I don't know then.* She looked around the cabin once more. Her face lit up again in realization. She lifted her finger and pointed to the old beat up chamber pot that they used to release themselves. Chloe burst out in laughter. Robert looked in Chloe's direction, but Chloe quickly looked down to fill the tin cup with water.

"Here you go, Mr. Preston. I'm afraid all we got is water," Chloe said, handing the tin cup to Robert.

Robert looked down at the cup, disappointed. "No wine? No beer? No tea or cookies? Your mammy here makes the best cookies this side of the Appalachia."

"I'm sorry, sir," Chloe said, looking down. "I'm afraid Mamas been busy with having that baby. She ain't had no time for cookies." Still sitting outside of Robert's view, Virginiamade an exaggerated face as if to say that what he had said was really stupid.

Robert turned back to Ester. "No bread either?" he asked. Ester shook her head no, while five-year-old Oscar, not ignorant to the conversation at hand, stuffed a piece of bread into his mouth.

Robert let out a boisterous laugh. "I suppose you're right. Well. Water will have to do then." Robert stood up from the chair he was seated in, raised his tin cup into the air, and said, "To Thomas. May he live a long and healthy life. May he be strong and work for the lush condition of our dear plantation." He looked at John and Ester, waiting for them to agree. They did not. "Here here!!" he proclaimed to himself and proceeded to sit down in the chair. He seemed intent to extend his visit to the cabin. Everyone else remained silent. John watched Robert wearily. Robert was a bit unpredictable in his moods. Happy one minute, a tyrant the next. Right now, he seemed pleased.

"By the way," Robert said, smiling down at his reflection in the water inside the tin cup. "I'm selling George over to Whitethorn."

CHAPTER 5

RAMBUNCTIOUS

Virginia, 1861

Eighteen-year-old Othello pushed a plow through the soil, tilling land on the plantation of a man named Thomas Wilson[1]. Othello was John's eleventh child. After the baby Thomas, John had three more sons, Granville, Wilson, and his youngest son Othello. In fact, John and Ester were grandparents now that Virginia had her first child, Della[2].

Mister, that's what they had started calling Robert Preston, had rented him to Mr. Wilson many times before, but Othello never complained because he had a reason to want to be at Mr. Wilson's plantation. Othello burst forward, running to plow the land that spanned before him. He quickly moved down the lane before he stopped, took his hat off his head, and turn around, laying one arm on the plow's handle. He bit his bottom lip and watched the woman walking slowly behind him, spilling seeds into the ground where he just plowed. She was a petite woman with her soft hair wrapped in a piece of cloth. She walked along the lane that he had just plowed in a rhythm that made her skirt sway from side to side like a dance.

"When you plow it too fast like that, these lanes really ain't deep enough," she said, smiling but not looking up at Othello.

Her name was Mary, and the budding romance between them was unmistakable. Mary was the reason that Othello never minded being rented to Mr. Wilson. When he worked here, he was able to spend a lot of time with Mary.

"I do that so I can turn around and watch you spread the seed in," Othello said, placing his chin on his arm that rested on the plow handle.

Mary looked up and cocked her head to the side in question. "You just asking for trouble," she said with a smile while looking over at the overseer who was in charge of watching them and ensuring they worked. Like most overseers, the man was impatient and would not hesitate to be violent. Right now, he was walking the field some feet away, too far to hear the conversation, but close enough to notice that Othello had stopped plowing if he looked their direction.

Othello turned around and looked at the man, and then he looked back at Mary. "It's worth it to watch you. You sure looking sweet today, Mary."

Mary stopped spreading seeds and placed her hand on her hip, and sighed. "That's cause I sure am sweet on you today, Othello," she said, smiling confidently before going back to spreading seeds.

Othello smiled. "Just today, Ms. Mary?" he teased her.

Mary continued to spread the seeds until she was close enough to Othello to be toe-to-toe. She looked up at him. "Every day," she said when she was close.

Othello slapped his hat against his leg in a gesture of happiness, turned around, and started pushing the plow again. Mary dug her hand in the apron she was wearing, pulled out more seeds, and continued to follow behind Othello's plow.

"Mary," Othello said, loud enough for Mary to hear him. "We

should get married," he said, saying each word between his grunts as he pushed the plow through the land.

Mary kept spreading the seeds, unaffected by Othello's announcement.

"You keep saying that, Othello. Ain't no marrying for the Negroes," she said.

"Ain't no legal marrying, but we can still get married. We jump the broom like our mommas and daddies," Othello said.

"My daddy ain't jump no broom with my momma, but that don't mean he ain't love her. She was his all the same," Mary said.

"Preacher man Aquilla," Othello said, referring to Mary's father, "had some type of marriage in front of God with your Mama. I'm sure ain't no preacher man going to try to live in sin. Ain't that what they call it? Living in sin?" Othello asked her.

Mary kept spreading seeds. "'Suppose you right," Mary agreed. "But how we gonna get married with you over there at Smithfield?" Mary asked.

"Mr. Ballard would let me come over to jump the broom with you," Othello said, stopping his plow again as he reached the end of the lane.

He tipped up the plow to place it on its pointed face, which allowed him to turn the plow and change its position to the next lane to plow in the opposite direction.

"Mr. Wilson won't allow it," she said, taking a peek over to the overseer again.

"He ain't gotta join in," Othello said, grunting again as he started the momentum of the plow forward. He found that getting the plow going was hard, but it was all about keeping it going once he did. The speed helped to get the plow to break through the weeds instead of getting trapped on them.

"You get your Sunday nights right?" Othello asked Mary. "Even Mr. Wilson give you some time on the Lord's day."

Mary nodded in agreement. "I get some of the evening on Sunday."

"Alright then. I can get Mr. Ballard to give me a pass to come to you a few Sundays from now," Othello said.

"I thought you said Mr. Ballard wasn't your master. That Mr. Mister is," Mary asked him.

"Just Mister," he said, correcting her. "His name ain't Mister, we just call him Mister. My brother said we ain't got no master, so we ain't calling no man no Master nothing. Mister's real name is Robert, but we can't call him that either. We can't call him Mr. Preston because that's what people called his daddy, so we just call him Mister. But, yes, Mister is the Master, but Mister Ballard is really in charge. If I get him to give me a pass..."

Mary stopped spreading seeds and stood still. Othello kept plowing forward, still talking to himself, until his voice faded so that Mary couldn't hear him anymore. In the middle of his conversation, he looked back to talk directly to Mary and realized that she was no longer walking behind him. He left the plow and walked back to her.

"You ok?" he asked.

Mary looked at Othello and studied his face.

"What ya'll doing over there!" the overseer yelled over to them.

"You really want to marry me that much?" she asked him in a bit of disbelief.

Othello smiled. "Nothing going," he yelled back, answering the overseer. "Just checkin' on Mary. Makin' sure she got what she need," Othello continued explaining to the overseer while smiling at Mary before turning around and going back to the plow. "Yeah,

Mary," he said, turning back to look at her over his shoulder. "You ain't get how much I love you yet?"

Mary blushed.

"I'll come on a Sunday, and your Pa can hitch us," Othello said. "Ok?" he asked again. Mary didn't respond. "Mary?" Othello said, now a bit unsure of whether Mary even wanted to marry him.

"Ok," Mary said in a small whisper. Then she smiled a big smile. "Ok," she said again.

———

A few days later, Othello stood outside of the blacksmith cabin on the Solitude plantation holding the reins of a horse. His older brother Thomas, now twenty-three years old, stood inside the cabin structure, banging away at a horseshoe. Othello was back at Robert's plantation working with his older brother Thomas. The plantation sat on what used to be a portion of the Smithfield plantation, but Mr. Preston had broken it off to give it to Robert as part of his estate[3].

Thomas' skin glistened with sweat as he held the horseshoe down with a clamp. With another swing of the hammer, Thomas blinked hard as his eyelids fought to get rid of a piece of dust that flew from the horseshoe into his eye. He turned the hand holding the hammer around and rubbed his eye with the back of the hand. Othello peeped around the horse's neck when the pounding sound of the hammer stopped.

"You done?" he asked his brother.

"Just about," Thomas said, blinking past his watering eye.

"You crying?" Othello asked.

Thomas smirked. "Nah. Why would I be crying?"

"I don't know," Othello said, shrugging. "Probably cause you still ain't fix that shoe, and I'm certain I see the second coming of Jesus off there in the distance it been so long."

"It's almost done. Just hold your horses," Thomas said.

Othello looked down at the horse, which turned around and looked at Othello as if acknowledging the bad joke. After a few more hits with the hammer, Thomas put down the clamp and carried the horseshoe, a few nails, and the hammer over to the horse.

"Can you hold the reign and hold his leg?" he asked Othello, placing the hammer on the back of the horse so that he could free his hand to adjust the horseshoe he was holding into a better position to put it on the horse. "Pick it up from the other side, so the hammer don't..."

Before Thomas could finish his sentence, Othello bent over to grab the horses' leg, and the hammer slid off, aiming right for the back of Othello's head. Thomas caught it in midair before it made contact. His quick reaction made Othello look up, and Thomas made a loud exhale out of his nose. The horse turned to the side again to look at Thomas as if to say that he was pretty sure that only *he* made sounds like that.

"I was going to say grab it from the other side so the hammer don't slide off but..."

"Thomas! Come here, boy! I have news! I have news!" Thomas and Othello's work was interrupted by the screams of now fifty-three-year-old Robert in the distance. Hearing Robert's booming voice, Thomas rolled his eyes and continued to put the horseshoe on the horse.

"Here, boy!" Robert called again.

"You'd better go," Othello said.

When not on the Wilson plantation, Othello always stayed close to Thomas. He was always a figure by his side. Thomas smiled at his little brother. He was fairly sure Othello stuck around for the entertainment, and here comes a new show.

"If you don't go, he'll just get angry, and you're hardly back to normal as is. You still can't even lift the ax all the way when you choppin' after he let Waller go at you and beat you down the way he did," Othello said, referring to Mister having Mr. Ballard's son Waller beat him a few weeks ago.

Thomas put down his hammer and slapped Othello on the back.

"Ah, don't worry about me. It looks worse than what it is. I just let that old man think I'm hurt, so he feels better about himself. As long as he thinks he's doing something, it's easier for us," Thomas said, trying to reassure Othello.

"Easier for us," Othello murmured, putting down the horse's leg. "But not easier for you."

Ester approached from around the structure holding Virginia's daughter Della on her hip. "Go 'on. Don't leave Mister waiting for too long," she said intervening before there was an issue. She knew her son and knew that he often did things that brought Mister's anger down on him. She had been nearby working with the flax when she heard Mister's voice calling for Thomas. As usual, she jumped up to come over and make sure that Thomas made his way over to Mister to answer him.

Thomas walked over to his mother and kissed her on the cheek. "Mama," he said in greeting as he walked past her towards the sound of Mister's yelling. As soon as Mister was in his view, Thomas saw that Waller was with him. Waller met Thomas' eyes and smiled. Thomas twisted his mouth and mumbled under his breath until he was interrupted by Robert yelling louder. Having to deal with just Mister was one thing; having to deal with Waller, who was learning to be just as bad as his uncle, and was doing whatever he could do to prove it, was not something that Thomas was counting on when he began his way over to Mister.

"Thomas! Boy, if I have to..." Robert's threat is interrupted by the appearance of Thomas in his line of view.

"Ha! There. Boy! I got news!" Robert said, slapping Thomas on the back. Thomas flinched.

Robert paused and looked at Thomas as if in regret, but then his face sobered from the hold of empathy, and he smiled.

"Aw, you ain't heal yet, boy! Waller ain't get you that bad. Your Mama the best dang nurse round here! She ain't heal that yet?"

Waller took that moment as an opportunity to tap the switch that he held in his hand against his cheek. He was taunting Thomas with his recent experience, and with the possibility of more damage. Robert removed his hand from Thomas' back.

"That last beating wasn't that bad. Waller's young, he don't have the strength in his hands like I use to have in mine," Robert said before pausing, waiting for a reaction from Thomas, as if he expected Thomas to agree. A flash of several emotions crossed Robert's face: concern, regret, and then content. "We keep going like this boy, I'll be sure to beat your way into our Lord's heaven; spare the rods spoil the child. God would be pleased. He would be pleased!"

Thomas wiped his mouth with his hand as if removing words before they escape. "You need me, sir?" Thomas asked in brief annoyance. Robert paused as if considering Thomas' tone and whether it was inappropriate.

"Yes. News. The news! I've just been named Colonel of the army of Virginia, boy! The 28th Virginia Infantry Regiment. I will lead those boys. You hear about that war with the Yankees[4]?" Robert asked.

"Yes," Thomas said, cocking his head to one side. "The one that is trying to free us?" his eyebrow raised.

Robert paused. "It's not just about the Negros, Thomas. It's about freedom…." Robert realized what he has said. "Freedom for States. States should be free to run themselves?"

Thomas raised his head to the sky. "Yes," he said, as if trying to maintain patience. "Freedom." Thomas' face changed as he noticed the irony. "Well, thank you, sir," Thomas began with sarcastic joy, "for telling me the news! I am sure thankful that I should know that you are fighting for your freedom, but not mines."

"Your freedom!? Freedom from what, boy! You're mines. I take good care of you. I don't even treat you like the niggers. I let you leave Solitude and Smithfield and go work the railroad and other plantations. We let your daddy go run errands for us for days at a time. Your daddy, the one that went over to the river to pick up my grand-daddy's headstone for his grave; took him two days to do it![5] And you do good boy. You do real good! Everybody talks about you on that railroad. People got to pay good money to get you. You ain't no nigger like the rest of them, boy. You ain't like the rest of them."

Thomas stared back at Mister. He was unsure what to say and if there was even anything that could be said to him to get him to understand.

"Well, I'm glad to hear, sir," Thomas continued. "I hope you don't die."

"No. You wouldn't want your *master* to die, would you?" Ballard, now fifty-seven years old, said, appearing as if from nowhere. His voice seemed to take an immediate effect on Robert's joy, extinguishing it with gusto. Waller crossed his arms in annoyance. He disagreed with his father on how to deal with the slaves. Waller had no intention of spending his life dealing with backhanded comments about loving the slaves as his father had been.

"No, sir," Thomas said, immediately sobering past his sarcasm.

"Congratulations, Robert," Ballard continued, looking at his brother. "I hear you will be serving the great state of Virginia. What an opportunity to have an accomplishment!" Ballard said, genuinely happy for his brother, his words ending with a pointed look at Thomas. Thomas raised one eyebrow.

"Something funny, boy?" Robert said to Thomas, indicating his patience was not as kind as it was before Ballard's arrival.

"No, sir," Thomas replied, not appearing the slightest intimidated. It was clear that he was familiar with Robert's shift in behavior when others were around and his erratic mood swings. Ballard gazed at Thomas for so long that awkwardness began to unsettle Robert, who was about to speak up when Ballard looked over to his son Waller and smiled.

"Hey, my boy!" he said, walking forward to greet his son.

"Uncle's going to fight for Virginia, and so am I," Waller declared as a greeting.

Ballard continued to smile at his son while bracing both of Waller's arms in an embrace.

"Virginia would be lucky to have you, son! You make me proud," he said tapping Waller on both his arms before turning his attention back to Robert. Waller shook his head in disappointment. He thought the old man was so oblivious. Everybody thought his father was so smart because he was a lawyer and held those seats in the Virginia Congress, but Waller thought his father wasn't very good about seeing what was right in front of him.

Ballard looked back to Thomas. "Have you heard?" he began before turning his attention back to his brother. "The Negros of the south have been running to the Union? They run north *and* west. They join the Union, and they become freemen." Ballard paused again. "Have you heard?" he said, pointedly turning back to Thomas as if trying to speak to another cause. Robert looked between Thomas and Ballard, clearly unsure and uncomfortable in the subject.

"Yes, I've heard," Robert said. "I am a Colonel, aren't I? But my Negros wouldn't run. Thomas wouldn't run. I take good care of my niggers."

"I don't know," Ballard said, turning his attention back towards Robert. "I don't know how much a man can enjoy slavery."

"Niggers ain't men, though," Robert said as a matter of fact.

Ballard pondered for a moment.

"Would you, Thomas?" Ballard asked.

"Would I, sir?" Thomas asked, pretending that he did not know what Mr. Ballard was asking him.

Robert quickly stepped forward towards Thomas and punched him in the face. "You'll show me respect, you little runt!! Would... you....run!?" he screamed in Thomas' face.

Thomas rubbed his face, robbing Robert of any real reaction to his assault. Unhappy with Thomas' nonchalance towards his uncle's efforts, Waller jumped forward with his switch and swung it at Thomas. Thomas caught Waller's arm and ripped the switch from his hand.

"You ain't never do nothin' to me that I ain't let you do," Thomas whispered to Waller in a deep voice as he threw Waller's switch to the ground.

"Pa! You see that, Pa!?" Waller said, grabbing his wrist in pain, looking at his father, and pointing to Thomas. "That nigger assaulted me!"

Ballard stood in shock. "Were you going to hit him, Waller? I told you we don't abuse the slaves here on Smithfield. I made our cousin leave because he raped one of our girls," Ballard said to his son as if seeing him for the first time.

"You gonna make me leave, Pa?" Waller said with a sneer.

"No," Ballard answered, shaking his head. "But I don't understand what is going on? The Fractions are a good family. They do
the work we tell 'em. They don't give us any trouble at all."

Thomas looked at the ground and gave the same sneering look as
Waller to no one in particular. He knew he had already pushed his
limits, so he did what he often promised his mother that he would
do- stay calm, pull back, and swallow his pride. "That's the only
way you can stay safe," his mother would often plead with him.
He just didn't like when people said things like that, making him
sound like a happy slave who just lived to do his Master's bidding.

Ballard stretched out his hands in presentation. "I don't understand what's going on?" he said, although he fully understood
what was happening. What Ballard really wanted to know
was *why*.

Robert, his mood changed again, waved his hand at Ballard and
Waller in dismissal. "Forget all that. Waller's right, niggers got to
know his place," he said dismissively. "Now I want to know if
Thomas has thought about leaving," Robert said, walking closer
to Thomas.

"Well, I ain't thought about it until just now, sir," Thomas said to
Robert before looking over to Ballard.

"You still *ain't* thinking about it," Robert said, moving quickly
forward toward Thomas, intent on attacking him.

"If you cannot be a man of moral," Ballard demanded, clearly
speaking about Robert's behavior, "at least be a gentleman of
decency!"

Robert stopped in his tracks and looked over at his brother. He
puckered his lips as if tasting something sour and nodded frantically, as if trying to compose himself. "It's just," he began to say,
clearly trying to gain control. "Right now, I need him to go back
and work the railroad. We need that railroad running for the war.
The Union's been using the railroad to stay ahead of us all the

time. They've got a whole system in Tennessee. I've got Thomas here, and he's the best I have at it. You damage him, you damage the war[6]."

"I'm afraid you are the one attacking him to do harm. I simply share information that one would find interesting," Ballard said. "A human being has options," he said with finality towards Thomas.

Thomas listened with intent and hearing loud and clear the message left for him. There was freedom in Tennessee. He didn't need to know anything else.

———

"Thomas! Thomas!" Othello moved quickly behind Thomas, who appeared to be moving frantically towards the old cabin. "Thomas, wait up!" Othello pleaded. He waved for their brothers Granville and Wilson to follow. "What did Mister say? What did he say?"

"It's not what Mister said," Thomas answered Othello once he was able to match his stride. "It's what Mr. Ballard said."

"What did Mr. Ballard say?" Othello asked, grabbing Thomas's arm to make him stop walking.

"He pointed me to where we can go to leave this place," Thomas replied.

"What?" said Othello.

Thomas looks around, paranoid about being overheard.

"Come on. We're going out to the field. I want to talk to Mama and Pa about it. I think we can all go together," he said, starting to walk again.

"Go where?" Othello asked, following Thomas, more afraid than confused.

"Hold on," Thomas said, putting up his hand to Granville and Wilson. "Stay here and keep working. We can't all go."

Thomas continued on, not waiting for Granville and Wilson to agree or disagree. He moved quickly down the dirt path and through the trees. Othello was following close behind. They passed a few of the enslaved packing away material, and another leading horses. They began to walk past the Preston family cemetery when Thomas stopped and looked around. The view from the hilltop cemetery gave Thomas an idea.

"Which way do you think is north and west?" he asked Othello. "I'm thinking that way," he said, simultaneously pointing in one direction, while Othello answered, pointing the opposite direction.

"And there's my first problem. Don't worry, I'll figure it out," Thomas said.

Before the brothers reached the fields, they saw John and Ester moving past the slave quarters. With Della tied to her back, Ester looked up at the brothers rushing towards them and raised an eyebrow.

"Why do I know something is wrong?" Ester asked, wiping her hands with her apron.

Othello followed closely behind Thomas as if to proclaim support before even knowing the plan. Ester pointed them to their old cabin, indicating that they should go inside. The brothers and John follow her directive to go there to talk. When they walk in, their feet track in dirt.

"Come on, Thomas, I just cleaned these floors!" Virginia gasps with impatience as they entered. "Sorry, Ginny, but," Thomas started to explain. He hesitated to get his thoughts together and to allow his mouth to catch up with his thoughts.

"Wait a minute, Thomas," Ester said, placing her hand in the air to indicate *stop*. "What did Mister do this time?" she asked.

"Mister?" Thomas asked, confused, before he realizing the last time his mother saw him, Mister had called to him. Thomas waved his hand dismissively. "Nothing, Mister don't want nothing. But Mr. Ballard. Man! Mr. Ballard. He told me where we can leave for. All we have to do is go…"

Upon hearing the word "go," Virginia stood up as if angry. Thomas looked over to her and her sudden motion. He stopped talking, and everyone followed his gaze and looked at Virginia, waiting for her to say something. Realizing that she had the full room's attention, she looked at Ester, pleading for her to say something sensible. Ester wiped her hand on her apron but didn't say a word. Virginia crossed her arms on top of her chest and waited for the rest of Thomas' speech. Thomas remained quiet, staring at the old floor of the cabin in contemplation.

"Go where?" Ester asked, breaking the silence of the room.

Thomas looked at Othello with an expression that showed that now he was a little unsure of how the family would react because of Virginia's reaction. Just a few seconds ago, he was sure that the whole family would be happy about the possibility of leaving.

"When," Thomas began, the excitement slowly returning to his heart. "When I was with Mister, Mr. Ballard came. He said that Negros are running north and west."

Ester interrupted Thomas. "We know that, Thomas," Ester said, "We've been running north for years now."

"Yes," Thomas continued. "But now, Negros are running north *and* west, and the Union is letting them fight in the war."

"Fight in the war?" Othello asked. "You mean we can kill us some slave masters?"

"I guess. But that's not the point," Thomas smirked at Othello. "We go and fight. We're free when we fight, and when the Union wins, everybody's free. Everyone. EVERY…ONE!"

"You going?" Othello asked Thomas.

"I want to go. I'm going to go," Thomas replied.

"When we going?" Othello asked.

Just then, Granville and Wilson walked into the cabin. Thomas looked over to watch them enter. He bit his bottom lip in frustration.

"I told ya'll to keep working," Thomas said.

Granville and Wilson looked at each other. "We want to know what's going on too," Wilson said.

"We'll fill ya'll in later. Somebody gotta be out there working though," Othello said.

"Tell us what's going on first," Wilson said, crossing his arms over his chest.

"They talkin' bout leaving," Virginia announced.

"It's going to take some planning," Thomas continued. "There's plenty more to find out. Mr. Ballard gave us some clues, but we have to find out the rest. Virginia can listen while she's working inside of Smithfield. I'll go work the railroad, like Mister said. And…"

"Wait," Ester interrupted him. "Mister sending you out again to work for others?"

"Yes, Ma'am," Thomas answered her. He wasn't half as bothered with the idea as Ester was.

"It ain't safe out there," Ester said, wiping her hands with her apron.

"I'll be ok, Mama," Thomas said. "I just…I work the railroad. I'll figure out from the work which way it's going, and from there, I figure out which way is north and west".

"We don't have to wait for no railroad work," Wilson said, rolling his eyes. "We can leave tomorrow. Remember Pa told us the sun rises in the east and sets in the west. We just got to pay attention tomorrow to where the sun rises, and then we know which way is the west. And we know the Yankees is north. We know which way that is. We go the other way from the sunrise." Wilson said. Granville nodded in agreement.

"It ain't just that, Wilson," Thomas said. "Look. When they build stuff, one of the things they do is find the safest land to use. You can't just go walking round without a pass. It ain't safe. If I work the rails, then I find out the best route; both the route that is away from them and the route that is safe out there in the woods."

"Man! We don't need no route," Wilson said again.

"Don't ya'll go doing nothing crazy," Ester said to Wilson. "Listen to your big brother. From that work Mister got him doing, he knows more about what's out there than you two."

Wilson didn't answer his mother. He left his intention unsaid and hanging in the air. Virginia just looked at Thomas, and he returned her stare. They stood there studying each other for a long time. Othello looked back and forth between the two of them, waiting for one of them to break the silence. He was really waiting for Virginia to tell him he was crazy and *ain't no way she was getting involved in this scheme.*

"Ok," Virginia said, surprising everyone. "I just have one question," she continued. "What about us? What do you think Mister will do to us once he knows you're gone? What will he do to aalllll of us?" she asked, waving her hand around in a circular motion indicating the entire family.

"I'm not worried about Mister. You shouldn't be either," Thomas replied.

"All of us don't have the grace of being *special* to Mister," Wilson said, delivering what was meant to be a low blow to Thomas. "Don't matter to me, though. I'm leaving too."

"ENOUGH!" John demanded, walking fully into the old cabin. Before now, no one seemed to have noticed that he stood next to the door of the small cabin space. Immediately the conversation was over. Ester looked around the room, taking stock of each of her children.

"All of my children. MY children," Ester demanded. "All my children are MINE!" she said again before she was interrupted by the cabin door opening. Chloe rushed in, another woman tailing behind her.

"Guess whose Master is here for a visit with Mister!?" Chloe said, bursting into the cabin. Her giant smile melted away when she noticed the mood in the room. She halted her stride, stopping herself from fully entering the room. Othello looked towards the door and saw Mary walking in with Chloe. He gave her a short wave and smiled.

"I'm sorry, Mama," Wilson began. "That's not what I meant. I'm just talking about how…"

"Enough," Ester said wearily, placing her hand in the air as if to say stop. "I'm old, Wilson. I'm old, and I'm tired. I'm old, and I'm tired, and Thomas is a man now."

"Mama," Wilson pleaded, losing all the energy he had to fight the advice of his brother.

"My daughters are beautiful women," Ester continued, waving to Virginia and Chloe. "My sons are men," she said, looking at Thomas, Othello, Granville, and Wilson. "And your lives are yours," she said, taking two steps over to Thomas and cupping his face in admiration and love. "Your Pa will take care of me. Mister can't do more to me than he already has".

"But it's not just you, Mama," Virginia explained, stepping towards Ester. "Mister will come for all of us," she paused, taking in her family in the cabin and looking at everyone. She paused as if thinking about it. "But I'll take the risk. I don't think Mister would give up Mama's cookies or my minding that house, even if he mad at Thomas." Virginia moved away from Ester towards Othello. "But you just going to leave Mary?" Virginia asked him, waving a hand in Mary's direction with a smile on her face.

Othello paused. His face and his mind now a blank slate.

"Only for a short while," Othello answered. "Besides, I'm going to marry her first. Ain't that right, Mary?"

Mary smiled. "Where you going?" she asked.

"We running north *and* west to where the Union is," Othello answered.

"Oh," Mary said. Her eyes wandered around the small room in thought. "I think you should go. You should go, and then you'll come back for me, right?"

"Yes, 'cause you'll be my wife. I gotta come back for my wife, right?" Othello answered with a smile.

"Is there anything I can do to help you?" Mary asked.

"Just stay quiet and unseen until I come back for you," Othello said. "That way, you can stay safe."

"Alright now! Come on out here! Mr. Preston has an announcement to make!" A voice screamed outside, booming through the cabin and interrupting the moment. Ester wiped her hands with her apron, a nervous tick she had developed over time. It showed more often by the mention of Mister. John noticed her anxiety and moved to hold her hand.

"Come on out!" the voice yelled again with a heavy bang on the thin cabin door.

Everyone in the cabin moved to exit the room. They were greeted by the face of the slave overseer, a setting sun, and the approach of a warm night. Thomas assessed the scene. He saw Robert sitting on a horse, surrounded by two other men, his brother-in-law and his nephew. All of the other enslaved on the plantation had already gathered. Mister had apparently saved their family for last. Mister and the others seemed quite pleased with themselves and their current performance. They were there to deliver a warning to anyone thinking of running away to the war[7].

"I have reason to believe," Robert began, appearing like a deranged Santa Claus, "that it may be in the best interest of us all, some more than others," he stated pointedly at Thomas, "to remind you that running away is NOT an option." He continued speaking now to everyone. "Should ANY of you merely attempt to run. No. No, wait, attempt is not the right word. Should ANY of your merely *think* to run, you and your family will suffer under the wrath of 'ol Theodore here," Robert said, pointing to the overseer. "And Ol' Theodore there is eager for some...exercise. Now, whether you think of running north, west, into the ocean, doesn't matter. I will find you. I will make a boat from the bones of your dead mammies and sail the rivers until I find you. Do I make myself clear!?"

All the enslaved look at each other and nod with murmurs of, "Yes, Sir."

"Good!" Robert said with a giant smile. He looked towards Thomas. "Very good," he said before he and the other men turned their horses around and left.

"This don't change nothing," John said to Thomas. This was the first comment that John had made on the subject of running.

"No. It don't change nothing," Thomas smiled and then laughed, drawing questionable looks from those around him. "He can't do nothing with me!" Thomas said again in silent triumph. "He KNOWS it."

"So we going? You sure?" Othello asked.

"Yeah," Thomas said in finality.

Othello turned to Mary. "You're gonna end your days as a free-woman. I promise you."

Thomas turned around to see Ester standing there smiling, part of her apron balled up in her hand.

"Ok," she said as if pep-talking herself. "Ok," she said again as she released her apron and clapped her hands together.

William "Ballard" Preston ((November 25, 1805 – November 16, 1862)[8]

Robert Taylor Preston (May 26, 1809 - June 20, 1880)[9]

Thomas Fraction would be 21, M (Male), B (Black) in this 1860 Slave Schedule for Robert T. Preston (line 18). Othello maybe the 18 year old, M (Male), B (Black) on line 21.[10]

CHAPTER 6

VIRGINIA

Virginia, 1862

Thirty-three-year-old Virginia leaned on a large wooden table at the lower level of the Smithfield house. Down in the lower level was a kitchen where the enslaved cooked for the Preston family[1]. A woman named Flora was preparing the supper to serve to the house. She was slicing meat and placing the slices onto a platter. Virginia eyed a piece of fat from the meat that was sitting on the table. She noticed how it glistened in the light, appearing wet due to a layer of warm, melted fat. She leaned forward and held one finger in the air over the meat fat.

"You plan on using this for something?" she asked Flora, pausing before placing her finger on the meat fat that she was reaching for.

"I might ask Master Preston if I can take it for some stew. 'Pending on what he says, I might do something with it. Why? You dry?" Flora asked, noticing Virginia's hand positioned with just one finger over the meat fat. Virginia nodded. "Go on then," Flora said, nodding her head towards the meat fat. "If you just looking for a little, you'd be fine, I could still use it."

Virginia gave Flora a small smile and slid her finger across the top of the meat fat. She lifted the finger that was now covered in the glistening melted fat and rubbed it across her full lips. She reveled in the moisture that it added there. She rubbed her lips together to spread the grease around. Virginia had always wondered what she'd look like in lipstick. Curiosity got the best of her once when she was younger and caring for Mr. Ballard's children. She was all but twelve or thirteen when she was charged with being a child-minder for the Preston family. She went from cleaning the house and emptying chamber pots to taking care of children before she had started her own monthly menstrual. So one day, when she was in the house, and Mr. Ballard and Ms. Lucy had gone out for a social call, she picked up the lipstick on Mrs. Lucy's vanity, rubbed some of the color on her finger, and spread it on her lips. She remembered being in shock at how it had transformed her mouth. Ms. Lucy and other women like her had such thin lips, and she had never seen color like this on lips like hers. She thought it was beautiful but had never done it again, even though she liked to remember that moment when she used the meat fat to help keep her lips from drying.

After she spread the meat fat on her lips, Virginia rubbed one hand on the table where Flora had removed the last of the meat to the platter, covering her hand in the melted fat residue that was there.

"You 'gon smell like meat all day," Flora warned her.

"No matter," Virginia said. "It's supper now. They won't notice I smell like the meat when they eatin' it. They going to think the smell is coming from their plates."

Flora nodded in agreement.

Virginia looked around. "Imma go up and make sure the place settings is right," she said, lifting herself off of the wooden table. "And I'll help Ms. Lucy get herself ready for dinner. You settled here, right?" she said to Flora, who nodded in agreement again.

Virginia made her way up the narrow steps of the slave entrance into the dining room. She walked into the dining room and circled the dining table, checking the placements for perfection. She checked the buffet to ensure that it was ready to receive the pastries and desserts for the meal's end. She made sure that the fireplace's dish warmer at the was there and already warmed and ready to receive any dish that was best served hot. Once she was satisfied that everything was in place, she walked towards the master bedroom that was connected to the dining room. She stopped at the doorway and waited for Mrs. Lucy to acknowledge her presence and ask her to enter.

Fifty-four-year-old Lucy Preston sat in a rocking chair in front of her fireplace. She rocked back and forth and stared at the fire as if in deep thought. It seemed to Virginia that lately, all Mrs. Lucy did was sit and think. Virginia laced her hands together and sat them in front of her as she stood waiting patiently to be acknowledged. Her mother was right. Even though people and several enslaved surrounded them, women of the house always seemed lonely. Lucy looked up at Virginia.

"You know, Ballard told me once that it was your grandfather that made this chair," she said, lightly tapping the armrest of the rocking chair with the palm of her hand.

Virginia nodded. "Yes, ma'am."

Lucy sighed. "He's a good man. Don't you think?" she asked, referring to her husband, Ballard.

Virginia nodded. "Yes, ma'am."

"He's good to you people," Lucy said, smiling up at Virginia.

"Yes, ma'am," Virginia agreed again.

"Have you come to prepare me for supper?" Lucy asked.

Virginia nodded. "Yes, ma'am."

"I suppose you should come on in then," Lucy said, waving Virginia forwarded.

Virginia entered the room and began to organize Lucy's space. She straightened the bed and began to organize the vanity.

"Mrs. Lucy. What color you thinking for supper tonight?" Virginia asked, referring to the lipstick that sat on the vanity. Based on the conversations that Virginia heard when the woman sat for tea, Mrs. Lucy was ahead of the trend, using lipstick from Paris when it was still considered a little scandalous to wear it here in the States. Virginia remembered Mrs. Lucy explaining that the key was to keep the colors soft so that it wasn't as noticeable, "Just enough to keep the other girls envious," Mrs. Lucy had chuckled while sipping her tea.

"A simple rose will do," Lucy said with a sigh.

Virginia searched through the multiple options of lip color until she came across three versions of pink. She hesitated for a second before remembering that whenever Mrs. Lucy talked about the color rose, she meant the lighter color, the one that almost matched the shade that her lips already were.

Just then, Lucy's son Waller walked into the front entrance of the house. From where the master bedroom was positioned, when someone entered through that front door, they could be seen from the master bedroom. Waller surveyed his surroundings and paused when he met Virginia's eyes. He turned to Virginia and placed his hands behind his back. He walked innocently into the master bedroom and bent over towards his mother to greet her with a kiss on her cheek.

"Mother," he said as he lifted himself to a standing position. He turned to face Virginia and stood there silently while looking her over. "You've slathered yourself with fat again," he said as a matter of fact. It wasn't a question. It was meant to be delivered in a way that Virginia could not mistake that he didn't like when she did it. "You smell like supper," he said, curling his nose in disgust. "Wipe it off."

Virginia sighed deeply and placed the case of rose lipstick that was in her hand back down on the vanity. She picked up her apron and proceeded to rub the meat fat off of her hands. Once she finished, she stretched out her hand to pick up the rose lip color again.

"Your lips," Waller reminded her. "Clean it off your face too," he demanded.

Virginia slowly pulled back her hand from picking up the lipstick, picked up her apron, and wiped at her lips to remove the meat fat.

"Why do you do that anyway?" Waller asked, the malice gone from his voice. In that moment, he reminded Virginia of the little boy that she had raised.

"Keeps the skin from drying, Mr. Waller," she answered him.

"Is that the Negro secret?" Lucy asked in wonder as she lifted her own hands to see the millions of tiny cracks in her own skin. "I've often wondered how my hands and my face look like a lifetime of labor like I've been the one that's slaved all my life. This whole time you've been covering yourselves in meat fat. Is that a savage tradition from Africa?" Lucy asked, genuinely in awe.

"I suppose so, Ma'am. I learned it from my Ma. Maybe she learned it from hers," Virginia answered Mrs. Lucy.

The room went quiet as no one said anything else. Waller looked around the room as if looking for something. Virginia knew she needed to get Mrs. Lucy ready for supper, but instead of proceeding on that task, she linked her hands together and rested them in front of her, waiting for further direction. She had raised Waller, so she knew him better than he knew himself. He was looking for a conflict, and any move she made, he was going to find a way to make it into something more than it was. So instead of continuing on to prepare Mrs. Lucy for supper, she stood there waiting for direction. There couldn't be a conflict if she did exactly what she was asked to do.

"I'd like to try it," Lucy announced. She seemed to be unaware of the awkward tension in the room.

"You'd like to try what, Mother?" Waller turned to ask her. She was still sitting in her rocking chair.

"The meat fat! I'd like to try it," Lucy said to Waller as if she didn't understand why he didn't understand what she was saying. "Virginia. Go get me some," Lucy demanded. Virginia's eyes went wide, but she proceeded to leave to go back down to the kitchen to get Mrs. Lucy some meat fat.

"Absolutely not!" Waller interrupted. "Virginia, stay," Virginia stopped walking. "Mother, I came in here to discuss business affairs with my father, and you want to talk about covering yourself in animal fat like a…" he was at a loss for words. He turned his attention back to Virginia as if she'd help him remember the words he was looking for. "Virginia can cover herself in animal fat because it's meaningful for her," he continued. "Science has proven that the Negro is a close cousin to the ape. Primitive things like that are in her nature."

Virginia raised one eyebrow. She tucked her lips into her mouth to keep herself from explaining to Waller the many times she had to stop him from eating his own feces as a child, but she thought it best not to start a *"who's really an ape"* conversation. She decided that doing that wouldn't help the situation.

"An ape!" Lucy declared, insulted. She struggled to stand from the rocking chair where she was sitting. "Would I have left an ape to care for my own child!?" she said, looking up at Waller, expecting an apology.

Waller rolled his eyes at his mother. "I don't mean that she *is* an ape mother. I mean that in comparison, she's closer to an ape than she is to a White man, even to you!" he explained.

Lucy walked away from Waller over to Virginia. "Ginny. Sit," she said, pointing to her vanity.

"Mrs. Lucy, it's not proper to…" Virginia began.

"Sit!" Lucy demanded.

Virginia sighed again. She often found herself in the middle of an argument between Mrs. Lucy and Mr. Waller. It was their way to spend quality time together. Mr. Ballard was slowly transferring all the Smithfield business and the estate to Mr. Waller because he was the oldest son. Sometimes Waller liked to talk things through with his mother since a large part of what Mr. Ballard had outside of Smithfield came as part of the estate of Mrs. Lucy when they married, though he'd never admit that to the other men.

Mrs. Lucy stood in front of Virginia so that her body was positioned between her and Waller. Her old hands shifted through the lip color on the vanity until her eyes lit up with mischief and amusement.

"This," Lucy began, "is what will prove that you are a woman like my husband says," Lucy said, grabbing Virginia's face and spreading lip color on her lips. When she was finished, she stepped back and smiled at Virginia. "Stand up and let Waller see you."

As Virginia stood up, Lucy stepped to the side. Waller looked at Virginia with no expression on his face. The room was quiet, and he swallowed hard.

"Could an ape in lipstick drive you to silence?" Lucy said, happy that her point had gotten the reaction she wanted.

"It's because I can tell she has on the lipstick. You know that lipstick is scandalous. It's for harlequins and whores," he said in a whisper.

"Are you calling your mother a whore, Waller?" Lucy said, cocking her head to the side., "Because if you haven't noticed, that color comes from my vanity."

"No, mother. I am not calling you a whore," Waller said apologetically.

"Then my point is made," Lucy said, proud of herself. She held out the lipstick that she had applied to Virginia and placed it in Virginia's hand. "You keep this," she said. "If ever someone tells you that you are not a woman, you put this on and declare it!" Lucy said as she grabbed the rose lipstick that Virginia was preparing to apply to her before Waller entered, spread the color on her lips, and left the room to arrive at supper.

Virginia watched Mrs. Lucy leave and concluded that the woman had lost her mind. There was no way that she was going to run around Smithfield, or any place for that matter with lipstick. Any intelligent, enslaved woman knew it best to try to stay unnoticed. She looked over to Waller, who was still staring at her, and then she looked into the vanity mirror that she was still standing in front of and studied herself. Virginia already thought that she was beautiful. The lip color just reminded her of a painting. She dared not smile at herself as she looked over to Waller.

"Take it off," he hissed. "You may not be an ape. But you're not a woman either," he said as he exited to the dining room.

Virginia sighed. Once again, she was caught in the middle of a temper tantrum between Mrs. Lucy and Mr. Waller. She shrugged her shoulders, lifted her apron to her mouth, and removed the lip color. She didn't really like the color, anyway. She still thought that the one that she tried when she was twelve years old was better. The memory made her smile at herself in the mirror.

A few minutes behind Waller, Virginia entered the dining room, preparing to serve the house their supper. Mrs. Lucy was at her seat, surrounded by her other children Ann, James, Lucy, and Jane. Virginia met Mrs. Lucy's eyes as the woman watched her, still amused by their most recent interaction.

"Would you like warm apple pie this evening, Mrs. Lucy?" Virginia asked her.

"You should address me first," Waller said. "I'll be the next head of this house. You should address me first," he continued saying, adjusting his body in his dress coat to improve the fit.

"Would *you* like warm apple pie this evening, Mr. Waller?" Virginia asked him.

He nodded.

Virginia went over to the buffet where the desserts were and picked up an apple pie. She moved over to the fireplace to place it in the small metal container that was there to warm food or keep warm. As soon as she slipped the pie into the container, the main door to the dining room opened, and Mister and Mr. Ballard walked in. Waller stood to greet his father and uncle and then turned to one of the enslaved to instruct them to begin serving. As usual, the men talked about current events as the woman made small talk about whatever came to mind. Gossip and business talk would come after supper when they gathered in the drawing-room for tea and coffee. Virginia stood back, listening to the events from the men as she did her part for Thomas' escape plan. She was serving slices of the warm apple pie when a heavy knock came from the main door to the dining room. At the unexpected interruption, everyone stopped speaking and paused.

"Everyone knows this is the supper hour," Lucy said, confused as to what could be so urgent.

Ballard stood up as one of the enslaved men went to the door to answer it. As the door opened, Theodore, the overseer for the enslaved ,stood in the doorway.

"I'm sorry to interrupt supper," the man began, removing his hat from his head. "I just," he hesitated.

Virginia squeezed the serving knife in her hand. Something was wrong, and she knew it. The only time an overseer was nervous was when they failed at their job, and the only way an overseer can fail at his job was to lose a slave. Either someone was dead, or someone was missing. Virginia prayed that someone was just missing. Robert sat at the table, continuing to eat. He seemed disinterested in the news and didn't rise out of his seat. He took a large bite of pie before leaning far enough back in his seat to slightly turn around and look at Theodore.

"Come out with it, Theodore. What is it? Which of the niggers tried to leave?" Robert said nonchalantly.

"Two of the Fraction boys," Theodore continued. "We noticed they was missing. We tracked them down. Looks like they tried to leave, but we found their bodies in the river and..."

Theodore was interrupted by the sound of the serving knife that Virginia was holding crashing to the ground. She held her breath. Robert stopped in the middle of another large bite of pie and put down his fork. He stood up and turned towards Theodore in an angry fury.

"Which Fraction boys!?" Robert yelled at Theodore, his face turning red with fury.

"Wilson and Granville, sir," Theodore answered. "We brought you their bodies.²"

CHAPTER 7

THE PLANNED AND UNPLANNED

Virginia, 1862

Thomas stood on the grounds of Solitude, finishing up heavy labor to improve the house so that Mister could have more room to do nothing, as Thomas liked to call it. Even with Mister being a Colonel for the Confederate army, he still spent time here at Solitude. There were now at least four people between the Solitude and Smithfield plantations working with the Confederates: Mister, Mr. Ballard, their cousin Mr. Buchanan, and Mr. Ballard's son, Waller. Thomas had heard that Mr. Buchanan was back at Smithfield and was serving as a Colonel for the Confederate army after Lincoln put him out of Washington for sending guns down here to the south when he was the Secretary of War for the United States[1]. According to Virginia, when she was in the house, all Mr. Buchanan talked about was how he "Didn't do no wrong." She also told them about how Mr. Buchanan said that he had to arm the Whites since that incident with Nate Turner showed him that. "Negroes wanted to kill all the Whites so they don't have to work no more." Thomas shook his head in disbelief, remembering how he felt when Virginia told them this story. All he could think about was how they just didn't get it, how all of them couldn't see that it wasn't about not working; it was about being free to work your own, earn your own, and be your own man. He thought Mr. Ballard understood that until Virginia told them that Mr. Ballard would be the one to write up the law so that the state of Virginia would no longer be part of the Union, and everyone there would fight for the Confederates.

"I don't know why he did it if he was going to walk around Smithfield all depressed like a dying dog because of it," Virginia had said.

Thomas shook his head, nonverbally admitting that he was disappointed by Mr. Ballard.

"I know why," John had said. "I was a child with Mr. Ballard. I watched him grow as I grew. I watched him struggle with becoming the man that Mr. Preston wanted him to be while being the boy who loved his Negro mammy so much he promised to free her almost daily and send her back to Africa, 'though he never got the chance to."

"Oh. He had the chance," Thomas said, not willing to discount Mr. Ballard's reluctance to use his own power. "He might not have been able to pass a law to free 'em, to free us, but he could have freed Fanny and Jack with a few words from his pen. But he didn't. He could give us papers to free us. But he don't."

"And his son Waller growing up to be like Mister. Going around giving us trouble," Othello said.

"Waller's just angry," John tried to explain on Waller's behalf. "He thinks his Pa spent more time caring about the Negros than him. He never understood the idea of a man's lifework. I felt the same about my Ma taking care of Mr. Ballard and Mister when I was younger. The older I got, the more I understand it was her work- she ain't have no choice."

"They had a choice," Othello murmured, referring to Mr. Ballard and the rest of the Preston family's freedom of choice when Fanny did not have that freedom.

"Not as much as you'd think," John said, hoping that the small statement provided enough of an explanation.

———

"So, where are we supposed to go?" Othello asked, interrupting Thomas' thoughts and bringing him back to the present.

"What?" Thomas asked, realizing for a moment he was lost in a daydream.

"I mean, how are we supposed to know *where* to go? Or even *when* to go?" Othello asked again. "You know...when we..." Othello looked around paranoid to be overheard.

"Leave," Thomas said, seeming unafraid of the invisible threat. "When we leave?" he said again as a matter of fact.

"Sure," Othello said. "But, how do you know where to go?"

Thomas thought for a moment realizing he didn't have an easy answer.

"Well," he began. "Mister said something about the Union in Tennessee. I suppose that's where we go."

"How are we supposed to know how to get to Tennessee?" Othello asked.

"Othello. I'll figure it out," Thomas laughed, picking up a bucket off the ground. "I'll figure it out, ok. Mister got me working on the railroad again starting tomorrow. I found my way out of Virginia, and now I just have to get us to Tennessee. If he says that the Union has the railroad and they're in Tennessee, I think that the railroad will tell me how to get there. We can probably either follow the tracks, hide in a car, or walk until we come across Union soldiers and ask to join 'em. I'll figure it out."

Othello smiled at Thomas as if relieved of a weight. Thomas turned and focused on the work at hand as his smile turned into a serious expression of thought. How *would* they get to Tennessee? The last word was that there were Union soldiers in Virginia, but it seemed unwise to run through the Confederate Army to reach the Union. The smartest way seemed to be the railroad. He'd have to spend his days working the railroad trying to find a passage. There had to be a way.

"Thomas. Come here, son."

Thomas' concentration was broken by the southern drawl of Mr. Ballard. He had lost the gusto in his voice, and these days almost everything was said in a sigh.

"Come here, son," Ballard said again. Thomas walked over to Ballard, still holding the bucket that he had in his hands. "Walk with me," Ballard said, turning around to walk away from Solitude.

Ballard began to walk down the road. He and Thomas walked in silence for a moment in the direction of Smithfield. Thomas could see Ballard's horse tied to a post a bit of the way down. Ballard placed his hands behind his back and looked ahead in thought.

"While I know that you can't read," Ballard said, breaking the silence. "But this here," Ballard said, placing a tightly folded paper in the palm of Thomas' hand, "is what I'd like to call…a map to liberation."

"Yes, sir," Thomas said, taking the small square of folded paper in his palm and tucking it in his thick coiled hair. He noticed, like Virginia had recently described, that Mr. Ballard looked worn down. The bags under his eyes were a shade of blue, his lips were dry, and he just looked tired.

"I am afraid that secession was required," Ballard continued, beginning to walk down the path again. "Do you know what secession is, Thomas?"

Thomas shook his head.

"Secession," Ballard began to explain, his mood a bit more perked with his eagerness for the opportunity to teach. "Secession is when this fine state of Virginia and all her holy glory decided that it wants to function as its own government. Its own country of sorts. It would no longer be part of the Union that my father's father fought so nobly for during the Revolutionary War because the Union wants too much control over the states. Lincoln doesn't understand that the states will abolish slavery on their own terms and at the right time. Things have to align before the Negroes are granted freedom," Ballard continued partially ranting, partially warning Thomas. "Apparently, in some states, including Virginia, it is fitting," Ballard continued on, "to rob others of their freedom to ensure our own. Some demand this thievery of freedom under the guise of safety. And I fear that I will not be able to do what I have worked to do, to emancipate the slaves in my lifetime. I have thought that, if I agree with secession, if I am loyal to Virginia, I can at least keep the beast on a leash when I have failed to keep it caged." Ballard stopped and turned his full attention to Thomas. "But you, boy. You're brave. You don't need me to give you your freedom," Ballard said, placing one hand on Thomas' shoulder. "You, boy, can *fight* for it."

"Yes, sir," Thomas said, a bit in awe of Mr. Ballard's speech. "Yes, sir, I can."

"But keep in mind, boy," Ballard said, holding a stern stare at Thomas. "I have *no* idea where you got it from." Ballard straightened his back as if returning to his world. "Well," he said, backing away from Thomas with a voice that sounded like he had been asleep for hours. "Back to it then."

"You need help on your horse, sir?" Thomas asked him, noting his lack of strength.

Ballard nodded in agreement. Thomas walked closer to Ballard's horse and went to bring his hands together to lock his fingers to give Ballard a boost. That motion made him realize that he was still holding the bucket. Thomas put the bucket on the ground, locked his fingers together, and bent down to indicate to Ballard to place his foot there for a boost. Ballard placed one foot in Thomas' hand and then hesitated while he gathered the strength to climb onto the back of the horse.

"Don't you worry about it, Mr. Ballard. Just a small push, I'll get you the rest of the way up there," Thomas said. Ballard looked at Thomas with a small smile before pushing himself lightly. He landed his chest against the saddle as Thomas grabbed him and pushed him the rest of the way onto the horse. "There you go, Mr. Ballard," Thomas said, patting the side of the horse. He focused on the horse's long lashes instead of Mr. Ballard. He's seen this type of thing before. He always had a good instinct for an end, and he felt like Mr. Ballard was approaching his.

Ballard gave Thomas a slight nod.

"Yes, sir," Thomas said, still staring at the horse. He nodded back to Mr. Ballard before walking back to where he had placed down the bucket, picking it up, turning around, and returning to the house to finish his work.

When Thomas arrived back to the side of the house, Othello was leaving out of the small doorway of a structure on the side of the pond that was used to keep things cold.

"So," Othello said, trying to lead Thomas into providing an explanation. He grabbed a large milk container that was sitting outside of the doorway. He placed his hands on each side of the container and braced himself to pick it up, but hesitated. He looked up at Thomas, waiting for an explanation of what Mr. Ballard wanted him for.

"He gave me something, said I need to read it," Thomas said, answering Othello's unasked question.

"So?" Othello asked again, now leaning his weight on the container but still not lifting it.

"So I can't do it here," Thomas said in a condescending tone. "Being I'm not supposed to know how to read or even have whatever it is that Mr. Ballard just gave to me."

Othello nodded in agreement. "You'll read it later?" he asked.

"Yeah," Thomas said.

"This 'bout to be a long day," Othello added, picking up the milk container like it was the heaviest thing in the world. Thomas laughed.

———

Hours later, Thomas and Othello quickly marched towards the old cabin. Night had fallen, and the sound of all the creatures that belong to the moon could be heard. The day had ended, and Thomas was eager to read the paper that Mr. Ballard had given him. He didn't have much time to read the paper and plan the escape with Othello and the others before having to leave for work on the rail at sunrise. When they entered the cabin, they saw that Ester was already there, settling down for the day. She was wiping her hands with her apron and looking around the cabin as if taking inventory of whether or not everything was in its place before she ended her day. When she was satisfied with the state of things, she turned around and looked down on the floor in the corner of the room. Virginia's new baby, Sarah, was lying there watching all of Ester's movements.

"So what is it?" Othello asked, turning to Thomas.

"What is what?" Ester asked, picking up baby Sarah and moving to the other corner of the room to sit in a chair that was there. She took a quick peek over at Virginia's oldest daughter, Della, who sat on the floor playing with a blanket.

"Mr. Ballard gave Thomas something. We think it's supposed to help us," Othello announced.

Ester straightened her back with interest.

"From Mr. Ballard or Mister?" she asked skeptically.

"Mr. Ballard," Thomas answered, sitting on an old stool next to his mother. "Enough about that though, Mama. How you feeling?" he said, leaning his elbows on his knees so that he could lean in and gaze closely at his mother.

"Like I'm well on my way to my own freedom," she said with a smile. "I just hope those pictures in the Smithfield house ain't right, and I don't get right up to heaven's doors and see a whole lot of White faces that look like Mister waiting for me."

Thomas gave a slight laugh. "That'd be hell, Mama, and we all know you ain't going there." The cabin filled with an awkward silence. "I wish you wasn't going anyway," Thomas said as if wishing on a star. Ester grabbed his hand and squeezed it slightly. The sad mood was interrupted by their older brother Oscar opening the cabin's front door and walking in.

"Ya'll talking about how beautiful my Momma is again?" Oscar said jokingly.

"When she's beautiful, she's my Momma. When she's mad, she's your's," Thomas responded.

Oscar let out a laugh and gently tapped Thomas on the shoulder with his fist. It was a light chastisement meant to jab at Thomas playfully. "How you feeling, Mama?" Oscar asked Ester, noticing her appearance.

"She talking about dying again," Thomas answered for her. "I don't like it."

"I know, baby," Ester said, cupping his cheek. "I'm ready to go, though," she said, folding her hands together and plopping them down in her lap. "And don't worry," she continued, "I feel fine. I'm just old. It's time 'cause I'm old. I wasn't supposed to live this long!"

Thomas gave a small chuckle and stood while slightly squeezing his mothers' legs. "You ain't old Mama; you're a fine wine." Ester blushed a bit.

"Can we get to what Mr. Ballard gave you?!" Othello exclaimed, throwing his arms in the air. "I mean, I love you, Mama," he continued, "but this thing has been on my mind all day! It's been *hammer hammer* Mr. Ballard, *saw saw* Mr. Ballard."

"Mr. Ballard gave you something?" Oscar asked.

"Yeah, I think it's some information 'bout leavin'," Thomas said.

"I need to know if I'm packing or staying!" Othello continued, impatient that Thomas still was not reading the note.

Thomas rolled his eyes at Othello. "What you think you packing? What do you have worth weighing you down?" Thomas asked.

"I don't know," Othello said, "but I need to know if I need to put some thought into it."

"Oh, Lord," Ester said, shaking her head at Othello. "Thomas, Lord Jesus on Heaven, promise me you will take care of your brother."

"I'll never let him leave my side, Mama. Don't you worry about it," Thomas answered her.

"Hey," Othello said, faking indignation. "I'm not a chil'. I can manage. Now…what do you have?"

Thomas dug into his hair before a panicked looked came across his face. He dramatically searched around, looking on the floor and under the stool where he had been sitting.

"On no," he whispered.

"What!" Othello exclaimed, exasperated, "You lost it!?"

"No," Thomas said, teasing Othello. "It's right here." He opened the palm of his hand to show the small folded piece of paper there.

"So what is it?" Othello asked again.

Thomas took out the tightly folded piece of paper and began to unfold it. He was surprised to find that it was a fairly large piece of paper that Mr. Ballard folded tightly into a small coin size square. Thomas took the paper over to the candlelight so that he could see it clearly.

"What's it say?" Ester asked.

"It say," Thomas began reading, slowly allowing himself a moment to figure out each word as he came across it. "100 Colored Men Wanted. Officers & Clerks for United States Colored Regiments, Organizing in the South-West. These Men are Enlisted under SPECIAL Ah…" Thomas paused.

"Ah..?" Othello asked.

"Sorry," Thomas corrected himself. "This one is tricky. Sometimes it's hard because the letters together make a different sound than when they are apart." Thomas adjusted the paper in his hands and leaned in closer to the candlelight as if the fire would help him remember how the letters worked. "Ah..ority? Authority?" Thomas looked up to Ester and Othello, proud to have figured it out. "These Men are Enlisted under SPECIAL AUTHORITY from the War Department-must be able to Read and Write Fluently, and must be Men of Intelligence." Thomas looked up at Othello again. "It tells us where to go."

"That don't sound like where to go to me," Othello said skeptically. "I can't really read and write that well. Not like you."

"But you are a man of intelligence. I'll take care of the rest," Thomas said. "There's more here," Thomas continued. "A lot more. I'll have to take my time to read it. But it tells us where to go, and it says we get money to do it."

"Hallelujah," Ester whispered, tears swelling in her eyes. "We serve a good God."

The joy in the cabin was interrupted by the sound of fast-approaching sobs and screams. Everyone in the cabin looked at each other as if the other knew what was going on. Suddenly Virginia burst through the cabin door. Her face was in grief-stricken horror. She was gasping for breath. Thomas immediately took in the scene and looked his older sister over, trying to determine what was causing her grief and her being out of breath. If Mister had touched his sister, he'd kill him. He had reserved himself for that a long time ago.

"Mama!!!" Virginia yelled in between her gasps and tears. "Mama!!" she screamed again, running to lay her face in Ester's lap. "Oh, God!" she screamed again.

"What is it, child?!" Ester asked, afraid to know the answer. She struggled to lift Virginia's face from her lap. "What is it!?" Ester asked again, desperate for an answer. Seeing their mother distraught, Virginia's children began to cry.

"Granville and Wilson!" Virginia gasped in sobs.

"Oh God, my God," Ester said under her breath, her hand over her mouth.

"What about Granville and Wilson?" Thomas asked, taking on the task of getting the information from Virginia.

"Thomas," Virginia said as if hoping that Thomas can change what she was about to tell him. "They just brought their bodies on a wagon. They found them in the river. They tried to leave but couldn't get across the river. They drowned, Thomas! They drowned!!!"

Nothing but the sound of Virginia's tears filled the room as everyone else fell into silence at the news. Ester stood up and took two steps towards the door before she stopped. She froze in place, not saying a word or shedding a tear.

"I told those boys to wait!" Oscar said, stomping his foot on the old cabin floor.

Thomas moved quickly over to Virginia and fell to his knees to hug her tightly. He looked behind him and up at Ester. "Mama." he said with a light voice. He didn't know what to say to help her.

Othello moved to place his back against the wall of the cabin and slid down it to sit on the floor as if defeated. Ester suddenly staggered to lean against the wall as if she couldn't hold herself up a moment longer. Oscar ran over to hold up his mother, and she finally began to sob.

"They should have waited for the plan," Othello whispered to no one in particular. "They should have waited for the plan."

Thomas and Oscar made eye contact. "Thomas," Oscar began, "we stick with the plan as soon as you think you found a route. I test it. If Virginia reports back that Mr. Ballard received a letter from me, you know your route is safe, and ya'll can come along and follow. You hear me?!" Thomas nodded in agreement. "You hear me, Othello?! You don't go runnin' like that. We get a plan! We stick with the plan!"

This flier is one of the many fliers that were used during the civil war to recruit slaves and freemen to the Union army. Thomas Fraction may have been able to acquire one of these fliers for him to know where to go in Tennessee[2]

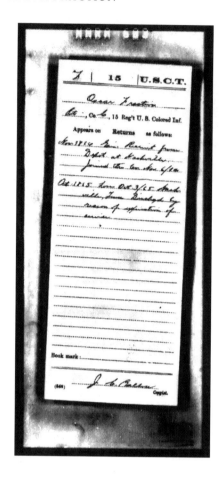

Oscar Fraction Union Army Service Record. He enlisted in September 1864. While he was recruited and stationed in Nashville, TN, Oscar would live out the remainder of his days in Ohio.[3]

CHAPTER 8

THE ROUTE

Virginia, March 1865

"I hope the weather stays good for you," thirty-year-old Virginia said, breaking the silence in the old cabin as twenty-five-year-old Thomas poked away at a fire. She sat on the floor holding her latest child, baby Wilson. She hugged the baby as she thought about her dead brother, who she had named him for. It had been a little over two years since Granville and Wilson died and a few months since Thomas and Oscar thought they had finally figured out a safe route to get to the Union army. Oscar had left in the middle of the summer of last year, and Virginia had finally reported that the House received a letter from him, so that meant that the route that they charted worked.

Thomas stared into the flames as if looking for other answers. It was late in the evening, and he could hardly sleep. Virginia was there at the cabin, determined to spend one more day with her brothers before they attempted to leave the plantation. Her children, Della, now five years old, Sarah, now three years old, Josephine, two years old, and Wilson, who was just born, were with her. She had seen the Misses at the house read a letter from

Oscar, which meant that the route was safe. Othello, now nineteen-years-old, wanted to leave the next day, but Thomas thought it was better not to make it so obvious and to wait a bit. There wasn't a point in running if they would just get caught for being sloppy.

Thomas stood up, broke his gaze from the flames, and took baby Wilson out of Virginia's arms to hold him. He looked over his shoulder to where Chloe sat on the floor wrapped in an old blanket. She picked away at the small cotton balls that covered the blanket showing the blanket's age and dependability. Thomas smiled at Chloe and sat next to her on the floor. His thoughts were overwhelmed with decisions, hesitations, fears, and sadness. The worry for his mother and father when he leaves, whether Chloe would feel abandoned, and whether Virginia would be ok in the Smithfield house.

Othello leaned against the wall next to Mary. They had indeed been married while working on Mr. Wilson's plantation, just as they had planned. She had started using his last name, although they weren't considered legally married by the law of the state of Virginia[1]. Othello took Mary's hand and smiled at her.

"You still have the paper?" Mary asked, referring to the flyer that Mr. Ballard, God bless his soul, had given to Thomas those years ago. Mr. Ballard had died shortly after he gave Thomas the paper. He just became sick and died there in the Smithfield house. Othello nodded. "Good!" Mary said, smiling at him. "You'll come back for me, ok," Mary said while squeezing Othello's hand. It wasn't a question-- it was a declaration. "Running is the easy part; I'll need you to survive that war too," she half-laughed uncomfortably.

"I just," Othello began finally speaking. "I just want life to be fair and easy. Just once. Just for a little while."

"Well," Mary said with a smirk. "Make sure you come back to me. And I'll be sure to be fair and easy. Just once," she said. Othello laughed. "Just for a little while," Mary continued.

"You ready?"

Othello and Mary were interrupted by Thomas, who was standing at the edge of the room with a few small possessions tied in a piece of cloth.

"You know," Mary said to Thomas with a smirk. "I can still find you a wife before you go if you want. Plenty of the girls would be willing. All that talk about my husband's big brother gets annoying."

Thomas smiled. "It's hard to think about that right now. Ain't got no time for it." He sobered, thinking about this being their last goodbyes. He was excited about the prospect of freedom, but he was also sad because of the circumstances of having to leave his family here. He was afraid of what was out there, about running into some White men that were just interesting in the entertainment of "hanging niggers." He was afraid of being captured and resold to someone else. He was afraid of what would happen if someone besides Mister caught them. He was afraid of getting lost trying to get to Tennessee. He was afraid of the war. But even with all of that, what Thomas wasn't afraid of, were the possibilities.

Othello kissed Mary one last time and studied her face. "I'll be back for you, you hear?"

———

Not long after they left the plantation, Thomas and Othello found themselves walking silently through trees and bushes. Both of them were deep in thought and trying not to make any sounds that could be heard by anyone nearby. There seemed to be no one around but the two of them.

"We probably should have waited for better weather," Othello whispered, noting the cool temperature of the night. "At least we wouldn't have to worry so much about the cold. We should have left with Oscar. It would be warmer all the time. I hate the cold."

Thomas didn't respond. He hated the cold too, but hated both slavery and Mister even more. Mister *was* the cold as far as Thomas was concerned.

"I should have worn more clothes," Othello continued to complain.

"You don't *have* more clothes," Thomas reminded Othello still moving forward.

"Nah, but maybe I could've taken one of Granville's shirts," Othello stated. The reminder of Granville made him sad. Othello looked down at the ground and tried to think of other things to take his mind off Granville and Wilson's drowning. Suddenly, Thomas stopped walking. Othello looked at him and saw the stark seriousness on his face.

"Why..." Othello began to ask.

"Just shhh," Thomas said, slightly annoyed.

He continued to stand still, causing Othello to do the same. Neither of them moved a muscle as they listened closely to the woods around them. Othello looked over at Thomas' face, waiting for an outcome because Thomas was obviously hearing something that Othello wasn't. Thomas motioned to Othello to follow him. He moved carefully past a bush and towards a large oak tree. As they approached the tree, Thomas leaned against it as if attempting to use it as a shield. Othello did the same, although he wasn't sure what was going on. Thomas stared at the sky, trying to convince himself that if he couldn't see whatever it was he heard, it couldn't see him either. *Or maybe he was praying*, Othello thought to himself as he watched him. Suddenly Othello jerked his head to the left as he finally heard what he suspected Thomas had already heard: footsteps. Othello's eyes grew wide, and he looked at Thomas for instruction. Thomas closed his eyes in silent prayer. The footsteps stopped. Thomas opened his eyes and looked at Othello, who was suddenly snatched away by what seemed like the night. At the same time, an arm came across Thomas' neck, holding him tightly against the tree.

"I told you, boy," Robert began. "I told you no one leaves. Didn't I tell you, boy?"

Thomas peered down at Mister, the expression on his face not fearful, regretful, or in panic, but angry. Robert looked over at Othello, who was struggling at the hands of two men holding him. One of the men held a rope tied into a noose. He placed it around Othello's neck but did not tighten it to fit.

"I give simple instructions. Simple instructions that I don't think are hard to follow!" Robert said, a bit annoyed. He placed the hand that was not holding Thomas over his heart as he went on. "I do what is best for you, Thomas. You are mine. My responsibility. Mines to guide and mines to protect. It is a foolish man that doesn't protect his property."

"I am not your property," Thomas said through a choked throat.

"Oh, but you are," Robert said, matter of factly, as a big smile formed on his face. "But don't get so caught up on words. Look at my actions. I am trying to protect you, Thomas. Do you know what's out there? If I didn't find you first," Robert began preaching like a worried parent. He stopped and twisted his face as if to dread the thought. "Out here, unless I send you, unless I send word, unless you have papers with my permission, you are just another nigger that can hang at the end of that noose," Robert said, indicating the noose around Othello's neck. "I ride around and see these niggers hanging on these trees like Christmas lights. I don't care otherwise, but I can protect you. And I will if you follow my instructions. I will protect you because you are mine." Robert paused, waiting for a reaction from Thomas. Maybe a sign of…understanding? Agreement? Maybe, even gratitude? "Now, what are you running off for?" Robert asked him. He waited for Thomas' answer, but he didn't say anything, he just stared back. Robert slapped Thomas across the face. "I'll ask you again, where're you going?" Robert probed further. Thomas still doesn't answer. He knew that Mister already knew where he was going. Robert stared at Thomas again. "You running off to join this war? Do you even know what you are running to? I've been running into these battles and into this blood for four years now, boy. Trust me, you have it better here with me. These soldiers are brutal when it comes to the niggers. They are not just trying to shoot you down, boy. They want to chop you into pieces. That's what I do to 'em when I catch 'em[2]." Robert stared at Thomas again. "So come on, we're going home." Robert turned away from Thomas, slowly loosening his grip on his neck, preparing to let him go. One of the men holding Othello released him, while another continued to hold on to the end of the noose around his neck. The man proceeded to walk over and grab Thomas.

"Give me this," Thomas whispered in a voice that only Robert could hear. Robert stopped loosening his grip on Thomas' neck, but he didn't tighten it back to a choking position.

"Wait," Robert said to the man walking over to grab Thomas, not taking his eyes off of Thomas.

"Give me this," Thomas continued. "I've done what you asked all my life. I've taken all that you could throw at me. I've been denied all my life, all while I hated that part of me as much as you hate the nigger in me. But..." Thomas continued, determined not to let the burning in his chest and throat get the best of him. "But give me this ... Please ... give ... me ... this."

Robert stared at Thomas, shocked to hear Thomas plead with him. He took it as a submission. Finally, Robert closed his eyes and, for a second, looked as if he had just tasted the sweetest fruit his tongue had ever tasted. Thomas stared at him, trying to hide his hate. He didn't know if Mister was feeling satisfaction like a sweet taste, or disgust like a bad smell. Not knowing what to expect, Thomas braced himself, but Robert let him go.

"You want to do this?" Robert said in a whisper that only Thomas could hear. "Fine. But if you go," he continued, "and try to come back here, you're mines, and I will kill you."

Thomas looked at Robert, neither agreeing nor disagreeing.

"Where are you going?" Robert asked him again. Thomas still didn't respond. He did not want to admit that he was not completely sure. "New York or Tennessee?" Robert asked again, trying to show his knowledge of all things concerning the war. "That's where the niggers go, so where are you going?" he asked again. Thomas still didn't respond. "No matter," Robert began. "I'll find you either way. But I can't make sure you're safe out there, boy. You hear me!?"

Thomas looked at Robert. "I need my brother," Thomas began, not removing his stare from Robert to look over at Othello. "I have a better chance if I have my brother." Thomas said, hoping that Mister's obsession with his safety will keep Othello safe.

Robert once again transformed into a jolly Santa Claus, stroking his long white beard while considering the prospect. He looked over at Othello. "You keep him safe," he began talking to Othello. "Or by God, nigger, I will make your life a living hell."

Othello nodded, unsure if he should say anything else. The two men holding him removed the noose from around his neck and let him go. He nor Thomas said another word as they watched Mister pulling at his pants to adjust the fit, turn around in a circle as if taking in the scene, and then walk away to mount his horse. The men that were with him followed him, mounting their own horses.

"So you just letting them niggers go?" one of the men asked Robert. "Then what was all this for?" he asked.

"He's doing what I tell him," Robert said. "Everyone does what I tell them, don't be mistaken. But if you see them again, bring them back to me," Robert said while digging his heels into the side of the horse, urging it to move, and grabbed the reins for the horse to turn around. "No harm to Thomas," he continued looking at the other men. "You bring him back to me."

Othello waited until he could no longer hear the hooves of the horses before turning around to face Thomas. Thomas still stood at the tree. His back was straight, but his fists are tight as he stares down at the ground.

"You ok?" Othello asked him. Thomas didn't respond, but Othello could see Thomas' fists were clenched in such a way he was sure that Thomas' nails were likely stabbing his palms. Othello moved a bit closer. "Thomas?" Othello asked again. "You ok?" When Othello was close enough to see Thomas' face clearly, he could see tears falling to the ground.

"I hate him," Thomas said in a whisper. "I hate him."

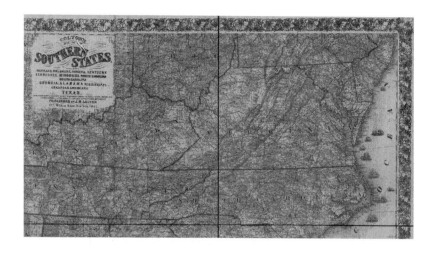

This map from the year 1864 shows where in Virginia the Smithfield Plantation was compared to where Nashville, Tennessee is. Nashville is where Thomas and Othello would be stationed. [3]

VOLUNTEER ENLISTMENT.

STATE OF _____ TOWN OF _____

I, _____ born in _____ in the State of _____ aged _____ years, and by occupation a _____ Do HEREBY ACKNOWLEDGE to have volunteered this _____ day of _____ 1865, to serve as a **Soldier** in the Army of the United States of America, for the period of *THREE YEARS*, unless sooner discharged by proper authority: Do also agree to accept such bounty, pay, rations, and clothing, as are, or may be, established by law for volunteers. And I, _____ do solemnly swear, that I will bear true faith and allegiance to the **United States of America**, and that I will serve them honestly and faithfully against all their enemies or opposers whomsoever; and that I will observe and obey the orders of the President of the United States, and the orders of the officers appointed over me, according to the Rules and Articles of War.

Sworn and subscribed to, at _____ this _____ day of _____ 1865; BEFORE _____

I CERTIFY, ON HONOR, That I have carefully examined the above-named Volunteer, agreeably to the General Regulations of the Army, and that, in my opinion, he is free from all bodily defects and mental infirmity, which would in any way disqualify him from performing the duties of a soldier.

EXAMINING SURGEON.

I CERTIFY, ON HONOR, That I have minutely inspected the Volunteer, _____ previously to his enlistment, and that he was entirely sober when enlisted; that, to the best of my judgment and belief, he is of lawful age; and that, in accepting him as duly qualified to perform the duties of an able-bodied soldier, I have strictly observed the Regulations which govern the recruiting service. This soldier has _____ eyes, _____ hair, _____ complexion, is _____ feet _____ inches high.

_____ Regiment of _____ Volunteers, RECRUITING OFFICER.

(A. G. O. No. 74 & 75.)

Thomas Fraction Volunteer Enlistment into the Union Army's United States Colored Troops-Sworn into service in Greenville, Tennessee April 25ᵗʰ 1865. Notice in the middle of his signature an indication of an "x" and the words "his mark". This was a technique during the period where a person that could not write would place an "x" in front of a witness that would indicate their signature. We will learn later that Thomas may have pretended to not know how to read and write. This may have been in fear of the repercussions of the period where a slave being able to read and write was either not allowed, frowned upon, or against the law.[4]

Thomas Fraction Military Declaration of Recruit, April 25, 1865[5]

4 | 40 | U.S.C.T.

Thomas Fraction

, Co. *K*, 40 Reg't U. S. Col'd Inf.

Appears on

Company Descriptive Book

of the organization named above.

DESCRIPTION.

Age *25* years; height *5* feet *5* inches.

Complexion *drk*

Eyes *drk*; hair *drk*

Where born *Montgomery Co. Va.*

Occupation *Farmer*

ENLISTMENT.

When *April 26*, 186*5*.

Where *Greenville, Tenn*

By whom *Col F. W. Lister*; term *3* y'rs.

Remarks:

Steel

(383ø) Copyist.

Thomas Fraction Military Company Descriptive Book[6]

F. | 40 | U.S.C.T.

Thomas Fraction

Pvt. , Co. *H*. *40*. Reg't U. S. Col'd Inf.

Appears on

Company Muster-in and Descriptive Roll

of the organization named above. Roll dated

Greenville Tenn. 6 May, 1865 .

Where born *Montgomery Co. Va*;

Age *25* y'rs; occupation *Farmer*

When enlisted *26 apl*, 1865.*

Where enlisted *Greenville Tenn* *

For what period enlisted *3* years.*

Eyes *dk* ; hair *dk*

Complexion *dk* ; height *5* ft. *8* in.

When mustered in *26 apl*, 1865.

Where mustered in *Greenville Tenn*,

Bounty paid $ 100; due $ 100

Where credited *1 C. D.*;

Company to which assigned *H*.

Remarks :

* Muster-in and descriptive roll shows enlistment of all men of this company as of same date. See enrollment on subsequent card or cards.

Book mark : •

G. E. Dayton

(356f) Copyist.

Thomas Fraction Military Company Muster-in and Descriptive Roll[7]

Thomas Fraction Military Company Muster-in and Descriptive Roll[8]

Othello Fraction Volunteer Enlistment into the Union Army's United States Colored Troops. Sworn into service in Greenville, Tennessee April 25th 1865[9]

Othello Fraction Military Company Muster-in and Descriptive Roll[10]

Othello Fraction Military Company Muster-in and Descriptive Roll[11]

CHAPTER 9

WELCOME TO TENNESSEE, BOYS

Tennessee, April 1865

O thello stood in the large doorway of the wooden car of the old train. Both he and Thomas had boarded the train at the direction of the Union general that they had eventually met when they approached the Union army camp back at the Virginia and Tennessee border. They and about fifty other men were sent to Nashville, where they were told they could enlist in the Union army.

"You boys up to it?" the General had asked them. "We started with about 300 Negros wanting to follow up and join us, and once the supplies got low, they went back to their Masters. So you up to it?[1]" They were.

Othello lifted his hand over his eyes to block the bright sun. "Geez," he said, waiting for his eyes to adjust so that he could see his way down off the railcar. He and Thomas were the last two men to get off from the group of Negros that had made it to the camp to enlist. Thomas approached Othello from behind and gave him a slight push to urge him to get off.

"Get moving. Let's not start off falling behind," Thomas said, brushing past Othello. "Remember what I told you. Keep up with me, don't leave my side until I figure all this out."

Othello nodded and proceeded to get down off the train car after Thomas. The ground was like wet clay, and Othello could immediately feel the cold on his feet. "First thing. Can we get some of those army boots?" he said.

"Plenty of dead men to get them off of," a man said, passing by Thomas and Othello. He stopped in front of Othello, recognizing the opportunity to scare someone with the prospects of war. "Yeah. Might find a boot with a few toes still in it."

"That's alright," Thomas interrupted him. "Show me the foot, and I'll take the boot. Dead man ain't got no use for it. I'm sure he won't mind."

"Oh, yeah!" the man said, looking over Thomas with approval. "Hey! I'm Preston!"

"For God's sake," Thomas said, rolling his eyes at his seeming inability to escape anything "Preston." Othello laughed.

"Ah, you one of those ox Negros, huh?" Preston said. Othello looked over at Thomas as if he thought at that moment Thomas actually turned into an ox. "You know what an ox Negro is?" Preston asked Thomas.

"No," Thomas said pointedly. "But I can't say much about me caring to know either. Come on, Othello," Thomas said, grabbing Othello by the forearm to drag him to follow the crowd of men that they had arrived with the enlistment line. Preston proceeded to follow along.

"An ox Negro," Preston continued, oblivious to Thomas' disinterest, "is one of those big and strong niggers. The ones that get away with so much 'cause the white man's kinda scared of him. He ain't gonna tell him that, though." Thomas kept walking, still not interested in the conversation. "Where you coming from, ox?" Preston asked.

"The train," Thomas said.

Preston stopped walking and laughed.

"Ah! You's a funny ox! Ain't never met no funny ox! I know why YOU joining the Union army. I joined to stick to Governor Harris. You know he took a state vote for secession, and even though he was outvoted, he still seceded Tennessee. Papers said he was outvoted by sixty thousand. SIXTY! Then gonna tell me and all the other boys round here that we gotta fight for the Confederate.[2] I said, 'Nah way, he don gon crazy. I ain't fighting for treason and rebellion. And I sure ain't fighting to keep slaves that I ain't got'." Preston stopped to finally take a breath.

The crowd of men they were following proceeded to make a line. Thomas pushed Othello forward to line up ahead of him.

"You know they try to tell us your people better off as slaves? They tell us in Africa, you would be monkey savages eating raw meat and running from lions. They tell us ya'll happy."

Thomas looked at Preston from the corner of his eyes, one eyebrow raised. He didn't turn his head in his direction, though. Preston noticed that the statement about Africa got his attention.

"Yeah, I seen enough colored men in the colored infantry to know ya'll ain't now and ain't never been no happy."

Thomas dropped his head down so that his chin touched his chest. Preston could see that he had almost talked Thomas into defeat.

"So you just gonna sign up for the Army, huh? Ain't no point now," Preston continued to Thomas.

Thomas stared at the ground, contemplating how to get rid of Preston. Maybe he could lose him in the crowd, or act like he was sick, or stuff his ears with...

"The worst of it is probably over. Lincoln done freed you. You can go back home now and be a free man," Preston continued talking.

Thomas looked over at Preston and stared at him for a long moment before giving him a short laugh that obviously meant nothing funny had occurred. "How long you been here?" Thomas asked him.

Happy that Thomas was finally engaged, Preston smiled in satisfaction. "Since August last year. I done seen some battles, I done seen some blood man. Ain't no joke."

"You mean to tell me you been in this war since August, and you still believe that these southern White men just gonna take Lincoln at his word and just walk away, huh?" Thomas said, tilting his head to the side in question. "You think they just gonna say..."

Othello suddenly turned around to face Thomas and Preston and cut in with a dramatic performance of a White southern plantation owner. "My word!" he began exaggerated, "Why good 'ol Lincoln has declared the slaves as free. By golly, why didn't he say that earlier? Is that what we were fighting for this whole time?" He gave a hearty fake laugh.

Thomas smirked at Othello. "And now all the slaves'll say..."

Othello cut in again, "Geez, Laudy!! We's free now. Massa get that notice from Missa Lincoln, and we's be free. I's gonna get me one of dos' there donkeys, get me some land, and grow me some tobacco. Yes, laud, I'm gonna be rich like them there White men. Alls gonna be good now. I's sho' glad Lincoln signed that paper."

"Yeah," Thomas said back to Preston, the smirk gone from his face, "because this whole time. All these years, all they was waiting for, was a piece...of...paper".

Suddenly a Union Army General stood on the desk at the front of the line and called everyone to attention. "Your attention, please. Men! Gather yourselves! Your attention, please!"

Everyone looked up at the man on the desk. He looked down at the buckle of his Union Army belt and fiddled with it for a second before looking up at the crowd. He lifted his hands up to his head and straightened his hat. His eyes were rimmed with red. Thomas wasn't sure if the man was tired or crying.

"It is my duty to inform you all, White and Colored, that on April 14th, Lincoln was shot and killed in Washington." The crowd immediately exploded with conversations. Thomas stared ahead again.

"Calm yourselyes!" the General standing on the desk yelled until everyone was quiet again. "Don't be discouraged. We have also taken Fort Sumter in South Carolina and are preparing to take North Carolina. We continue to pressure the Confederates to surrender, and we will deal with the guerillas as they come. You are all still needed."

Thomas looked over to Preston. "I don't blame you for hoping, though," Thomas said to him. "It would have been nice if all it took was a piece of paper."

Preston moved his gaze from the General to Thomas. "Welcome to Tennessee, boys," he said, reaching out his hand to shake Thomas.'

May 1865

Thomas stood outside, staring into the darkness of the South Tunnel in Tennessee. He and Othello were part of the 40th United Stated States Colored Infantry[3] and were assigned to guard the railroad[4]. They were told during assignment that their skills and experience in the railroad and in labor made them great assets to not only keep it safe, but to provide repairs when needed[5]. They were told that this particular railroad was an important tool for the Union army to provide supplies to the regiments by moving materials using these tracks between Louisville and Nashville[6].

Every so often Thomas would look above the tunnel to the greenery. He was doing his duty of guarding the railroad and the tunnel that it passed through, but after days of no action, he was mostly testing his eyesight. The Confederates in the area had all surrendered, but the guerillas in the area[7], who were ex-confederate soldiers, were always looking to keep the fight going[8]. Reports from Tullahoma had come in that a gang of fifteen guerillas were killing men, robbing families, and raping woman. There was even a report of a gang that raped a sixteen-year-old girl in a room with the body of her dead cousin who they had killed[9]. The President keeps telling the Generals to let these guerilla men go if they take the oath to be loyal to the United States, but their actions showed time and time again that their word meant nothing. No matter, as the General complained, they had to write to Washington to get permission to hang these men[10].

"They're demons incarnate," General George Thomas once said.

The darkness of the tunnel was thick like oil, but the greenery above it sat in the bright, welcoming light of the day. *Dark and light. Dark and light,* Thomas thought to himself as he shifted his eyesight back and forth. It was becoming a bit of a game to see how fast his eyes would adjust to seeing as far into South Tunnel as he could after it had been looking at the light of day. Realizing he was beginning to develop a bit of a headache, Thomas looked at Othello.

"Come on," Thomas said. "Let's walk around a bit; check stuff out."

Othello pushed himself off the rocky wall he was leaning against, stomped his army booted feet on the ground, and flung the coat to his uniform dramatically. Thomas looked at Othello, half amused, half annoyed.

"Stop doing that," Thomas said.

"What!?" Othello smiled. "I like the uniform."

They walked towards a lower part of the stone wall that made the tunnel and use it to climb to higher ground. They often used this valley of a hole in the wall to climb up to the top for a better view of their surroundings. From what Thomas had been told, the valley in the wall was from an attack two years earlier when the Confederate army managed to capture the soldiers there and destroy the tunnel by setting a train full of hay on fire and then pushing the train into the tunnel. The fire set the support beams of the tunnel on fire, and the tunnel collapsed[11]. The Union had managed to rebuild the tunnel, and now they were guarding it. *There's no way those Confederates are going to capture me if they come back here*, Thomas thought to himself. There was no way they were sending him back to Mister, or, as he had heard that they call him in the Confederate army, Colonel Bob[12]. Thomas started laughing to himself.

"What's so funny?" Othello asked, following close behind Thomas.

"Colonel Bob," Thomas laughed. "BOB," he said again, as if burping the name. "Where did they come up with that, anyway?"

"I know," Othello agreed, obviously not finding the name Bob half as funny as Thomas did.

"It's like they don't know the man! Seriously!" Thomas continued. "When they say he reminds them of Santa Claus' that gets me the most."

"I know," Othello agreed again.

For a while, Thomas and Othello walked silently along the tunnel. Both of them would scan around the greenery at the top of the tunnel while occasionally looking down at the other men standing in front of the tunnel and along the path of the railroad. Everything was quiet and still. *All of the action must still be deeper south,* Thomas thought to himself. That was fine with Thomas. As far as he was concerned, the action could very well stay in Alabama and Mississippi. Othello was eager for a fight, but Thomas wasn't.

"What is that?" Othello said in a whisper as he peered through the greenery. Thomas looked in the direction of Othello's gaze. Thomas saw there was movement up ahead and quickly realized it was Confederate soldiers he was seeing. Suddenly, he heard sounds of pistols and screams coming from the lower tunnel. They were under attack by guerillas.

"Get out your gun, Othello!" Thomas screamed to his brother, "And find a tree!! Take cover!"

Othello did as he was told, and Thomas did the same, following his own directives. They both began to aim their guns and shoot from behind the tree.

"It's some more of them niggers over there!" a guerilla soldier yelled.

"Then go and get them," they heard another answer.

Othello looked at Thomas for instruction. He didn't think that they were outnumbered too badly. Like the other reports of inter-actions with the guerilla soldiers, it was probably about ten men, and it sounded like down below the other men were in their own fight. Othello kneeled down with his gun in a firing position, waiting for Thomas to say something regarding what he thought they should do. He took a quick peek over at Thomas before refo-cusing and shot at a guerilla soldier riding quickly towards them on his horse. A bullseye hit, the soldier fell from the horse.

"Good idea!" Thomas said to Othello.

"What?" Othello asked. "I didn't say anything."

"We have to get out of here," Thomas said, lifting his gun and taking another shot. "We're going to take their horses. Then we can give them to Captain Nicklin[13]."

Othello's eyes brightened as he understood Thomas' plan. "Get a horse," he said to no one in particular. "Ok, I can do that," Othello refocused on his gun and fired another shot into the distance. It was answered by a soldier's scream.

"You already got yours," Thomas said, nodding to the horse from the first soldier Othello shot.

Othello looked over at a horse who was standing just far enough to be safe from the gunfire; the horse stood if it were waiting for orders. Othello looked back at Thomas with a face that said that he thought that Thomas had lost his mind if he thought he was running through bullets to that horse.

"You can make it," Thomas said. "Go ahead. I'll shoot so you can run," he said, focusing on his gun and shooting into the distance.

"Got dang, nigger!" a guerilla soldier screamed. Thomas shot again. "Got dang it!" the guerilla soldier screamed again. "That was my leg!"

"What about you?" Othello asked, not seeing a way out for Thomas.

"I'll get my horse," Thomas said.

"Got dang nigger!" the guerilla soldier continued to yell.

"Call me nigger one more time!" Thomas yelled into the distance, threatening the voice of the guerilla soldier out there.

"Dang, NIGGER!!!" the voice yelled. "Nigger, nigger, nigger, nigger."

Thomas shot again, hitting a tree near the man.

"Dang it!" the guerilla soldier snarled.

Not far behind the voice, Thomas could see more guerilla soldiers coming. Othello looked at Thomas as if about to argue.

"Go on," Thomas urged. "I'll be fine."

Othello nodded and ran towards the waiting horse. Thomas began firing towards the guerilla soldiers so that they had no choice but to take cover instead of shooting at Othello. Othello made it to the horse, jumped on its back, and moved it behind a tree. Quickly, he pulled out his gun and held it in a ready position.

"Go!" Othello yelled to Thomas.

Thomas placed the strap to his gun over his head so that the gun hung on his back. He waited behind the tree, hoping he had gone unseen. With an obvious intent of getting to Othello, a guerilla soldier on a horse proceeded to gallop past Thomas, who immediately grabbed the man by his leg and jerked him off the horse. Before the soldier could get back to his feet, Thomas jumped on the back of the horse and turned the horse around towards the soldier, who was in the process of standing back up on his feet. Thomas turned the horse around so that he could kick the man in the face. The man went down and didn't move. Thomas turned around to see another man approaching him. He raised his gun in warning.

"Ah ah...stop," Thomas said.

"I got one over here too!" Othello yelled from behind Thomas. A guerilla soldier stood before him with his hands raised in the air.

Thomas moved his horse so he could see both of the guerilla soldiers. "Aight now," Thomas said, his tongue licking his bottom lip as if he could taste sweetness in the circumstances. "Aight now, just stop right there," he said again, his voice a deep baritone. He was so deep in the moment that his words expressed his thick Appalachian accent. The guerilla soldier noticed.

"Ah, geez. A Appalachia nigger. From the Virginian hills! You miss working those lead mines, nigger!?

Thomas didn't reply. The other guerilla soldier being held at gunpoint by Othello chimed in.

"I think you right, Beauregard. He shaped like a labor nigger."

"Give a nigger a gun," the guerilla soldier at Thomas' gunpoint said, "he think he's a man. You a man now, nigger? Why don't you come down here and fight me like a man?"

"I wouldn't do that," Othello said, his voice muffled by his hand that was close to his face as he held his gun nice and steady. "I hear my brother is what ya'll like to call a ox nigger".

"What's an ox nigger?" the soldier in front of Thomas asked, confused.

Thomas flung his gun to his back, jumped off his horse, approached the man, and punched him in the face-one, two, three, and then the guerilla soldier was out cold on the ground.

"Ox nigger," Othello said again.

"I really hate ya'll niggers," the soldier at Othello's gunpoint said.

———

Back at the camp, Captain Benjamin Nicklin recognized the urgency in Thomas and Othello's approach. He abandoned his task and moved quickly towards them, ready to hear a report as soon as they were in hearing range.

"Now, boys!" he urged. "What's going on?".

"Sir," Thomas began, catching his breath. The horse had done all the running, but his adrenaline was in full force. The entire gallop back, Thomas was waiting for a bullet to hit him in his back. "Sir," Thomas began again, "over at South Tunnel. Confederate guerillas attacked again. About ten of 'em. I think they wanted to tear up the track, burn the ties, and just try to kill their way through again".

"The other men?" Nicklin inquired.

"Guerillas still alive were captured, sir," Thomas stated. "We have two wounded."

"Captain Cleveland!" Nicklin screamed.

"Yes, sir," Captain Cleveland replied, coming up behind Captain Nicklin.

"Get some of your men if you can and get down to the South Tunnel. See if we can keep the rest of those men alive," Nicklin said, appearing tired of the continuous battle for a war that was already won.

Captain Cleveland gathered 40 men of his First Tennessee Mounted Infantry[14], and they road quickly back to the South Tunnel on their horses. Othello seemed in shock as he held his gun as if to strangle it. Thomas looked ahead with no expression on his face. Nicklin noticed the expressions on both of their faces.

"First battle?" Nicklin offered. Thomas nodded in agreement. "First kill?" Nicklin asked further. Thomas nodded.

"I don't actually know if I killed anyone," Thomas said. "Othello there," Thomas looked at his brother, "I'm sure he did."

Nicklin looked over to Othello. "I'm not going to tell you it gets easier, boy," Nicklin began, "but you certainly realized, whether it is right or wrong, it is you against them. Someone's going to die. Just wasn't you today."

———

July 1865

Othello stood next to Thomas, waving away an annoying fly that was buzzing around his face. He and Thomas stood behind General Johnson. They were in Fayetteville, Tennessee, on the plantation of William Bonner to look into a case of an illegal whipping and a group of Federal Home Guards that seem to have overstepped their boundaries and duties[15]. General Johnson was acting for the Military Commission Courts Martial and didn't seem too enthused to be there.

The General removed his hat from his head and started to fan himself with it. He was already dripping in sweat as he sat on a wood crate underneath a large tree. "Mr. Bonner. Give me your statement. Tell me your case," he said out loud to no one in particular, though the statement was for Mr. Bonner. Another Union soldier, Charles, sat on another wood crate, paper and pen in hand, preparing to dictate the statement that Mr. Bonner and the others were going to give. Thomas, standing behind General Johnson, watched the man who received the whipping. He stood over to the side, obviously still sore. His name was Henry. Watching the man in that condition, especially after Lincoln's proclamation, made the muscle in Thomas' jaw jumped.

"Yes, sir," William Bonner said in response to General Johnson's request. "Um, my name is William Bonner. I reside in Lincoln County near Fayetteville, Tennessee. I know the boy present," William nodded to the whipped man. "He calls himself Henry Bonner. He has been my slave for more than fifteen years."

"Why do people take the name of their Master?" Othello whispered to Thomas. "I'm glad we don't call ourselves no Preston," Othello continued. Thomas smiled.

"Currently, Henry is working for me," William Bonner continued his testimony. "I have about twelve workers, but this man has always been a very sullen and contrary darkey." With an intense stare at Bonner, Thomas crossed his arms over his chest. William Bonner watched Thomas, nervously cleared his throat, and continued. "On the evening of the 3rd of July, a conflict with a colored woman named Mary occurred, and when I went to the fields, this darkey," William nodded towards Henry, "approached me on the difficulty. We exchanged words, after which I went to town. I saw Captain Shipp, and I made a statement to him because he is the Provost Marshall. Captain Shipp said he would send a guard down and have the things corrected. He sent two soldiers and Captain Adkins of the Home Guards, along with the Captain's two brothers, Joe and Jim. We went to the plantation about seven o'clock in the evening. The whipping was then administered on this boy by the Federal Soldiers and Captain Adkins."

A soldier brought Henry forward and lifted his shirt to show the evidence of the whipping on his back. Othello made a hissing noise at the severity of the beating. "Dang," he whispered. Thomas tensed and blew air through his nostrils like a dragon. He bit his bottom lip.

"Is it possible for the darky to take a seat?" William Bonner asked General Johnson.

"Henry?" General Johnson asked. "I think a better view of his whipping is when he stands."

"No, not Henry," William Bonner said. "That one," he said, pointing at Thomas.

General Johnson continued to fan himself, turned slightly, and looked up to see Thomas. Thomas made eye contact with the General and raised his eyes brows in question. General Johnson turned back to William.

"What's wrong with Thomas?" General Johnson asked.

"Ox nigger," Othello whispered so only Thomas could hear him. Thomas smirked.

"I'm attempting to give my testimony, and the darky there looks like we have a problem," William Bonner said.

General Johnson turned and looked up at Thomas again. "He doesn't look like he has a problem to me," General Johnson said, seriously studying Thomas' face as if there was something there that he couldn't see.

"I'd just feel better if he knew his place," William Bonner continued.

General Johnson turned back towards William. "Fine," he said, annoyed with Mr. Bonner and the heat. He looked up at Thomas again. "Thomas, if you please," Thomas pointed to himself in fake surprise. "Apparently, yes," General Johnson answered with a sigh.

Thomas looked around, exaggerating as if he were lost. He noticed a tree stump and pointed at it as if to ask. *Should I sit over there?* General Johnson nodded in agreement. Othello bit his lip to avoid laughing and proceeded to follow Thomas over to the stump. Thomas nodded once to General Johnson in agreement before slowly walking over to the tree stump and taking a seat.

"There," General Johnson stated to Mr. Bonner. "Now, please, proceed."

William Bonner ran his fingers through his wild hair. "Now, I call that a very severe whipping," he admitted, pointing back to Henry, "but I did not think he was whipped so bad, but I couldn't tell because it was dark out, I could not see. We were all armed and a little excited. I do not remember what I said to the boy, and I cannot say whether I said I would blow his brains out or not." Othello's eyes went wide. Thomas leaned forward, placing his elbows on his knees. "When I first went up to the house," William Bonner continued, "the boy Henry was tied to a tree by his hands being fastened around the tree. I did not count the licks. I think it might have been about one hundred; perhaps there was more." Othello whistled in disbelief. **"**The boy did not threaten my life or threaten me with violence at all," William Bonner admitted. "But from his attitude and the presence of the other Negroes I saw, I thought the Negro a dangerous man[16]."

"So Henry's an ox nigger?" Othello said under his breath, stroking his chin with his fingers as if there was a beard there. "Well, that makes things more...interesting," Thomas looked up at Othello as if to silently say, *stop it*. Othello shrugged in innocence.

"How many men did you lose or, how many of your men were beaten in your efforts to tie him to a tree...in the dark?" General Johnson asked.

"I...I don't...well. None, sir," William Bonner answered.

"Well, what kind of dangerous Negro is that!?" General Johnson said. He breathed in frustration, removed his handkerchief from his pocket, and wiped his face. "Mr. Mullin!" General Johnson yelled, waving the next witness into his view. "Your testimony, please."

Another man stepped forward. "Um, my name is Matthew Mullins. I belong to company "C" 5th Tennessee Cavalry. Um, on the 4th of July, I was at Fayetteville. I went out to William Bonner's plantation with Tyler Harrison of my company. We were joined by two other men when we arrived to William Bonner's house. The whole party proceeded to the Negro quarters, and we took out one of the Negros." Matthew pointed to Henry. "We tied him fast to a tree and fastened his hands on the other side with a bridle reign and whipped him about three hundred yards from the quarters. We did not count the blows, but I think they could not have exceeded one hundred and fifty. The Negro howled, but he did not curse anybody while we were whipping him. We whipped him for saucing his master, William Bonner..."

"He no longer *has* a master," General Johnson said as a matter of fact and a bit bored.

"Uh. Yes, sir. Of course. Um, we were sent out under the charge of the Home Guard Captain and were to do what he directed, and he directed the party to whip the Negro. Captain Shipp ordered myself and private Harrison to report to the Captain of the Home Guard for this duty. I have known other soldiers sent out before to settle difficulties like this where Negros have been whipped by soldiers. The Negro did not use any disrespectful language to William Bonner or any other person present in my presence at this or any previous time[17]."

Everyone was quiet for a moment. "Is that it?" General Johnson asked.

"Yes, sir," Matthew Mullins responded.

"Have you something else?" General Johnson asked William Bonner.

"No, sir," William Bonner responded.

"Well," General Johnson began as he stood up. "It seems to me this is a case of mistaken identity. Mr. Bonner here still believes he is a Master, but Henry here knows he's no longer a slave. I suggest the next time you two talk it out. But, then again, I suppose it was up to the Home Guard to know this." General Johnson adjusted his pants and belt. He took a deep breath, obviously tired of these conversations. "Considering, as Mr. Mullins has pointed out, this isn't the only time I've heard of these cases with the Home Guard ordering whippings. It seems we have a problem here." He waved his finger at Thomas and Othello to follow him. "I'll deal with Captain Shipp. But Mr. Bonner, you are fined $50 for the whipping. And Charles," Captain Johnson said, pointing to the soldier taking the statements, "draft a letter from me to Washington. These Home Guards are ordering all these whippings that are being reported from the communities. I consider them of disloyal character and will issue an order that they all be disbanded unless they are assigned and organized by the government. Any further action taken as a Home Guard is grounds for legal action.[18]"

General Johnson moved to his wagon and climbed up to the seat. Charles, not far behind him, climbed up to take the horse's reins. Othello and Thomas followed to board the back of the wagon where the supplies were.

"Stay strong," Othello whispered to Henry as he walked by him. "We are with you. Remember that ox niggers gotta stick together."

"What?" Henry said, looking at Othello.

"Nothing," Thomas said, walking past Henry. "Take care of yourself."

Othello and Thomas boarded the wagon.

CHAPTER 10
FURLOUGH

August 1865

Since the day that Thomas and Othello joined the Union army to fight in the Civil War, they had been serving in the 40th U.S. Colored Infantry. Most of their days were spent patrolling, protecting, and every so often, fighting with ex-confederate guerilla soldiers who still weren't ready to accept the Confederate defeat in the war. Both Thomas and Othello had been punching and shooting their way through numerous towns and plantations. They saw first-hand the government's struggle in providing clear rules and laws about how to treat the newly freed citizens of these United States[1]. On a few of their patrols, they had come across people, both Negro and White, that generally wandering around wondering what they were supposed to do next. Many of the Whites, who were accustomed to slaves performing even the most basic duties of cooking and cleaning, now found themselves in a position to have to do it themselves and lacking the skills to actually do it. The formerly enslaved were trying to figure out how to become self-made and were wary about what Lincoln's proclamation really meant. They were unclear of their position in society, their rights as people, and even their status as citizens. Many of the former enslaved were misguided by bitter Whites who gave them misinformation, telling them that Lincoln's proclamation just meant they were no longer slaves, but it didn't grant them any status. As a result, many of the former enslaved allowed themselves to be treated the same as before since they did not understand what Lincoln's proclamation meant. That was the bigger question that even Thomas had, what did Lincoln's proclamation really mean?

One day Preston, the first soldier that Thomas and Othello met at enlistment, approached them frantically, waving a paper in the air for them to see. "Boys!" he yelled, running up to them. "You see what the Freedmen's Bureau is giving out to the Negros and Masters in Clarksville!? I think the Negros being set up with a bad deal over there with the proclamation," Preston said, still waving the paper in front of Thomas' face. Thomas turned away, wincing as Preston waived the paper too close and too frantically for Thomas to actually see what the paper was. Frustrated, he grabbed the paper from Preston's hand.

"I can't see nothing if you just waving it around like that," Thomas said to him.

Preston grabbed the paper back. "Give it here. You can't read it, no how. Let me read it to you."

Thomas looked at Othello from the corner of his eye, and Othello smirked back at him. "Yeah," Othello said with a smile. "You can't read it no how. Let Preston read it to us," he teased Thomas because he was still pretending that he couldn't read and write.

Thomas sighed and looked back at Preston. "Alright. Go 'head and read it. What's it say?"

"It's rules of employment for slaves that's now free," Preston began. "They get a bad deal, Thomas. It says: One: one-half of the wages of the employee will be retained by the employer until the end of the contract for its faithful performance. Two: the employees will be required to rise at daybreak, each one to feed and take care of the stock allotted to him or perform any other business that may be assigned to him; to eat their breakfast and be ready for work at the signal, which will be given when the sun is half-hour high. All time lost after the signal is given will be deducted. Three: no general conversation will be allowed during working hours."

"Well. I'm out," Othello said, referring to the rule of no conversation during working hours. "That's a worse deal than before. At least Mister let us talk while we work."

"Oh...there's more," Preston continued. "It goes on and says, Four: bad work will be assessed at its proper value."

"Who decides what bad work is and what the value is?" Thomas asked.

"It don't say," Preston said, "but I bet you can guess."

"And I can guess how often the work will be said to be 'bad,'" Thomas said, running his tongue across his teeth.

"There's still more," Preston continued. "Says, Five: for disobedience one dollar will be deducted. BUT," Preston said, emphasizing the word, "Six: neglect of duty and leaving without permission will be considered disobedience." Thomas shook his head in disgust. "Says, Seven," Preston continued. "No livestock will be permitted to be raised by the employee; if they do, they will be charged for it. Eight: apples, peaches, and melons, or any other product of the plantation taken by the employee, will be charged for. Nine: the employee shall receive no visitors during work hours. Ten: three-quarters of an hour will be allowed during the winter months for dinner, and one hour and a half during the months of June, July, and August. Eleven: impudence, swearing, or indecent and unseemly language to, or in the presence of the employer or his family, or agent, or quarreling or fighting, so as to disturb the peace of the plantation, will be fined one dollar for the first offense, and if repeated, will be followed by dismissal and loss of such pay as shall be adjudged against him by the proper authority. Twelve: all difficulties that may arise between the employees shall be adjusted by the employer, and, if not satisfactory, an appeal may be taken to an agent of the U. S. Government or a magistrate. Thirteen: all abuse of stock, or willful breaking of tools, or throwing away gear, will be charged against the employee. Fourteen: good and sufficient rations will be furnished by the employer, not, however, to exceed six pounds of bacon and one peck of meal per week for each adult. Fifteen: house rent and fuel will be furnished, free, by the employer. That's a good one," Preston said, noting the free rent and fuel.

Thomas looked skeptical. Preston was desperately trying to find a silver lining.

"There's twenty-one of 'em," Preston said. "The one about the free rent and fuel was fifteen. Sixteen says no night work will be required of the employee, but such as the necessities of the plantation absolutely demand—such as tying up fodder, firing tobacco, setting plant beds afire, securing a crop from frost. Seventeen: a cheerful and willing performance of duty will be required of the employee."

"Wait," Othello said. "They require us to be happy?"

"Seems so," Thomas said.

"Eighteen," Preston continued on. "Stock must be fed and attended to on Sunday."

"I thought they wanted us to stay away from the livestock?" Othello said. "Didn't they say they deduct a wage from us for doing that back at number eight or something?"

Preston shrugged his shoulders, indicating that he didn't know.

"Nineteen," Preston continued on. "The women will be required to do the cooking in rotation on Sunday. Twenty: the employee will be expected to look after and study the interest of his employer; to inform him of anything that is going amiss; to be peaceable, orderly, and pleasant; to discourage theft, and endeavor by his conduct to establish a character for honesty, industry, and thrift. AND twenty-one: in case of any controversy in regard to the contract or its regulations, between the employer and the employee, the agent of the Bureau for the county shall be the common arbiter to whom the difficulty shall be referred.[2]" Preston looked up at Thomas. "What you thinking?" he asked him.

"I'm thinking they still trying to have slaves. All those times you just read they say that we could have our wage taken if the employer doesn't like…" Thomas raised his hands, intending to tick off a list and then thought better of it. He threw his hand up in exasperation. "Anything! The employer just has to claim he's unhappy about anything, and he doesn't have to pay you!"

Othello shrugged his shoulders in carelessness. "Eh," he said. "We knew it was going to be a bad deal. Are we really surprised?"

Thomas took a deep breath. "No," he said, defeated.

"So. What's a Negro to do?" Preston asked Thomas as if he expected Thomas to speak for all Negros everywhere.

"First, we find out if those rules are just Clarksville, or if that is everywhere, 'specially Virginia," Thomas began. "And if it is, then we just have to get our own plantation."

"Where we going to get a plantation?" Othello asked in disbelief. "If Mr. Ballard was still alive, he'd probably let us work to get some. But this is Mister we talking about."

"If we can't get no plantation," Thomas said, "then we get ourselves jobs in something we know we good at. Something we know we will do perfectly."

"The rails?" Othello asked.

"Probably," Thomas answered.

"I don't really work the rails. That's your thing. I'm good at farming and stuff,." Othello said.

"We'll figure you out," Thomas said. Othello nodded in agreement.

Preston looked down at the paper in his hand with the rules and began to fold it up to put it away. "Remember when I first met ya'll?" he asked both of them. "Remember what you told me, Thomas? You said things take more than a piece of paper." Preston slapped the paper in his palm. "It ain't nothing but a piece of paper, Thomas. I got to believe there's enough good people out there that won't treat you people like that, even if the paper say that they can."

Thomas looked at Preston, clearly not as hopeful as he was. Experience had told him otherwise. "I hope you right," he said to Preston, intended on ending the conversation there.

———

July 3, 1865

A few days later, Thomas sat on the ground under a tree. It was a hot day, but as long as he sat there, the weather was bearable. He had his boots hanging from small branches of the tree so that they could get some fresh air. He wasn't ashamed to admit that they smelled. Othello sat to his right, his legs in a crossed position so that his elbows rested on his knees. His chin was in his palm as he attempted to read a letter from Oscar.

"I think I get it for the most part," Othello said to Thomas, still staring at the letter. "I don't know all the words, but I think I got most of it. So he's in Ohio now?"

Thomas nodded. "Yeah."

Othello went silent again as he continued to stare at the letter. "Why Ohio?" he asked Thomas, handing him the letter.

Thomas took the letter, folded it, and tucked it into his military bag. "He said when his infantry was sent there, he thought it wasn't all that bad. He's staying because it's North, and, when he was there, he found out that Ohio freed their slaves before Lincoln's proclamation[3]. About 60 years ago. He said if we had been living there, us, Pa, Ma, and everybody would have been free already. He said he ain't going back to Virginia. He don't trust them. He said he went home on break, he called it a furlough, I asked one of the others here what that meant, and they say the army gives you a break to go home and call it a furlough; anyway, he said he tried to go home on break, and Mister went crazy before he could even get close, so he spent his 30 days up in Roanoke."

Othello stared at Thomas with a blank expression on his face. "All that was in that letter?" Othello asked Thomas.

"Well, not all in this one letter. This one is just about being in Roanoke. The rest of what I said I put together from the other letters," Thomas answered.

Othello nodded. "Can we get one of those furloughs? I'd like to go see my wife," he said with a smile. "Now that we free, Mary can probably be my wife under the law. I need to find out how to get that done."

Thomas nodded in agreement. "I think so. Next time we can get some time with the General, I'm going to ask. I ain't going though if I can't get you one too," Thomas said. Othello nodded in agreement.

Their conversation was interrupted by a man approaching. His hat sat on top of his head in a position so that it didn't fit snuggly, allowing fresh air to run over the man's head. They could tell the man was trying to wear the hat as required while also dealing with the heat.

"Private Fraction," the man said as he approached both Thomas and Othello.

"Yes, sir," they replied together.

The man smiled slightly. "I mean the big Fraction. Sorry. I'm not too sure how to separate you two when you are together."

Othello rolled his eyes. "He ain't *that* much bigger than me."

"Don't worry about it," the man said, looking at Othello. "I think we're about to clear that up shortly." He looked back at Thomas. "General Johnson would like to see you." The man looked at Othello again. "Why don't you come along? I'm sure you'd like to be there."

Thomas and Othello looked at each other, confused. Thomas was more paranoid than intrigued, and Othello was more intrigued than paranoid.

"Yes, sir," Thomas agreed with the man. He grabbed his boots, put them on, and stood up. Othello, already standing because his shoes were on his feet, followed the man and Thomas to the General's tent.

"Private Fraction and Private Fraction!" General Johnson greeted them as they entered the tent. "Come on in, boys, this won't take too long."

Thomas and Othello fully entered the tent and stood before the General's desk at attention. To the General's left and right were two Colonels. Thomas had a past with these two men. They were assigned to work with the Colored infantry but made it very clear that they didn't like it unless the Colored troops were assigned laborious and cleaning duties.

"Niggers are good at cleaning and lifting. They made a mistake when they let ya'll do things that make you think you equal to Whites," one of the Colonels once said to Thomas after the General gave Thomas an assignment other than labor.

The General walked from behind his desk to stand in front of Thomas. "Thomas, I'm on my way to Washington, so I'll be leaving this station in a few months. I won't be returning here. I'm going to finish out my duties there until I retire. Slavery no longer exists in the land, and the farther we get away from it, the more hideous it seems. While it existed in the South, the Southern people were hardly responsible for it. The slaves had been handed down from parents to children, and they represented just so much money, and few felt able to cut themselves loose from the degrading institution. But the country is freed from the disgrace, and all men North and South rejoice thereat.[4]" General Johnson paused as he turned around, his back to Thomas. He leaned forward and grabbed something from his desk. "I did not want to leave before doing this." General Johnson turned around to face Thomas, a military pin in his hand, "For your skill, experience, and performance in the United States 40th Colored Infantry, I hereby promote you to Sergeant.[5]" General Johnson placed the pin on Thomas' coat. Thomas' eyes went wide. Almost as wide as Othello's smile.

"Oh! WHAT!?" Othello screamed, throwing his arms in the air. "WHAT!?" he said again, laughing out loud with a huge smile on his face. "You just made a Negro a Sergeant!!" he said, rushing over to congratulate his brother.

"That's what I said," grumbled one of the Colonels standing to the side. He was obviously not happy about this.

"You'll be given the command of about twenty men, and it's your duty to make sure they are taken care of and understand the jobs they are assigned," General Johnson said, patting Thomas on the chest.

Thomas looked down at the pin on his coat. "Uh...thank you, sir," he said in a small voice.

General Johnson grabbed Thomas by the shoulders. "You deserve it, boy. You're a fine soldier and a clear leader."

Thomas grabbed his coat to lift up the pin to get a better view. "I ain't never..." he began and stopped. He didn't know what to say, he was speechless.

"Let me see," Othello said, turning Thomas around to get a look at the pin. "Gah lee" he said, shaking his head in disbelief.

"I agree," the Colonel said to no one in particular. "I can't believe it either. It's like I said, General Johnson, with all due respect, to reward him for doing his duties seems a bit overcompensating. If you're going to reward him for being a Negro, there are several hundred others, including Private Fraction here, that I'm sure are more than open to a promotion."

General Johnson turned around to look at the Colonel. He stood there for a moment, not moving and not saying a word. The General was considering how to handle the Colonel and his clear insubordinate action towards his decision to promote Thomas. General Johnson ran his fingers through his beard.

"His promotion," he began to the Colonel, "is in recognition of his ability to perform his duties above and beyond, and in the midst of the pressure that is put on him by you and others who don't even want to afford him the opportunity to be his best, yet he manages to do it, anyway." The General walked toward the Colonel to stand in front of him and the second Colonel, who agreed that Thomas was undeserving as a Negro. "Might I recommend that both of you come to terms with these outcomes? Upon my departure, it would not be wise for you to lead regiments that you intend to destroy from the inside simply out of social habit. Thomas is a skilled soldier and an excellent resource for you to have. Don't throw that away because you don't like the hue on his skin."

The Colonel, obviously not convinced, proceeded to redeem himself, at least, as a soldier. "Yes, sir," he murmured to the General.

Thomas knew better. He knew that this situation between him and the Colonels wasn't over. This was especially true since the

General was leaving the regiment. General Johnson returned to his desk and leaned against it, watching Thomas and Othello.

"You boys will do alright," General Johnson said, crossing his arms over his chest. "Where do you plan to go after this?" he asked. He thought for a moment before he stood straight and went around his desk to go shuffle through the papers that lay on top of it. "If this has it right," he said, picking up a sheet of paper and holding it close so that he could read it, "when you enlisted, you dedicated three years." He looked up at Thomas and Othello. "Both of you. Is that right?"

"Yes, sir," Thomas and Othello answered at the same time.

"When your time is up, are you going back to Virginia? Or are you going North? Enlisting for more time?" General Johnson asked.

"Virginia is my home," Thomas answered first. "I'm going home."

"The South is hanging niggers from trees," one of the Colonels answered. "You better off going up North."

Thomas ran his tongue across his teeth, slightly bit his bottom lip, and looked straight ahead to the tent wall. "They always been hanging niggers in the South. That ain't nothing new," he answered, not looking at the Colonel.

"Didn't you have a brother write you a letter telling you that he already ran up there to be safe?" the Colonel asked Thomas.

Thomas recognized the insult in his statement. He was calling Oscar a coward. "My brother went North because he said those White men up there is smarter than the ones in the south," Thomas answered him. "They figured out freeing the Negro was to their benefit 60 years ago…sir," Thomas added the formal acknowledgement to be able to deny the return of the insult.

"Well, I'm going back to Virginia," Othello said, interrupting the tension. "I got me a wife back there that I have to get back to. My sweet Mary is waiting for me."

"Be sure to remarry so that it is legal," General Johnson reminded Othello. "You want it legal. You'll have a pension that may help later." The General shuffled papers on his desk around again. "How about a 30-day furlough?" he offered them, still looking down at the papers on his desk. He found a piece of paper and began to write. "A much-deserved break," he said while he continued to write, "and Othello can use the time to remarry his wife...Mary? You said her name was?"

Othello nodded and looked at Thomas. He was happy that they were being offered the furlough without having to ask for it.

"You'll have to wait a while," the General added. "I can't release you until other soldiers on furlough return. We need to keep a functioning regiment. We'll end up leaving around the same time. When you see me leaving is when you can go. "

"Yes, sir, thank you," Thomas said to the General.

General Johnson handed Thomas the paper that he just completed granting Thomas and Othello their furlough, congratulated Thomas again, and sent them on their way. Exiting the General's tent, Thomas began walking to the courier's tent.

"Where you going?" Othello asked.

"I'm a get the courier to take a letter for me. We going to answer Oscar, and we going to write home and tell Ma, Pa, and Virginia that we coming to visit," Thomas answered him.

As they approached the tent, they saw the courier placing the strap to his bag over his head.

"Mr. Jessie," Thomas said, making the man turn around to look at him. "I'm glad I caught you. Can I get you to add two more letters on your trip? They real quick letters if I can get you to just take a minute."

Jessie looked at Thomas, a bit annoyed.

"Half one day's rations when you return if you do this for me," Thomas offered Jessie.

Jessie smiled and rummaged in his bag until he found two sheets of paper. "Alright then," he said. "Come on in."

Thomas and Othello followed Jessie into his tent, where Jessie went over to a corner and pulled out a small folded wooden desk. He unfolded it and placed a pen and ink pad on top of it.

"Alright. Where's the first one going?"

"Ohio," Thomas answered.

"Your brother Oscar again?" Jessie asked.

"Yes, sir," Thomas answered.

"Simple enough," Jessie said. "What you want it to say?"

"Oscar. I've got a furlough--both me and Othello. We going home to see the family. We will write to tell you how everyone is feeling. I got promoted to Sergeant," Thomas said, dictating to Jessie.

Hearing about the promotion, Jessie stopped writing, "Sergeant?" he asked Thomas.

"Sure did," Othello answered.

"Couldn't have happened to a better nigger," Jessie said with a smile. He continued to write. When he finished writing the letter, he folded it up and placed it in his bag. "The other letter?" Jessie asked, moving the other sheet of paper towards him.

"Virginia. Smithfield in Montgomery County. The Preston family house and plantation," Thomas said.

"I know the place," Jessie answered, writing on the paper. "What do you want it to say?"

"Family, me and Othello are coming home to visit. Oscar is still in Ohio. He ain't coming, but he love you. See you soon," Thomas dictated to Jessie.

"Ookaaaaaay," Jessie said, stretching out the word until he finished the last stroke of his pen. He took the note, folded it, and placed it in his bag. "That's it, right?" Jessie asked again.

"Yes, sir, that's it," Thomas said. "Thank you, Jessie."

"No need," Jessie said. "Here's hoping when I get back, our rations include some meat," he said with a smile.

———

About two weeks later, Thomas marched behind an ex-confederate guerilla soldier who he and his regiment had recently arrested in the local town. The men had been terrorizing the local stores in the area and were guilty of looting and setting fires. The regiment, including Othello, lined up the guerillas in an open area of the military camp while they awaited General Johnson to come and determine the sentencing for the men.

General Johnson came from around one of the tents flanked by his Colonels. He stopped a few feet away from the men that were lined up and called for them to come closer and line up where he stood. All the guerilla men moved except for the one standing in front of Thomas, his back to him.

"Go on now," Thomas said in a low voice so only the man could hear him. The man didn't move or turn around to look at Thomas. "Go on now," Thomas repeated himself.

"It'll be a cold day in hell 'fore I take orders from a nigger," the man said. He still did not turn around to face Thomas.

"Is there a problem over there, Thomas?" General Johnson called over to him across the distance.

"No, sir," Thomas yelled back over to the General. He looked at the man in front of him. He was rather small and light. The effects of war taking away any size and health that the man likely had years ago. "This here Confederate prefers a personal ride," Thomas continued yelling across the distance to the General.

"Well, do oblige him if you could, Sergeant Fraction," General Johnson yelled back across the distance.

"Sergeant?" the man questioned in a squeak as Thomas grabbed him by the back of his shirt and, almost lifting him completely off the ground, dragged him over to the lineup.

"I have to admit," began one of the Colonels standing next to General Johnson, "I still don't like him being a Sergeant, but it becomes tolerable to see the reaction on those Confederate soldiers' faces when you say it."

Thomas continued to drag the man, his arms wailing in the air as he yelled for Thomas to release him. When Thomas got the man to the lineup, the man turned around.

"Don't you ever touch me again, nigger," he screamed like the devil and spat in Thomas' face.

Thomas took a deep breath and then grabbed the man by the front of his shirt. The man braced himself, waiting for Thomas to punch him. The Colonels, also eager for Thomas to lose his temper and threaten his position, waited for his reaction. Instead of hitting the man, Thomas, still holding the man by his shirt, lifted him until the man's shirt reached his face. He wiped off the man's spit, then flung the man to the ground into the dust. Thomas hesitated, he wanted to walk away because he felt like he'd probably kill the man if he didn't, but he knew his duties as a Sergeant required him to stay and continue to lead his men. General Johnson closed the small distance and walked over to the man on the ground. He bent down, resting his weight on his toes.

"So, just to be clear," General Johnson began saying to the man. "You were caught terrorizing a town, trying to burn it down, assaulting woman, and you've spit in this man's face," he said, pointing to Thomas, "but you believe that *he* is the one less than human here? I've said it before, and I'll say it again. You, and men like you, are the devil incarnate."

The guerilla on the ground smiled. "Thank you kindly for the compliment," he said with an evil smile.

General Johnson stood back on his feet. "Get these men over to holding," he said, indicating a direction with his head. The regiment led the captured guerillas away.

A few feet away, Thomas noticed Jessie, the courier, standing there. When Thomas met his eyes, Jessie waved Thomas over to him. Thomas looked to General Johnson. "Requesting to be dismissed, sir." Thomas asked the General. Speaking with his Colonels, the General looked to Thomas and agreed, and Thomas walked over to Jessie.

"I have a letter for you," Jessie said to Thomas as he approached.

"Oscar wrote back that quickly?" Thomas asked, confused.

"No," Jessie said. "When the Virginia courier took your letter to Smithfield, Colonel Preston required that he wait for his response."

"My letter was to my family, not Colonel Preston," Thomas said.

Jessie shrugged his shoulders. "I know, but I doubt the courier was given a choice," Jessie said as he handed the letter to Thomas.

Thomas took the letter and opened it. Before he realized that he should ask Jessie to read it, he caught a few words: kill, never, leave. Thomas quickly handed the letter to Jessie. "Can you read it for me?" he asked him.

Jessie took the letter but looked at Thomas for a moment before proceeding to read it. He noticed Thomas' reaction to the letter before Thomas had given the letter back to him. He could tell that Thomas could read at least some of the words, but he wouldn't tell Thomas that he suspected that he could read because it didn't matter to him. If all the Negros could read and write, that would mean less work for him because they could write their own letters, and he could simply deliver them.

Jessie looked at the letter. "It says, 'Thomas, my previous state-ment that when you left that you could not return still remains. You are not welcome here. Should you appear, I will consider it trespassing and will take action to protect myself and my property. This includes my property that your family currently resides. As an heir to Smithfield, as a Preston, this includes Smithfield. You are also not welcome there.'[6]" Jessie folded the letter and handed it back to Thomas. "I'm sorry," he said, handing the letter to Thomas.

Thomas stared down at the letter in his hand. "I'd like to answer," Thomas said, looking up at Jessie. "If I answer with you today, do you think he'll get the letter before I go on furlough?" Thomas asked Jessie.

"It's possible," Jessie answered. "Though not by much of an advance of a few days."

"That's fine," Thomas said.

Jessie began to walk back to the courier tent, and Thomas followed him. Once they entered the tent, Jessie pulled the folded wooden desk from the corner, and unfolded it. He proceeded to set up the pen and ink pad.

"Ok," Jessie said, rummaging to find a piece of paper in his pack. "I'm ready. How do you want to answer?"

Thomas thought for a second and said, "Say, Mister, I am a soldier and now a Sergeant. I am trained to fight. When I return to see my family, if you take action to harm me or my brother, I will not hesitate to protect myself.[7]"

Jessie was silent as he continued to write down what Thomas said. When he was finished, he didn't look up at Thomas but hesitated like he was thinking of what to say. Jessie placed his arms on the small folder desk, leaned against it, and looked up at Thomas.

"You sure that's a smart thing to say, Thomas?" Jessie asked him. "It seems like Colonel Preston don't want you on his property."

"No," Thomas said in disagreement with Jessie. "Colonel Preston still thinks my family is his property. I'm going to visit my family, not the plantation. All he has to do is stay away from my family, and he won't see me."

Jessie nodded in agreement.

"I suppose you right. I just don't think things will turn out good for you if you go. Sometimes you just have to accept things for the way they are and move on."

"I ain't never been that type of person," Thomas said. "Ain't about to start that now."

Jessie shrugged his shoulders. "Ok. Well, it's your life," Jessie folded the letter and placed it in his bag. "I'll take this with the next run."

"Thank you, sir," Thomas said with a smirk.

Thomas turned around and left the courier's tent. While walking back to the tent that he shared with Othello, he balled up Mister's letter in his hand. He was frustrated that Mister still thought he had control over them. He came here to join the Union to fight for their freedom, and Mister was denying him that before he even steps back into Virginia. At the approach to his tent, Thomas could see Othello there. He was searching through his military bag. With the sound of someone approaching, he looked over his shoulder, saw Thomas, and noticed his sober mood.

"What's wrong?" Othello asked him, turning back around to continue to rummage through his bag.

"Jessie's back. Mister made the courier wait for him to write a letter back," Thomas said.

"Mmhhmm," Othello said, urging Thomas to continue while still looking through his bag.

"He told us not to come," Thomas said pointedly.

Othello stopped looking through his bag.

"What?" he asked. "Why not?"

"He said we're not allowed on his property and if we come, we're trespassers, and he'll have to protect his property," Thomas answered.

Othello rolled his eyes. "Protect his property from what? We're not coming to attack his plantation," he began looking through his bag again.

"Our letter said that we are coming to see our family," Thomas said. "I think he still thinks that our family is his property."

"So we not going?" Othello asked him.

"Yes, we're going," Thomas said, "I already wrote a letter back through Jessie. I told him we still coming. That we trained soldiers now, so if he attacks us, we will protect ourselves."

Othello stopped looking through his bag again. "You answered Mister's threat...with a threat?" he asked.

Thomas shrugged his shoulders. "Look. Mister can't tell me I can't see my family. And after Lincoln's proclamation, he sure ain't going to tell me that my family is still his property."

"What if he really *really* meant the plantation when he said his property?" Othello asked.

"He didn't," Thomas answered. "First, my letter was to Pa and Virginia. They free people now, so he had no right to read the letter. AND, if he don't want to see us, he can just stay away from the cabins while we visit our family. He had no reason to write a letter."

"Yeah," Othello said with a sigh. "I guess you right. I guess we see what happens when we get there."

Thomas Fraction military muster showing Sergeant status[8]

CHAPTER 11

ISABELLA

February 1866

Twenty-two-year-old Isabella Tate walked along the dirt road, hustling along as quickly as she could despite the weight of the layers of clothes that she had on to stay warm. She had boarded a wagon in Gogginsville, Virginia, was let off here on this road in Rocky Mount, and was now walking along this road like Mr. Schaffer directed her to do. Unlike many of the enslaved, even after Lincoln's proclamation, she hadn't left the Tate plantation[1] because there was nowhere for her to go. She didn't know anyone in the area besides the other enslaved from the plantation because she really didn't talk to anyone too much. Isabella was known to stay to herself. Once Lincoln's proclamation was signed, Master Tate had announced that the enslaved could either leave or continue to work for him. Isabella decided to stay working. Most of the others left, none of them by themselves, and most of them went to go meet up with their families to plan together what they should do next. Isabella decided to try to also find family and decide what to do next. She only had one problem-she didn't know where anyone was. She didn't know her mother and father's name, and she didn't even know if both of her parents were Negroes, or if only her mother was a Negro and her father was a White man. Most other people tell her that her father must have been a White man because she was a mulatto, but she wasn't sure. All she was sure of was that she had a sister named Abby. Master Tate once told her that he saw her sister when he bought her at the slave auction when she was a child. He told her that he didn't want to buy them both, but he remembered the girl being labeled as her sister named Abby.

"Do you know who bought her?" Isabella had asked him.

"No," he answered her, "but I do remember only myself, Jones, Williamson, and Smith were there at the auction block at the same time. You'd best start searching with one of them."

Isabella had given that information to the man from the Freedmen's Bureau, a thirty-six-year-old man named Charles Schaffer when he set up his office in the church three months ago. The federal government had created the Freedmen's Bureau to help the transition of the newly freed into society, and with White society's inevitable acceptance of the newly freed into their new non-bondage role in their lives[2].

"We'll do all that we can," Mr. Schaffer had told her. "But we can't make promises. Putting together these slave families is almost an impossible task."

"I understand," Isabella said quietly. "I thank you for trying. If Abby's out there, she's all I know and got."

Mr. Schaffer looked at Isabella with a sad look on his face. "We'll try," he said again.

Now, months later, Isabella was walking to meet her sister. She went back to the church every week for three months, hoping there was news. There never was until this week. Isabella walked into the church and approached Mr. Schaffer. This time, instead of looking at her sadly, he smiled.

"There you are, Isabella. I was hoping this week wouldn't be the one week you'd given up," he said. "We've found your sister, Abby[3]."

At first, Isabella didn't react. She just stood there stunned. "I have a sister?" she asked quietly. "I got family?"

Mr. Schaffer nodded.

"Well, where is she? Does she know me? Does she want to see me?" Isabella asked him, the questions pouring out of her like water in a bucket full of holes.

Mr. Schaffer moved his hands as if pushing down an invisible door. "Calm down, Isabella," he said with a laugh. "Yes, she knows you. Yes, she wants to see you. She is in Rocky Mount, Virginia. Not too far from here. About a 3-hour walk south from here."

"You know the way?" Isabella asked.

"Yes," Mr. Schaffer said. "But there's a wagon that will leave in the morning on its way to Franklin County. It'll have to pass Rocky Mount. I've already asked the driver if he can take you as close as he can. He has agreed, but you must be at the depot at sunrise."

"I won't miss it," Isabella said with a smile on her face. "I'll be there bright and early, sir. Thank you," Isabella turned and exited the church with a spirit she had never felt before, a spirit of hope.

Now here she was walking where Mr. Schaffer and the wagon driver told her that her sister would be. She walked down the path until she approached a clearing of trees. There ahead of her was a small group of shacks and houses. A woman, Abby, sat on the stump of a cut tree knitting a garment. When she heard Isabella's footsteps, she looked up. She and Isabella's eyes met, and they both immediately recognized their resemblance to each other. It was unmistakable that they were sisters. Slowly, Abby placed her knitting to the side.

"Isabella?" she asked in a whisper, just loud enough for Isabella to hear. Isabella nodded in affirmation. "Isabella!" Abby screamed, lunging herself forward in a run to greet her sister. When they met, Abby flung her arms around Isabella and held her tightly.

"Abby, I can't breathe!" Isabella laughed.

"Oh! I'm so sorry," Abby laughed, letting Isabella go. She cupped Isabella's face in her hands and ran them up and down her. "You ok? You're well? You not hurt or nothing, right?"

"Yes. I'm ok," Isabella said.

Abby took a step back and looked Isabella over. She placed her hands on her hips.

"Well, Lord be," she said with a smile. "If you don't look just like me. You my sister, alright."

"You remember our mama?" Isabella asked Abby. "Do you think we look like her?"

"All I remember is her name," Abby said sadly. "Mama is Jennie. Daddy was called Banks. Not sure of too much else, though."

Isabella placed her fingertips on her lips in awe. "My momma name is Jennie?" she said in a whisper.

"Yeah, your mama's Jennie," Abby answered. She led Isabella over to the tree stump where she was sitting and knitting. She sat down and picked up her project, proceeded to knit before stopping, and balling up her project in her lap. She looked up, smiling widely, and stared at Isabella.

"What?" Isabella said softly, putting her hands on her face. "Is there something on my face?"

"Yes!" Abby said. "Me! I'm on your face!" She paused for a second. "I ain't never looked like nobody before," Abby smiled. "Well, whatever White daddy we got must have some strong blood."

"What makes you think our daddy White?" Isabella asked.

Abby looked at Isabella the way a dog looks at something that makes a strange sound.

"Look at us! We're not exactly, um, children of the earth," she said, referring to the rich dark brown color of the soil and sands.

"I don't know," Isabella said. "Maybe Jennie was light, and she's the one with a White daddy."

"Either way," Abby said, "there's a White daddy in there." She shrugged her shoulders. Abby stood up from the tree stump again. "Come on with me. Imma introduce you to some folks." Abby started walking, and Isabella followed. "How you doing up there where you at?" She stopped walking, and Isabella ran into her back. "Where *are* you at again?" she asked Isabella while starting to walk forward again.

Isabella started to walk again to keep up with her sister. "I'm still working for my Master," Isabella answered.

Abby stopped walking again, and Isabella ran into her back.

"You still working for your Master? Mr. Tate? Why?" Abby asked.

"I ain't got nobody down there. I ain't got nowhere to go," Isabella said. "What am I supposed to do?"

Abby started to walk again, and Isabella continued to follow. "Get yourself a husband. You ain't have no man jump the broom with you yet?"

"I don't talk to nobody," Isabella answered. "Talking to people is dangerous."

Abby nodded in agreement. "Well. You want to stop working for Mr. Tate. You either need a husband or a job."

"I got a job," Isabella said. "I work for Mr. Tate."

Abby shrugged her shoulders. "Well. If that is working for you, I guess that's fine."

Abby and Isabella approached a group of cabins. Abby grabbed Isabella's hand and started dragging her forward. Isabella, already struggling to move her feet to keep up with Abby without being dragged, tried not to stumble over her own two feet as Abby pulled her to increase their speed.

"Hey everybody!" Abby screamed. "She's here!" As they entered into a clearing of trees, Isabella looked around and saw a large group of people. They all burst out in greeting and walked over to welcome Isabella, and all she could do was smile.

———

May 1866

Isabella knocked lightly on the door to the chambers of Mr. Tate. She rubbed her sweaty hands down the front of her apron, removing the oil that was gathering there. She wiped the sweat off her forehead with the back of her hand and then rubbed her hands down the front of her apron again.

"Why's it this hot already?" she said quietly to herself.

She peered down the staircase, watching another man carry a large cooking pot through the house.

"Be careful with that there, Edward," she said to him from the top of the stairs. "That thing get a crack and ain't no using it for boiling."

"I know, Miss. Lizzy. I got it," he said, grunting from the heavy load.

Isabella turned her attention back to the door and tapped on it again.

"Master Tate," she said to the door. "Master Tate, I'm here to empty your chamber pot. You don't want it to start smelling in there now, do you?" Isabella could hear the old wood floors in the room creak. She heard a few footsteps and then Mr. Tate's voice.

"Come on in, Lizzy," Mr. Tate said through the door.

Isabella opened the door and proceeded to walk over to the corner of the room to grab the chamber pot. She kept her eyes to the ground, hoping not to catch Mr. Tate's gaze. As she bent down to grab the chamber pot, Mr. Tate called her name.

"Lizzy," he said. "Come on over here. I need to tell you something."

Isabella walked over to Mr. Tate. "Yes, Master Tate?" she said, her eyes still averted.

"Things are about to change around here. I'm knocking down those slave quarters to use the land for more farming, and a lot of these Negroes gonna have to go. I can't maintain my living and pay the Negros. It just ain't feasible," Mr. Tate said to Isabella.

"Yes, sir," Isabella said.

"Now I know you ain't got no family. So I set something up for you. You going marry my cousin's nigger boy. He's my cousin's blood, so I know he's a smart boy that'll be good for you," Mr. Tate said.

Isabella looked up at Mr. Tate.

"Master Tate, I don't..."

"Now, Lizzy," Mr. Tate interrupted her. "Ain't no choice. What else you going do? Free Negro men working plantations, and most of the plantations that are left are taking Negros they already had to employ. Ain't going be no place to hire you, so you need to marry one of the Negro men that'll be farming or working somewhere else."

Isabella, already well-conditioned not to question Mr. Tate, free woman or not, nodded in agreement. "Yes, sir," she said.

"Good! I'm glad you agree. The nigger boy's name is Lewis, and the nigger preacher is going to marry you two tomorrow. Mary will come and get you and take you over to Roda's house so ya'll can get hitched[4]."

Isabella nodded in agreement again.

"Lewis will be good. Since he's my cousin's nigger boy, my brother's sending him to Roanoke for some work. Better than farming. If he does good, you'll be living well," Mr. Tate continued. The look on his face was proud for this good deed that he was offering to Isabella.

Isabella nodded in agreement again. She stared down at the ground silently. Mr. Tate didn't say anything else, so Isabella peered up at him from under her eyelashes, her head still down. Mr. Tate was watching her closely.

"I told my cousin you're a pretty girl. Lewis a real lucky boy," He said.

Isabella swallowed hard.

"Go on now. Get the chamber pot," Mr. Tate said, sitting down in his chair and continuing to read his papers.

Isabella walked over to the corner, grabbed the chamber pot, picked it up, and left the room as quickly as she could. She moved down the stairs like a graceful wind, right out the back door of the house. She moved quickly past the other workers and stopped in a large clearing. She just stopped. She couldn't think anymore. She couldn't move anymore. She was confused. Could Master Tate just marry her off like that? Could he do that? She still didn't understand what freedom meant for her and all the Negros. She didn't think Master Tate would do this if he weren't allowed to. *I ain't never get in no trouble before*, Isabella thought to herself, *I ain't 'bout to start now.*

A woman walked over to Isabella, her head wrapped with a scarf. "You ok, baby?" the woman asked her.

Isabella looked to her right and saw Ida standing there. She was an older woman and one of the few people that usually spoke to Isabella. Ida was also one of the few people that Isabella would speak.

"Master Tate getting me married tomorrow. Some boy named Lewis," Isabella said.

Ida just watched Isabella. She was waiting to see how Isabella felt about it before reacting to it. It was obvious to Ida that Isabella was confused. When Ida didn't say anything, Isabella continued.

"Can Master Tate do that, Ida? Even with us free? Can he do that?" she asked Ida.

"I don't know," Ida answered honestly. "I been around long enough to see these White men pass a law they think they doing us good, but really it ain't good for us at all."

Isabella looked down at the ground again. "When I went to visit my sister Abby," Isabella began, "she said that one way to get out of here was to get married." Ida pressed her lips together. "I don't know what I'm supposed to do," Isabella said to Ida.

"I don't know either. But experience tells me, you'd better show up to where you are supposed to be tomorrow," Ida said, looking at Isabella sadly.

———

The next morning, Isabella found herself being led by the woman Mary to Roda's cabin. When they arrived, Mr. Tate was there, rocking back and forth from his heels to his toes. Next to him was another man that Isabella was assuming was his cousin.

"Ah! There she is!" Mr. Tate said, his arm stretched out to Isabella. He pushed the other man forward. "Didn't I tell you,

Walt? Pretty thing ain't she. Well behaved too. She won't give Lewis no issue. She'll be a good nigger wife."

The man, Mr. Walt, looked over Isabella that a prized cow in the county fair. "Good pick indeed, Tate!"

"Come, Lizzy," Mr. Tate said, waving her forward. "Come meet the boy, Lewis."

Isabella walked forward towards Mr. Tate. Behind Mr. Walt was a young boy. Isabella assumed that this was Lewis. He was a mulatto like her, but he was what they called "ginger"[5]. His hair was red, and so were the freckles on his face. He was a stripling of a boy, meaning that he was young. She could tell that he was young physically and mentally. From the look on his face, he was as trapped as she was. Neither of them said anything to each other.

Walt watched Lewis. "Well, say hello to your wife, boy!" Mr. Walt said, pushing Lewis forward.

Lewis walked forward but looked past Isabella into the trees. "Hello," he said shortly, like a young boy forced to greet an old wrinkled up grandmother.

Isabella looked at Mr. Tate. He gestured her forward, urging her to make conversation. "Um," Isabella said, turning to Lewis. "Good morning."

They both went silent again. Mr. Walt took an annoyed breath. He pulled his pocket watch out of his breast pocket, opened it, and checked the time.

Mr. Tate looked over to his cousin and noticed his impatience. "Well, let's finish this. I have other business," Mr. Tate said.

Mr. Walt and Mr. Tate walked into Roda's house. Isabella and Lewis just stood there silently. They didn't even look at each other. They stood there still as stone until Lewis turned towards the cabin and, without looking at Isabella, said, "You first."

———

Less than a week later, Isabella found herself in a room in Roanoke with her new husband, Lewis. Mr. Tate was right in that Mr. Walt was able to get Lewis work in Roanoke, and he had also set up a room for them to live. Isabella sat on the edge of the hard bed in the room, her hands clasp together. She wasn't sure what she was supposed to do.

"Master Walt said I need to be at the warehouse at 6 a.m," Lewis said to Isabella.

He was also sitting stiffly on the bed. They both looked forward at the door ahead of them. Since they had been married, they hardly ever looked at each other.

"I'll work the warehouse for a little while until I find something else," Lewis said.

Isabella nodded in agreement.

"I guess you can stay here and do whatever it is that wives do," Lewis continued. "I don't know what that is, 'specially in a room like this," Lewis looked around. "Maybe clean up or something?" he said in question.

Isabella looked at the ground. She shrugged her shoulders.

"I can find you something to eat for when you get back," she said. "I can do that."

Lewis nodded in agreement and then slapped his hands on his knees while he stood. "Ok. You can do that," he said. He walked over to the door, intent to leave for work, reached for the handle, and then paused. He looked back at Isabella, and for the first time, deliberately asked for her attention. "Hey," he said, calling to her to look at him. Isabella looked up. "I'll see you later," he said, smiling sadly. Lewis rushed out the door and never returned[6].

CHAPTER 12

HOME

Virginia, February 1866

Virginia Fraction, now thirty-one-years-old, held a pile of blankets in one hand while she tried to keep her balance as she bent down to pick up a tin cup off of the floor. She was at her father John's cabin, helping him to clean up a bit. Ester, their mother, had already passed away, and John was trying to maintain the best he could as a man who didn't do too much housework. If she were honest, she had been spending a lot of her free time here at Smithfield for another reason. She kept finding excuses to come over because she was waiting for Thomas and Othello to show up for their visit any day now. Today, it was Friday, early evening, and she planned to stay here today and tomorrow. She'd have to get back to Whitethorn by Sunday morning and have breakfast and supper ready for the Caperton family. Since Lincoln's proclamation, Virginia had started working at Whitethorn for the Capertons who are of the Preston family; they were cousins of the Smithfield Prestons[1]. The Capertons and other local families related to the Prestons were plantations that Mr. Preston, Mr. Ballard, and Mister often sent their enslaved to work for, so she and her family were familiar with the Prestons and their families.

When Chloe had received the letter from Thomas that both he and Othello were coming to visit and that Thomas was now a Sergeant, everyone was so happy and excited.

"You sure they coming?" Chloe had asked her one day. "Oscar wanted to come too," Chloe reminded Virginia, "but Mister didn't make it easy. So he never came."

"We talking about Thomas. He'll come just to make Mister mad. He don't care. Mister shouldn't have written that letter back to him. He would have been better off ignoring that Thomas and Othello was coming for a visit than to write a letter back," Virginia said.

Chloe nodded in agreement.

"Mr. Caperton ain't mad that you keep coming over here to Smithfield looking for them to show up?" she asked with a smile.

Virginia smiled back at Chloe. "Mr. Caperton don't mind. Long as I do what he got me doing over there, he's fine. I leave them two days' worth of meals, and I think the Misses likes to pretend that she makes the meals when she gives them to Mr. Caperton and the children."

Chloe laughed. "You should teach her how to do it," she said.

"That ain't proper," Virginia answered her. "I'll take care of it. The Misses can learn if she wants to, she can ask, but I'm not going to tell her she needs to learn it."

"Sarah still trying to get you to sit down and eat Sunday breakfast with her?" Chloe asked her, referring to one of the Caperton children.

Sarah liked to come to Virginia's cabin at the back of Whitethorn to sit down to have breakfast with her. Sarah and many others called Virginia 'Aunt Ginny.' Each time Sarah came, Virginia would lay out a lace white table placement and serve Sarah a wholesome breakfast, and almost every time, Sarah would ask Virginia to sit down and eat with her. Virginia always declined, telling Sarah that it wasn't proper[2].

"Yeah," Virginia answered Chloe, "but I don't 'cause it still ain't proper."

"How about Dan?" Chloe said, asking Virginia about her husband. Virginia had married Dan Capers[3]. He had been a slave at Whitethorn and had taken on a version of the Caperton name when he chose a surname after emancipation.

"Dan ain't sitting at the table either. Even if he wanted to, I'd tell him it ain't proper," Virginia answered Chloe.

"I get the feeling that this ain't nothing about being proper," Chloe said, looking at Virginia with a little skepticism.

Virginia smiled sheepishly. "My answer is still, it ain't proper."

———

John, now sixty-eight years old, slowly made his way down the road riding atop a small wood wagon pulled by a tired old horse. The small wagon he was on, and its tired wheels clanked as it hit the stones and ditches in the dirt. He enjoyed the solace of the ride and let the horse leading the cart take its time with the task of carrying him and the supplies he was bringing back to Smithfield. He was tired, his vision was blurry, his head was itching, and his hands were cramping when he held tightly to the reins. This cold weather didn't help his hands either.

"At least it's not snowing," John said to himself.

It was a good thing that this horse was so well-behaved, and he didn't really need to place any pressure on it. The horse knew its way back to Smithfield, so there wasn't much leading that John had to give to the horse.

John's vision began to focus on two blurry figures walking along the road ahead of him. When he was close to the two figures, he yelled out "At your right," to indicate to the two figures that they needed to move further left to let him pass without being hit by the horse. He still couldn't see clearly. The two figures stopped, turned around, and just waited there. "At your right!" John yelled again, urging the two figures to move to the left to let him pass. Suddenly the horse increased its trot like the two figures were offering it the biggest bag of meal it had ever seen. "Whoa, Whoa!" John screamed trying to get the horse to stop. "Whoa, boy!" he cried again, but the horse kept lunging forwarding. When the horse reached the two figures, one of the figures started to laugh as he pet the horse along its neck.

"Hey, boy!" John heard the voice say. A man's voice. Wait, not just a man's voice.

John squinted his eyes to focus his vision better.

"Othello!? Thomas!?" John yelled, recognizing his sons.

"Yeah, Pa!" Thomas said, grabbing the horse's reins from his father. "What you doing out here by yourself. You can't see no more! Ain't nobody come with you?"

John laughed and starting to push himself to a standing position to get down off the wagon. His old knees making the task a greater effort than Thomas and Othello could imagine.

"Nah, Pa, stay seated. We'll come up," Othello said, climbing up the wagon.

Still holding the reins, Thomas followed him up on the wagon. The presence of both of them sandwiched John between them on the small wagon bench behind the horse. Thomas shook the reins to urge the horse forward.

John looked side to side between his two sons. "Look at my sons," he said with a smile on his face. "Your mama sure was proud. She would have been even more proud if she was here today."

Thomas looked down at his hands. "Yeah, I'm sorry we weren't here when she died," he said.

"Me too," Othello said sadly.

They all rode along silently for a while before John looked over at Thomas. Thomas looked back at his father from the corner of his eye. He smirked at him.

"What?" he said quietly.

"Sergeant?" John asked.

"Yeah, Pa," Thomas said with a smile.

"What you do as a Sergeant?" John asked.

"He's in charge of about twenty men, including me. He makes sure we do what we are supposed to do," Othello answered for Thomas.

"So you in charge!?" John asked, straightening his back in excitement and pride.

"No," Thomas said with a smile. "There are many people in the regiment more in charge than I am. I'm just in charge when there are more important things for them to be in charge of."

"They still dealing with Confederate soldiers in Tennessee?" John asked. "I hear there's small fights still going on as some of the soldiers are still fighting, burning stuff down, killing folks…" John faded off and stopped talking. He got lost in a daydream thinking about all the things he had seen through his life-the blood, the bodies, the folks hanging from trees as he ran the errands for Smithfield. "I can't believe I made it," John said in a whisper.

"Made it to what?" Othello said, looking at his father. He had leaned back in the wagon in a relaxed position.

John looked over at Othello. "My Pa and my Ma knew they wouldn't be free. Mr. Preston thought that the idea of freeing slaves was impossible. He said business wouldn't let it happen.

When I was growing up on Smithfield, Mr. Ballard used to always talk about freeing the slaves. He promised my Pa he'd get him free so he could go back home. Ester hoped that we'd be free after the war. Ain't none of them here today, but I'm here. I can't believe I made it. I can't believe I get to see it," John said, rubbing his two hands together. "Your children," he continued, looking between both of his sons. "Your children won't ever be a slave," he reminded them. "Your children will always be free. You have to make sure they remember this though, that they remember you, me, Esta, Oyewole, and Fanny. Make sure they remember us," he said, tears in his eyes.

"They'll remember, Pa," Thomas said, looking over at his father.

They rode along silently again until John slapped his knee. "I'm trying not to ask you no questions till we get back. I don't want you to have to repeat yourself," he said with a giant smile.

"We just around the bend," Othello said. "You can make it."

Thomas looked at his father from the corner of his eye. "You know what we use to do, Pa, when we use to run this errand?" he said with a smile, referring to the work that he and Othello used to do for Smithfield and Solitude.

"What?" John asked.

Thomas made three ticking sounds with his mouth, and the horse responded with a sound and wave of its tail.

"Hold on," Othello warned John, holding on to the side of the wagon.

"Gah!" Thomas yelled, and the horse lurched forward faster than it had ever run before. Thomas laughed hard. "You ain't had this horse running since we been gone, huh!?" he screamed over the loud sound of the wagon racing forward on the road.

Othello laughed hard and screamed. He was terrified and enjoying the ride all at the same time. John looked like he was holding on for dear life. As they approached Smithfield, Thomas pulled back the reins to slow down the horse. "Whoa, boy," he said with a laugh. "Good boy. Good job," he said, leaning forward to rub the horse. They continued to laugh at their father's terrified expression as the horse slowly trotted to the old cabin and stopped. It hummed in pride at its performance and turned its long neck around to look at Thomas. He smiled at the horse and rubbed its side again. "I missed you too," he said, smirking at the horse.

Virginia ran out of the cabin, Chloe not far behind her. "Those my boys!?" she screamed, running towards the wagon. "I know the sound of that crazy anywhere!"

Othello jumped off the wagon first and greeted his sisters, hugging them both tightly around their necks. "Aye!" he said. As Thomas helped John off the wagon, Virginia stood behind with her hands on her hips, waiting to greet him. When Thomas met his sister's eyes, he gave her a lop-sided smile. She smiled back.

"You did good," she said. "You look good. And just like Ma asked, looks like you took good care of Othello."

"Othello can take care of himself," Thomas said, grabbing his military bag from the back of the wagon.

"I'm sure he can," she said as Thomas walked towards her for a hug.

"Come on, ya'll," Chloe interrupted. "Can we go in the house? It's cold out here, and that fire in there is fresh."

Everyone followed Chloe into the cabin. Thomas and Othello placed their military bags in the corner and stood against the wall near the fire. They didn't sit in front of the fire to reserve the spot for their sisters and father. Chloe moved over to an iron pot.

"You came on a good day," she said. "I just finished making this stew for Pa. There's enough here. We should all be able to get some."

Thomas and Othello looked at each other and immediately ran over to the pot.

"Geez," Chloe said as she moved back to let Thomas and Othello grab two bowls to fill and begin to eat. "What they feeding you in the army? Pig slop?" she asked with a laugh.

"Something like that," Othello said with a mouth full of stew, the juice of the food running down his chin. He shrugged his shoulders. "You get used to it, though," he said, his mouth still full.

"Not a lot of flavor in the food," Thomas said. Unlike Othello, his mouth wasn't full, but the juice of the stew was running down his chin. John smiled, looking at his sons.

"Well," Virginia said. "When you finish, you can tell us all about it."

Othello continued to eat quickly, but Thomas slowed down. He wanted to savor the food and flavor, especially since he'd have to go back to Tennessee in less than a month. Although the furlough itself was thirty days long, they had to be back at the camp in that timeframe, too. This meant they only had a few days here at Smithfield.

Since Othello was eating so quickly, he finished his stew before Thomas did. He took a deep breath and sighed in satisfaction from the food. "I think army is army," Othello said, placing the bowl down on the floor next to where he was sitting. "Probably whatever you're thinking and whatever you've heard is true. What I really want to know about is what's being going on here, especially after Lincoln's proclamation. They treating you like free? A lot of freemen everywhere else ain't treated as free. Is Mary still at Mr. Wilson's plantation?" he asked.

Virginia shrugged her shoulders. "I'm working at Whitethorn. Chloe still here at Smithfield with Pa. We ain't seen George. And as far as we know, Mary still at the Wilson plantation."

Thomas swallowed the stew in his mouth. "What about Mister?" he said to Virginia. "How he treating you?" he continued, directing the question to Chloe since she would see him more often since she was working at Smithfield.

"He don't really get to treat me like nothing," Chloe said. "I'm not at Solitude. I'm at Smithfield."

"He still spending lots of his time at Smithfield, though?" Thomas asked.

"Yeah," Chloe said. "But I can ignore him like we usually do. He really leaves us alone with you gone." Chloe picked at the hem of her dress. "Sorry about his letter to you," she said. "I didn't mean for him to see the letter you wrote us. I was just so happy about it, I was trying to show it to some of the people at Smithfield who miss you as much as we do. They ask about you all the time. Want to know if you and Othello is alright. Waller saw the letter and told Mister," Chloe said, referring to Ballard's son.

Thomas placed his bowl down on the floor. He had finished the stew and figured if he put the bowl down, he wouldn't crave more. It wasn't working.

"It's ok," he said to Chloe. "I ain't paying Mister no mind. We probably be on our way out of here before he even knows that we here."

"We are *not* wasting this family time talking about no Mister," Virginia interrupted. "How about you tell us what a Sergeant is, Mr. Army Man," Virginia said, joking around with Thomas.

"It means he's in charge of about twenty men, and he makes sure we know what we are doing," Othello explained to everyone in the room.

"So you in charge?" Virginia asked the same question that John asked earlier.

"No," Thomas said.

"Sometimes you are," Othello corrected him.

"I'm in charge of something when that something is not important enough for the people in charge to be in charge of," Thomas corrected.

"That's still in charge," Othello said, shrugging his shoulders.

Thomas shrugged his shoulders in return. "I'll tell you what Sergeant means. It means that some of the people in charge give you a hard time because they don't like that you a Negro in charge. It means people spit on you, and it means that ex-Confederate soldiers fight even harder when you try to arrest them because they are trying to burn down entire towns, breaking into stores, stealing things, and raping women. That's what Sergeant means," Thomas said.

Othello looked at Thomas in disbelief. "All that's not because you a Sergeant. That's cause you a Negro. I'm getting the same thing, and I'm not a Sergeant."

"True," Thomas agreed. "Except if they spit on you, you can hit them in the face," he said with a smile. "I have to stay calm and controlled."

"Yeah," Othello agreed. "Glad I'm not you."

"I do have something for you," Thomas said to John. He stood up and walked over to grab his military bag. He dug inside the bag and pulled out three dollars.

"I wanted to give you some money," he said, handing it over to John. "I wasn't sure if you had any money. I know you supposed to be making a wage now, but there's some mix-up on the Confederate money and the Union money. I know the Confederate money ain't worth nothing no more, and I'm not sure if they have any Union money at Smithfield."

"They asked for forgiveness," Chloe clarified, referring to the ex-Confederates ability to ask for amnesty from the U.S. Government. "So the government giving them their money back."

"Oh, ok," Thomas said. "Well, you can still take it," he said, handing the money to John.

John took the three dollars and squeezed his son's hand.

"Thank you," he said in a whisper.

"I got three dollars," Othello said, hopping up to go to his bag. "But I want you to give it to Mary. I'm going to go and see her tomorrow and make my way over to the courts so we can report we married under the law[4].

Virginia clapped her hands together. "That's so sweet!" she said. "She's going to be mighty happy to see you. She told us about all the letters you been writing to her."

"Of course!" Othello exclaimed. "I love Mary! She's my wife."

John nodded in agreement.

———

A week later, Othello was outside in the cold finished up some repairs that he was completing on some of the beams outside of the old cabin. He figured that he'd find something to do to help his father while he was there, and this particular beam looked a bit weak and needed some repair. He noticed the cold air draft that the small holes in the beam were letting into the house. During the days that he was here, he had seen that his father would often just fall asleep in the old chair next to the fire and didn't really make too much of an effort to resolve the cold when he got comfortable. Othello was finishing the final steps of the repairs, just in time for dusk. The sun was going down, and his father would be coming in from his work at Smithfield soon. He grabbed the toolbox and began walking to go back into the cabin. As if speaking up the old man, he saw his father approaching the cabin.

"Hey, Pa," Othello greeted him. "I just patched up a few of those holes that was letting the cold air into the house. That fire should hold up better now."

John smiled and patted his son on the back. "Thank you, Othello. That's mighty fine."

Othello smiled. Together, he and John entered the cabin and were greeted by Thomas sitting on the floor writing a letter.

"Who you writing to?" Othello asked him.

"Sending a letter to Oscar letting him know how everyone is doing," Thomas replied. He went silent and kept writing.

"They know you read and write up there?" John asked him, referring to the army in Tennessee.

Thomas kept writing but answered his father. "I think some do and some don't. I'm not sure, really. Sometimes I have to say I don't know how; sometimes it don't seem to matter none, and other times, it seems to matter a whole lot. I try to figure it out 'pending on who it is."

John nodded in understanding. Thomas finished a few more sentences in the letter, folded it up, and tucked it into his military bag.

"I'll give it to a courier either when we find one on our way back to Tennessee or when we get back, and I'll give it to Jessie. I just figured I'd get it down now," Thomas explained, though no one had asked. He was interrupted by a knock on the cabin door. Othello walked over and opened it. It was a man name Hy. They had known Hy for some time, and Othello was happy to see him.

"Hey, Hy!" he said, grabbing the man's hand.

Hy smiled. "Hey, boys!" he said, stepping into the cabin.

"What you doing here?" Othello asked.

"I come to check on your Pa from time to time. I'm nearby working for Master Preston now," Hy answered. "Working for a wage now that we got Lincoln's proclamation." Hy said with a proud smile.

Thomas shook his head in disapproval.

"I know you don't like Master Preston," Hy said, looking towards Thomas. "I had to get a job where I could get one. Master Preston old, and he still got that plantation. He paying money. It's just me and him."

Thomas didn't respond or react.

"But I ain't here for that," Hy said. "I'm here cause I been over there working all day and at the creep of dusk, Waller, Mr. Ballard's son?" Hy said in question, making sure Thomas and Othello remembered him.

"Yeah," Thomas said, stretching out the word. "We know Waller."

Thomas wasn't too keen on Waller either.

"Well," Hy continued, "Waller came over to Solitude and told Master Preston that you and Othello was over here. I went around the back of the house, so it look like I was going another way, but I ran over here to tell you. Master Preston strapping up with pistols, and he, Waller, and his son-in-law on they way over here, he say, to kill you."

John struggled to stand up from the chair he was sitting in. No matter his age, he still had a trigger, and was adamant about protecting his children.

"Naw, Pa," Thomas said. "Go on and sit down. We fine. We just going to go ahead and leave. We would have had to leave in a few days to get back to Tennessee, anyway. We'll just leave a little early, so we don't cause you no problems." He walked over to his military bag and pulled out two pistols and a gun holster.

Hy whistled. "Gah!" he said. "They giving niggers guns in that Union army, huh? Two of um?" he asked.

Othello, following Thomas' lead and pulled a pistol out of his military bag.

"Nah. Privates get one. Thomas a Sergeant, he gets two." He followed Thomas' lead, put his gun holster around his waist, and added his pistol to the pocket.

Thomas adjusted his holster around his waist and threw his military bag across his shoulders so that his hands were free and his guns were clear from obstruction. He walked over to Hy and shook his hand.

"It was good to see you, Hy," he said. "You think you'll be around when we get back from serving. I'm coming back here. This my home, so I'm setting up home *here*," Thomas said, clearly making a point.

"I hear you," Hy said. "Just be careful."

Thomas and Othello said goodbye to John and asked him to tell Chloe and Virginia they said goodbye and explain why they had to leave so quickly.

"Don't take the main road," John told them. "That'll be the first place he look."

"What other way should we take?" Thomas asked John.

"I got a short path I take," Hy offered. "I can show you the way. You won't have to pass close to Solitude."

Thomas nodded in agreement, and he, Othello, and Hy left the house. When leaving the cabin, Thomas noted that the sun had almost completely set. These winter days were always short and cold. They walked along for a bit before Hy looked over to Thomas.

"They still enlisting Negros?" he asked. "I'd like to get me one of those guns."

"Depends on the regiments," Thomas answered him, "Not all of them are. Most of 'em are mustering out, ending." Hy looked disappointed but didn't say anything else.

They continued to walk along in silence, all three of them seeming in deep thought with something else when they were suddenly approached by Robert Preston, Waller, and Robert's son-in-law. Hy swore and immediately tried looking for an escape. Othello looked surprised, but Thomas didn't. The absolute absence of reaction and emotion on his face disappointed Robert. He wanted the fear that he saw on the other Union soldiers when his Confederate regiments came upon them. He wanted the averted eyes that the niggers he employed had when he came around. Thomas had neither. Robert looked over at Othello. Even Othello was different now. He looked surprised, yes, but he wasn't afraid. Robert shook his head and thought to himself, *it was a mistake to give these niggers guns and let them serve. They don't know their place no more.*

Thomas didn't say anything, but Othello took a few steps to be closer to him. He was positioning himself for a fight, as he had learned to do in the Union regiment. He was a skilled fighter now, just like Thomas had noted in his letter back to Mister.

Robert turned his attention back to Thomas. "You came back here," he said as a matter of fact. It wasn't a question, and there was no hint of disbelief in his voice. He made the statement like it was something that he wanted to point out to everyone because no one else was aware of it. Thomas didn't respond. "Why?" Robert asked him, his head cocked to the side in question.

Thomas licked his bottom lip and then bit it before raking his teeth across it and letting it go. "Like I said in the letter," he answered, "I'm here to see my family."

Robert stroked his beard. "I'm fairly sure I said that you weren't welcome to access my property."

"My...family...ain't....your...property," Thomas said, stressing each word.

"Everything within these lines is my property," Robert clarified. He looked at Thomas as if he was crazy for not understanding it.

"Lincoln's proclamation..." Thomas began.

Robert cut him off. "Oh, Lincoln's proclamation," he began, waving his hand in the air as if shooing off a fly. "What's it mean in the south? So, you're not a slave, but that doesn't make you a man or an equal. Lincoln forgot to define *what* you are. So for now, I get to define it." Robert began to stroke his beard again. "I think," he said and then paused. "I think you are a rotten criminal. A..." He looked up to the sky in an exaggerated gesture as if in deep thought, "trespassing thief," he finished his statement. He looked back at Thomas, at Othello, and then back at Thomas. "And based on those pistols on your hips," Robert continued, "I can't help but to feel threatened. This attempt on my life; this attempt to kill me has me so," he paused, *"DISTRAUGHT!"* he said with malice as he pulled out a pistol and cocked its hammer back.

At the same time that Robert pulled out his pistol to aim it at Thomas, Waller pulled out a pistol and aimed it at Othello. However, trained and experienced, at the second that Robert pulled his gun, Othello had pulled out his own and aimed it, and Thomas had pulled out both of his pistols and aimed them at Robert[5]. It was a Wild West scene in the middle of Blacksburg, Virginia, almost a century before the Wild West becomes the legend it would grow to be. Thomas had one pistol in each hand and cocked back his hammers with each thumb. No one made a move. No one pulled a trigger. Everyone stood completely still, pointing a gun at the other party.

"Make your move, boy," Robert said, urging Thomas to take action. Everyone continued to stand still, staring at each other, waiting for the other party to make the first move.

"Thomas," Othello whispered to his brother without lowering his pistol or taking his eyes off of Waller. "Don't do this," he continued. "You shoot him, they gonna kill you."

Thomas didn't respond. He just stared at Robert. This was an opportunity for him; He was a Union soldier and Robert was a rebel Colonel. Thomas could shoot him and show cause. Thomas could kill him, and the Union would know that it was self-defense.

"President Johnson is giving them forgiveness," Othello said as if he was reading Thomas' mind. "'Member what General Johnson said. These rebels are the devil incarnate, but the President still tells them, that all they have to do is take an oath, and he lets them go." Othello went silent for a second and then finished his whispered speech to Thomas.

"They lost the war," he said, referring to the Confederates, "but they got the White House."

Othello was right. Thomas exhaled and prepared to accept his defeat, but before he could make a move, Robert shot him[6].

CHAPTER 13

HANDCUFFS

It all happened so fast. Othello was standing there trying to talk Thomas out of killing Mister, and then Mister's gun went off. The gun was pointed at Thomas and the barrel was smoking, but Thomas didn't move. He just stood there. Othello was frozen in place. He didn't want to put down his pistol because Waller was still pointing his own pistol at him, but he wanted to make sure Thomas was ok. He must be ok if he's still standing, right?

Mister's eyes went wide in shock. "I...I...didn't..." Robert stammered. He looked at his nephew, Waller, and then sobered. Robert cleared his throat. "These niggers got to learn, right?" he said, his voice a bit shaky and unsure.

Robert looked back at Thomas. But Thomas just stood there; he wasn't moving at all, his pistols still aimed at Mister. Everyone just watched him until his hands began to shake, and Othello realized that he had stopped breathing. Thomas was holding his breath, until suddenly he exhaled and fell to the ground.

Robert took a deep breath. "Put down your gun," he said to Waller. "It's finished."

Othello kept his pistol trained on Mister while he stood in front of Thomas, who was lying down on the ground. He wanted to be a shield for him.

"Don't move!" Othello yelled. "Don't you move! Don't you…" he started to swear before he trailed off, tears choking his throat and blocking his words. The pistol in his hand started to go limp. "Thomas?" he said in a strained voice. He looked down at his brother.

Thomas was down on the ground, and he didn't move for the entire moment that Othello was holding his breath. He didn't realize he was holding his breath until suddenly Thomas moved to prop himself up with his elbows, and Othello exhaled loudly.

"The cock sucker shot me in the leg,[1]" he said, growling through the pain. He started crawling through the dirt to reach one of his pistols. "I'm killing the bastard."

Othello half-laughed in relief. Having already moved towards Thomas, Robert kicked away Thomas' pistols and stood to where Thomas laid on the ground and looked down at him.

"Now THAT," he said, pointing down at Thomas, "is where you belong. See. I could of killed you, but I didn't. You should thank me."

"Kill him," Thomas said to Othello, growling through the pain. "Seriously, I'm willing to die for it. Kill him," Thomas' nose flared in anger. Othello shook his head no.

Hy, mostly forgotten through the whole ordeal, moved forward to intervene. He finally felt like he could help. He knew he was better at playing the submissive Negro to Master Preston than Thomas was. Hy approached Robert, his hands outstretched in offering.

"Master Preston," he said, bowing down a bit. "Master Preston. Let me take Thomas. Me and Othello can take him off your property. He won't be a problem no more. You sho' showed him, Master."

Robert smiled. "Yes," he agreed, stroking his beard. "Indeed I did. But I don't think the lesson is done yet, though. I said I would kill him, but I'm not going to kill him, but he's going to jail." Robert looked back at Waller. "You got those chains?"

Waller nodded and came forward. He cuffed Thomas' hands behind his back and then proceeded to cuff Othello.

"Take 'em to the jail," Robert said to Waller and the other man that had come with them.

"Master Preston," Hy said, his hands still outstretched in offering. "Master Preston, you best let me take Thomas to get that bullet out his leg. If it get infected, you might kill him after all."

Robert thought about it for a second and then looked down at Thomas. "No. Let it stay in there," he looked down at Thomas. "You still a strong boy ain't you, Thomas?" He took a few steps to get really close to Thomas and leaned down to face him. "Once again, I bring you closer to God, nigger. That bullet stays right there. Just like communion in the church, 'this I do, in remembrance of me,'" he hissed, perverting the scripture of Jesus' last supper. "You will always remember *me*," Robert said, growling the words at Thomas, beating his chest with his fist like a deranged gladiator. Thomas didn't respond; he just watched Mister with hate.

"You want to help, Hy?" Robert said, standing up straight and turning back to the man. "Help him limp to the jail."

Hy nodded to Robert and moved forward to grab Thomas under the arm. He helped him stand up. "Put your weight on me," Hy urged Thomas. "Don't put it on the leg." Thomas nodded in agreement and grunted as they started moving forward.

———

Two days later, Thomas sat on the floor of a jail cell[2], the leg where Mister had shot him in an outstretched position before him.

His shirt was tattered because he ripped off a part of it to wrap the womb on his leg. As Mister directed, the prison had left the bullet in his leg[3] and had no intentions or plans to send a doctor to remove it and ensure there was no infection. He sat against the wall with the back of his head resting against it. His eyes were closed, and his face was tilted towards the ceiling of the jail cell. Othello lay on the floor of the cell next to him, fast asleep. Thomas listened to Othello's steady breathing as a sign that Othello had fallen into a deep sleep; he was dead to the world. Thomas was tired too, but he wasn't about to let both of them fall into a deep sleep so that someone could come upon them and do them harm. The Warden had told Thomas on the first day that they'd sit here until Mister was good and ready to decide what to do with them. Mister had no judicial authority here, but he had prestige based on the Preston name, and the Warden and the Magistrate did all that they could to be in Mister's good graces[4].

The silence of the room was broken by the sound of a door opening and someone approaching. Thomas put his senses at attention, but he didn't open his eyes. He wanted whoever was approaching to think he was asleep so that they would leave him alone. He was exhausted from dealing with the pain of the bullet in his leg.

"I'll be right outside the door," a man said. "These niggers try something, you just yell."

"Yes, sir," a woman's voice responded in a timid whisper.

Thomas heard the door to his cell open, and light footsteps approach. He still did not open his eyes. He heard his cell door close, footsteps leave the room, and the final door to the section where the jail cells were close. The room went silent again, but Thomas could feel someone near him. He raised one eyebrow in question and then opened one eye. Standing there before him was a young woman. She stared down at the ground, tapping her fingers against the bowl of hot water that she was carrying.

Thomas opened both of his eyes but just watched her, and he didn't say anything. She nervously looked around the floor of the cell before she looked up and saw Thomas looking at her. She was the most beautiful girl he had ever seen. He still didn't speak; he just looked at her.

The woman looked around nervously again, avoiding Thomas' gaze. Then she cleared her throat. "My name's Isabella," she said. "Isabella Ta…" she began, then she stopped. "Isabella Calloway, I think." She paused and thought for a moment. "Tate," she said. "My name is Isabella Tate."

Thomas raised his eyebrows in amusement. Her indecisiveness was endearing. He lifted his head off the wall to look at her better. "You still trying to pick a name?" he asked her, referring to the process of many of the newly freed people choosing a surname. Most took on the name of their former Master. This woman either wasn't sure what she wanted to do or had too many Masters to choose from. Thomas hoped it wasn't the latter.

Isabella shook her head and looked up at Thomas. "No. I already had one," she clarified. "My Master married me off and gave me a new name."

Thomas' heart dropped. "You married?" he asked, a bit disappointed. Then he felt confused. "How your Master marry you off? How does that work?" he asked, grunting through the pain.

Isabella looked down at the ground. "He told me I had to marry that boy 'cause that's what he wanted me to do. I don't know if I'm really married, though[5],[6]," Isabella answered, hugging the warm bowl of water to her stomach.

"You not sure of that either?" Thomas said, smiling at her with a small laugh.

Isabella took a good look at Thomas. He was handsome and strong, the kind of man that she normally would avoid eye contact with. Strong men were usually the scary ones; the ones that made her feel unsafe. She was a small woman, and small women, and their skirts were often unsafe around men like that. But this man was different. His eyes were kind when he looked at her. *Besides,* she thought to herself, looking at his leg, *he wasn't about to get up and come after her any time soon.*

Isabella made a small uninterested shrug of her shoulders. "My Master married me off to a young boy, sent us to Roanoke for his work. He went to work on the first day and ain't never come back. I stayed in the room at the boarding house his Master got us for about a week waiting for him to come back but," she said, not sure if she should finish. She realized that she was telling this man that she didn't know a lot about her.

Thomas waited for her to finish. "But?" he said, urging her on when she didn't continue.

Isabella sat the bowl of water down on the floor and started to remove her supplies from her apron. She sat next to the wound on Thomas' leg. "I waited a week, and he ain't come back. Eventually, the boarding house put me out. I been traveling around finding work where I can find it ever since. I'm here now," she said, referring to the jail. "Working as a chambermaid. It's what I'm good at."

Thomas looked around the jail cell, amused. "Well, please tell 'em I have some complaints about my room here at this Inn. My chamber ain't comfortable," he said with a smile, closing his eyes and leaning his head back against the wall.

Isabella continued to sit on the floor. She placed her hands on her thighs and stared at Thomas; she couldn't help but look at him. He looked serene and calm even though he was in this situation and was sitting on the floor of a jail cell shot in the leg. The Warden had even told her that the bullet was still in there, and while she was supposed to clean the wound and ensure it didn't get infected, she wasn't supposed to remove the bullet, not that she could. Isabella wasn't even knowledgeable enough to treat the wound; she was a chambermaid, not a nurse. She didn't do much of nursing while on Mr. Tate's plantation. The jail was just trying to clean him up because Mr. Schaffer from the Freedmen's Bureau was coming here to check on Thomas and his brother's case because someone came to his office and told him that two Negro brothers that were Union soldiers were being held in the jail for a crime they didn't commit. She didn't say anything. The silence made Thomas open one eye again to look at her. Isabella immediately looked down at the floor, embarrassed that she had been caught staring. Thomas opened both of his eyes but didn't remove his head from leaning against the wall.

"You have to excuse me, Ms. Isabella. This leg ain't right comfortable right now, so it's hard for me to be sweet on a pretty girl like you," he said with a small smile.

Isabella blushed. "I'm sorry," she said, embarrassed.

She lifted her hands to her head to fix her hair, making sure it still sat in the pins.

"Don't worry," Thomas said, adjusting to sit in a more comfortable position. The ground was hard, and he had been sitting there for a long time. The movement made a shot of pain run up his leg. "You looking pretty." He said with a strained grunt as he talked through the pain. He smiled at her and then had to laugh at himself for trying to sweet talk the woman while he was hot, sweaty, bloody, in pain, and he probably smelled too. Thomas' laugh made Isabella chuckle.

"No, I'm sorry 'cause they sent me in here to help you, and I ain't helping you." She looked down at his leg. "Can I unwrap this to look at it?" He did a quick nod in agreement. She started to peel back the piece of shirt that Thomas had torn off himself to wrap up his leg, stop the bleeding, and avoid infection if he could. "Now," Isabella said, talking to Thomas as she removed the bandage. "I ain't got as much nursing experience as some of the women on the plantation where I came from. But I'm all you got right now."

Thomas placed both his hands on the ground and lifted his entire body up to move his position again. Isabella looked up and hesitated for a second as she watched the muscles in his arms flex.

"I'm sure you do just fine, Lizzy," he said. "People call you Lizzy?" he asked her.

"Sometimes," Isabella said, continuing to address the wound.

"Which one you like?" he said.

"Either one do me just fine," she said.

"You gotta like one more than the other," he said. "Which one you like?"

Isabella went silent as she thought about it for a moment.

"My Master call me Lizzy," she said.

"I ain't ask you what your Master call you," Thomas said to her. He bent his head down so that his face was closer to her face, forcing her to look up at him.

Isabella looked up at Thomas and then looked back down and continued cleaning the wound. She was quiet for a bit before she smirked and said in a small voice. "I like Isabella 'cause it sounds like a song."

"It sure do," Thomas said, agreeing with her. He leaned his head back against the wall and closed his eyes.

Isabella cleaned away the blood, puss, and dirt from around the wound.

"They told me I can't take out the bullet," she said sadly. "Not that I could if they wanted me to."

Thomas just shook his head.

Isabella looked closely at the hole in Thomas' leg. "It hurts a lot, huh?" she said, looking up at Thomas.

He opened one eye again and looked at her, then smiled. He had forgotten how pretty she was that fast. His face brightened up as if seeing her for the first time again.

"Only a little," he said, grunting through the pain, trying to seem fine.

Isabella laughed. "Well, Mr. Thomas," she began, "since you don't have no pain, I guess this whiskey can go home with me," she said, pulling a bottle of whisky from her pocket. Thomas' eyebrows shot up. He looked at Isabella. "Or," she said, undoing the top, "I can pour some on the wound like this." She poured whiskey on the wound, hoping to help clean it and numb the skin around it. She then wrapped it with a clean gauze. "Then I can pour some whisky up here," Isabella said, moving forward to place the bottle to Thomas' lips.

She didn't mean for the moment to become intimate, but as soon as she touched his face to keep him steady while she placed the bottle up to his mouth, she found herself staring at him, and he stared right back at her. They watched each other as Thomas drank the whiskey. When she thought that he had enough, she pulled the bottle back. Thomas licked his lips to catch the excess whiskey and then looked down at Isabella's lips. He swallowed hard and loudly; he wanted to kiss her. Isabella cleared her throat and sat back.

She looked down at the ground again. "Mr. Schaeffer coming to see you tomorrow."

"Who's Mr. Schaeffer?" Thomas asked.

"The man from the Freedmen's Bureau. Somebody went to him and told him that they were holding two Negro brother Union soldiers down here at the jail for no charge," Isabella said, placing the whiskey bottle in her apron pocket. "I guess that's you?" she said in question to Thomas.

"Me...and him," Thomas said, pointing to his sleeping brother on the floor of the cell next to his.

Isabella turned her head around to look at Othello, still sound asleep on the other cell floor. "Which one of you is the older brother?" Isabella asked, looking back at Thomas.

"Ain't it obvious?" he said, smiling at her. "The one that knows better than to sleep that hard in this cell like that right now."

Isabella shrugged. "I don't know. You could not be sleep cause you hurtin'," she said.

"All the more reason to be sleep right now," Thomas replied.

" 'Bout right" Isabella agreed.

Both of them went quiet.

Isabella chewed the corner of her bottom lip. "Alright then," she said. "I think you alright now. 'Least that's the best I can do." She grimaced. "Sorry."

"You did fine," Thomas said, smiling at her.

He tapped his fingers on the hard ground. Isabella stood up and picked up the bowl.

"You be back tomorrow?" Thomas asked her as she walked towards the cell door.

"Lord willing," she said. Then she blushed, realizing how that sounded. "I mean. I suppose. Long as I work here," she smiled at Thomas.

"Well. Lord willing, I'm still alive tomorrow. I'll see you then, Ms. Isabella," Thomas said, smiling.

Isabella smiled and banged on the metal bars of the cell. The man came and let her out of the cell. She peeked back over to Thomas before leaving and smiled.

Thomas leaned his head back against the wall and closed his eyes. He let the smile remain on his face as he continued to think about

Isabella. The silence was interrupted by snickers of laughter coming from Othello. Thomas opened his eyes and looked at his brother. Othello, still lying on the ground, turned over to his other side to face Thomas and propped his head up with one arm.

"Is that a budding romance I see?" he said, teasing his older brother. "Is there finally a woman that broke through?" Othello asked without really expecting an answer.

Thomas grinned and scratched his chin. He didn't answer Othello, who just laid there smiling until he suddenly sobered, remembering Thomas' gunshot wound.

"You feeling alright?" he asked, the playful excitement gone from his voice. Othello looked over to Thomas' leg, indicating that he was concerned about the shot and the bullet that was still there.

"I'm alright," Thomas said in assurance. They went quiet for a moment until Thomas said to him. "Did you hear what she said about the Freedmen's Bureau?"

Othello shook his head. "I'm just waking. I only caught the end of your courtin'. First," Othello said with a smile, "what's her name?"

Thomas tried to stop himself from smiling, but that made the situation worse. Othello raised both of his eyebrows and tapped his chin with his finger.

"It's not working," Othello said, pointing out to Thomas that his efforts to not acknowledge his interest in Isabella were failing. "What's her name?" he asked again.

"Isabella," Thomas answered shortly.

Othello nodded. "I didn't catch a look at her. What she look like?"

"She was," Thomas hesitated. "She was beautiful," he finished. "I think she might be quiet. That's good after dealing with you every day," he said with a smile.

Othello faked indignation. "Hey...I," he began, intending to argue and defend himself. He shrugged in defeat. "I was going to argue, but you're right," he said. Thomas smiled. "Can't get the smile off your face, right? That's what it was like when I first met Mary."

Thomas scratched his chin again. "Othello," he said, trying to get his brother to focus on the matter at hand. "She said a man from the Freedmen's Bureau is coming here. She said someone told him that we were being held here for something we didn't do."

Othello nodded. "Hy," he said out loud what Thomas was already thinking.

"I think so," Thomas agreed. "The Warden sent her in here to clean my wound. She said they concerned about how I look to them."

Othello thought for a second. "She say when they coming?" he asked.

Thomas shook his head.

"No. I'm thinking they coming soon since they sent her in to clean me up. Maybe today or tomorrow?" Thomas said in question.

Othello sat all the way up and leaned against the wall. "'Suppose we wait then."

———

The next day Thomas arose to a man tapping him on the shoulder. He was still sitting up against the wall of his cell. He had not realized that he had fallen asleep but remembered why he did when he looked down to see that his shirt was wet with sweat. The man standing over him also looked down at his shirt, examining all the sweat.

"I think you might be fightin' off some kind of infection, son," the man said with a sad smile. "You seem to have a fever."

Thomas closed his eyes again, tired and unmotivated for any type of battle that this man in front of him was looking for.

"Your lips looking a little dry too," the man said, hitting Thomas' foot with his own. "Come on now," the man continued. "Take a drink so I can talk to you."

Thomas opened his eyes again and swallowed. The man was right, his throat was dry, and he was very thirsty. The man turned his back and then turned back towards Thomas with a small cup of water. He held it out to Thomas to take.

"Come on," he urged him.

Thomas swallowed again. "You mind telling me who you are, sir, 'for I go drinking something you offering?" Thomas said in a dry and tired voice. He closed his eyes again.

"My name's Charles Schaeffer, son," Mr. Schaeffer said to Thomas. "I'm from the Freedmen's Bureau. I need you to wake up now so I can talk to you. I need to see if I need to get you out of here."

Thomas lifted his hand up towards Mr. Schaeffer, palm up, asking for the cup of water without words. He swallowed hard. "I ain't sleep, Mr. Schaeffer. I'm just resting my eyes. It's easier that way right now if you don't mind." Mr. Schaeffer handed Thomas the cup of water. Thomas took the water and drank it down quickly. "Thank you, sir," he said, thumping the cup down as if it weighed a ton.

Mr. Schaeffer bent down to lean on his toes and to be face-to-face with Thomas so that he could look him over. "What's your name?" he asked.

"Thomas," Thomas said pointedly. He swallowed again. "Fraction." He finished lifting the tin cup of water and using it to point at Mr. Schaeffer.

Mr. Schaeffer looked at Thomas intently. "You drunk?" he asked with a smile.

"Just a little," Thomas answered. "Enough to take off the edge." He pointed down to the wound on his leg. "Isabella brings in whisky. It's all I got," Thomas continued to explain. Mr. Schaeffer looked down at Thomas' leg. "The bullet's still in there," Thomas said with a smile. He opened one eye. "Where is Isabella anyway?" He closed his eyes again. "I think she uses giving me the whisky as a reason to keep coming in here for a visit," he said with a smile. "She don't need no reason, though. I'm sweet on her. I do need to stop drinking it for a bit. Drunk *is* the next step."

"Can you answer my questions?" Mr. Schaeffer asked him.

Thomas nodded, his eyes still closed. "My speech ain't slurred, sir, and that's the sure sign of a drunk. I'm just warm and light. I'm aware," he assured Mr. Schaeffer.

"Ok," Mr. Schaeffer said, standing to walk to the corner of the cell and grab a small wooden chair that the Warden brought inside for him to use. He positioned the chair so that he could see Thomas and the cell that Othello was in. "I'm to assume you're his brother, Othello?" he asked, looking down at his notes without looking up at Othello.

Othello, who was already leaning his back against the cell gate that his cell shared with Thomas', raised one hand, wagged his index finger in the air, and said, "that would be me."

"Good," Mr. Schaeffer said, looking up at Othello. "Ok, boys. How about you tell me what happened, and I'll see if the stories match."

"Who came to you to tell you we was in here?" Othello asked Mr. Schaeffer.

"I tell you that after I have no reason to doubt what you tell me. How about you tell me your story first, then I'll tell you who came to see me?" Mr. Schaeffer said.

"We are in the 40th U.S. Colored Infantry; we stationed in Tennessee," Thomas suddenly began.

"He's a Sergeant," Othello said, his finger pointed in the air again, his back still to where Mr. Schaeffer and Thomas sat.

"Yes," Thomas agreed, nodding his head. "I'm a Sergeant."

"Really?" Mr. Schaeffer said in interest.

"Yes," Thomas said, popping his lips. "Well, I was. I doubt I will be anymore since they put me in this here jail," Thomas said, opening his eyes and waving his hands to indicate the prison. "Those Colonels just needed a reason. Now they got it."

"Don't worry 'bout that," Mr. Schaeffer said. "If what was said is true, you're innocent and will be released, and I'm sure your Sergeant status will be intact."

Thomas gave a half-laugh. "If you say so," he said with a smirk. He took a deep breath as if defeated. He was tired of fighting right now. "So," he continued. "We camped in Tennessee. We was given a 30-day furlough. I wrote a letter." Thomas stopped himself and opened his eyes to look at Mr. Schaeffer to see if he had noticed that he had just admitted he could write. Mr. Schaeffer was looking down, taking notes. "I mean, *I* ain't write the letter. I had Jessie write the letter. He's the courier at the army camp," Thomas corrected.

"Forget it," Othello said, waving his hand in the air in dismissal.

"Ah hell, you right." Thomas said to his brother. "I write. I write, and I read."

Mr. Schaefer peered up at Thomas without lifting his head. "You know that's fine with the proclamation, right?"

Thomas shrugged, uncaring. "So," he continued with a deep sigh closing his eyes again. "I got Jessie to write a letter home to tell my family we was coming home for a visit. Seems my sister Chloe went to spread the word, and Mister got a wind of the letter and..."

"Who's Mister?" Mr. Schaeffer interrupted.

"Mr. Preston." Thomas clarified. "Robert Preston, the rebel, the man that shot me."

"Your former…" Mr. Schaeffer began.

"Don't say it," Othello said, cutting Mr. Schaeffer off in warning.

Mr. Schaeffer looked over at Othello's back and then back at Thomas. "Your former Master?" he asked Thomas.

"And there," Othello said, shaking his head in disappointment.

Thomas opened his eyes and sneered at Mr. Schaeffer. "Ain't no man my Master," he said to Mr. Schaeffer, seeming to immediately sober. "Robert Preston is a man and a rebel soldier."

Mr. Schaeffer continued to take note. "I understand," he said. "But for the sake of the paperwork, I need to call him what he is…or was. What he was. I think it matters to the events." Thomas just stared at Mr. Schaeffer, who looked up at him after finishing his notes and smiled. "I'm just trying to help you, son," Mr. Schaeffer said.

Thomas laid his head back on the wall, still staring at Mr. Schaeffer. He closed his eyes again and continued. "Mister got wind of the letter and wrote me back at the army camp. He said we best not come back here, or he'd kill us. I wrote back that we was trained soldiers, and if need be, we'd protect ourselves if he show cause," he suddenly popped open his eyes. "You got any more of that there water, Mr. Schaeffer?"

Mr. Schaeffer stood up, placed his notes on the chair, and walked over to the water pitcher on the ground. He brought it over to Thomas and refilled his cup.

"You want water?" he asked Othello without turning around.

"'Yes, please, sir," Othello said, finally turning towards where they were.

After filling Thomas' cup, Mr. Schaeffer walked over to the bars. "This'll be a little tricky," he said, watching Othello maneuver his cup through the bars so that he could fill it with water.

"It's all right," Othello said as Mr. Schaeffer filled his cup. "You got it." When the cup was filled, he slowly and carefully pulled it back between the bars and began to drink.

Thomas took the last swallow of his water while Mr. Schaeffer picked up his notes to sit in the chair again.

"So we came home," Thomas continued. "We went straight to my Pa house. No harm to Mister. No return to his house or his crops. We just went to see my Pa 'cause my Ma is dead."

"And I went to see my wife Mary over at Thomas Wilson plantation," Othello said, providing more context.

Thomas nodded in agreement. "After a few days, our friend Hy came and told us that Mister found out that we was there and was coming to kill us. We said bye to our Pa and went ahead to leave, so we didn't cause no trouble for him."

"For who?" Mr. Schaeffer asked.

"For Pa. I ain't want to cause no trouble for Pa. So we left, and Hy said he could take us another path so we don't cross Mister and there wouldn't be no problem. We crossed Mister anyway, and Mister pulled out his pistol. When he pulled out his pistol, we pulled out our pistols. I went to tell Mister we was leaving and didn't want no trouble, and then he shot me. Threw me in this jail and told the Warden to keep the bullet in my leg, and I don't move until he want me to." Thomas closed his eyes again. "I suppose I'm sitting in here the rest of my life."

Mr. Schaeffer continued to scratch notes until he stopped, closed his notebook, and looked at Thomas and Othello. "So, you stories match Hy's," he said. "That's who came to see me. Hy."

Thomas nodded in agreement. "Good to know Hy is alright."

Mr. Schaeffer stood up. "I'll take care of this. You two take care of yourselves. This is an obvious case of self-defense. I should have you out of here in a few days."

"You don't know the hold that Preston name got around here," Thomas said to Mr. Schaeffer. "We ain't going nowhere 'til Mister say we do."

Mr. Schaeffer shook his head. "It might take some time. But like you said, Robert Preston is a rebel soldier. He'll need to apply for amnesty, or he'll lose everything. That means he'll have to do right," Mr. Schaeffer said.

Thomas, his eyes closed, lifted his hand to his forehead and gave Mr. Schaeffer a lazy soldier's salute. "I do appreciate it, Mr. Schaeffer," Thomas said.

―――――

July 1866

Thomas sat on a bench, handcuffed to a chain attached to the floor in the courthouse. He held the long chain and swung it back and forth, creating clanking sounds that filled the room. Mr. Schaeffer stood a few feet in front of him, speaking to the Magistrate. The Warden gave Thomas a look of warning for the annoying sound of the chain. Thomas smiled and dramatically grabbed the chain to stop it from clanking. It had been three months since they had been arrested,[7] and Thomas doubted that today would be the day that Mr. Schaeffer finally appeased the courts to get everything they required of them to prove their case. Never mind that Mister had presented no evidence to prove that they had made an attempt on his life[8]. Even Mr. Schaeffer had gone to the scene of the crime and found no evidence that Thomas and Othello had shot at Mister, which is what he was claiming.

"I saw no evidence that you had taken any shots at Mr. Preston. No bullet marks, no bullets on the ground. Either both of you are a bad shot, or he has told some untruths," Mr. Schaeffer told him.

On the good side, Thomas has had three months of daily visits to get to know Isabella. If he got out of here, he planned to take her with him wherever he ended up and marrying her. Othello sat on the bench next to Thomas. He was also chained to the floor. However, unlike Thomas, he was sitting still, slouched down in a sitting position so that his behind teetered on the edge of the bench seat, while his neck rested on the back of the bench so that his face turned up to the ceiling. At least Othello's wife Mary had come to see him many times since he had been in the jail. Thomas tilted back to look at his little brother. Their eyes met, and they gave each other a small smile. Then he turned around to the back of the room and up to the balcony where Mary sitting. She gave a small wave to Thomas. Thomas elbowed Othello and then pointed his attention to the balcony when he looked over to him. Othello looked up to the balcony, clearly seeing the view upside down. He gave a big smile and tried to lift his hands to wave at Mary. The chains yanked hard and gave a loud rattling sound.

"Ow," Othello whispered to the chains as if they consciously assaulted him.

Thomas began to turn back around when movement at the doorway entrance to the balcony caught his attention. He watched to see who was arriving. He thought that maybe it was Virginia or Chloe. A big smile came across his face when he saw that it was Isabella. She caught his eyes and waved before seeing Mary and greeting her with a hug.

"Would you look at that," Othello said, still viewing the balcony from upside down. "They friends already. Our children will grow up together."

Thomas turned back around towards the Magistrate with a smile.

In the past three months their trial had been postponed three times either because the Commonwealth's Attorney was too busy or the Counsel for the Prisoners was unavailable[9]. Mr. Schaeffer wasn't a lawyer, so he couldn't act as legal counsel, but he could work with the Counsel for the Prisoners if the guy ever showed up. Hy had been listed as a witness, but the courts refused to summon him. When Mr. Schaeffer asked why the courts said they couldn't handle the expense of bringing Hy to town to witness for a trial. Mr. Schaeffer was able to get the Freedmen's Bureau to foot the bill[10].

After being arrested, Mr. Schaeffer wrote to the Union Army infantry to inform them that they had been arrested after a warrant was issued for their arrest as deserters when they did not return from their furlough. Mr. Schaeffer had multiple correspondences back and forth with the infantry who, by July after their arrest, sent documentation to Mr. Schaeffer for both of them to sign for honorable discharge ending their service with the Union Army[11]. Thomas would never forget seeing his discharge documents.

"You can read that, right, son?" Mr. Schaeffer had asked him sadly.

Thomas stared down at the document and nodded without looking up at Mr. Schaeffer. He clutched the pen he was holding in his hand tightly.

"I'm so sorry. You was right about those Colonels up there," Mr. Schaeffer said sadly.

Thomas read the line again "Reduced from Sergeant to Private," it said simply[12]. They had given no explanation and no reason; they had just snatched it away. Thomas knew it was going to happen; he just didn't expect for it to bother him so much. *He* had finally been recognized for work that he had done, instead of Mister, or a Preston, or some other White man getting credit or accolades for his work; but they managed to take that too.

Now here they were, one year later. The Magistrate was finally there, the Commonwealth Attorney had shown, and the Counsel for Prisoners, who knew nothing about the case, it seemed, had arrived.

"I'd appreciate if this matter can come to an end today, your honor. It's been months, and each day that goes by where these young men are still held here for a crime that has not been proven that they have committed is a violation of their rights as United States citizens," Mr. Schaeffer said, providing his testimony to the Magistrate and the Commonwealth's Attorney.

The Magistrate looked at Mr. Schaeffer disinterested and fairly assumed by his discussion of Thomas and Othello's "rights." As far as the Magistrate was concerned, these niggers are better off in their place as slaves. The Magistrate tapped his fingertips on the judge's stand and looked at Mr. Schaeffer with amusement.

"Well, it's only right to give Mr. Preston an ample amount of time to prove his case. He's a busy man that needed accommodation," the Magistrate explained to Mr. Schaeffer.

Mr. Schaeffer nodded. "I'm sure you'll pass on my message to Mr. Preston that I appreciate his willingness to place his full attention to this matter, and note that he had no evidence before I proceeded to having the federal government petition to charge Mr. Preston with attempted murder of the boy, Thomas Fraction. I'd hate for his request for amnesty to be threatened by these events."

The Magistrate puckered his lips as if eating a sour pickle.

"So, if I have this right..." the Commonwealth Attorney inter-rupted, obviously reading the case documents for the first time. He was standing in front of the prosecution desk, his spectacles on the edge of his nose and one hand on his hip.

"These boys are Union soldiers who came home on a furlough, were tracked down by Mr. Preston, who shot one of them, but claims that he was molested and attempted to be killed by the Negros who," the Attorney turned a page, "had not even gone out to seek Mr. Preston for a confrontation upon their visit?"

Mr. Schaeffer looked over to the attorney. "That is correct."

The Commonwealth Attorney looked up at the Magistrate. "Your honor, is there a reason I have not seen these documents before now?"

The Magistrate straightened his back. "It was incomplete waiting for the evidence presented by Mr. Preston."

The attorney looked through the documents again. "The evidence that Mr. Preston now states does not exist?"

The Magistrate looked at the attorney with annoyance. "Do you wish to proceed with the trial or not?"

The attorney looked back at Thomas and Othello, who were sitting on the bench. Othello was still staring up at the ceiling. He had no expectation that this was going to end today. Thomas looked at the attorney and shrugged his shoulders as if to say, *It's up to you*. The attorney looked at Mr. Schaeffer dumbfounded and then back at the Magistrate.

"The State motions to dismiss, your honor," he said.

The Magistrate started to move like he was chewing on an invisible piece of tobacco.

"You sure 'bout that?" he asked the attorney.

"Yes, sir," the attorney said. "There's no case here."

"Motion granted," the Magistrate said, banging his gavel on the bench.

The sound of the gavel was loud, but Othello didn't move, and neither did Thomas, who now was looking out the window. They hadn't realized what happened until Mr. Schaeffer walked over to them, smiling.

"That's it, boys! Finally! You free to go," Thomas looked at Mr. Schaeffer and then at Othello, who sat up.

"That's it?" Othello asked. "We done?"

"That's it," Mr. Schaeffer said with a smile.

The Warden stepped forward, unlocked their cuffs, and left. Thomas rubbed his wrist and looked at them for a long time before saying to Mr. Schaeffer.

"What happens to Mister?"

"What do you mean?" Mr. Schaeffer asked, turning around to gather the papers he had laid out on the desk for the Counsel for Prisoners.

"When does he go to trial? When does he get arrested for shootin' me?" Thomas asked, finally looking up at Mr. Schaeffer.

Ashamed, Mr. Schaeffer didn't look up at Thomas as he said, "he doesn't."

"I got evidence. If he want evidence," he said, referring to the Magistrate. "I got evidence. He can dig in my leg, I got a bullet there for him."

Mr. Schaeffer didn't answer. Thomas stared at Mr. Schaeffer, waiting for something from him, anything. "So Mister get to keep his title, he gets to keep his land, he gets forgiveness from the Union, he just gets to keep going on like he ain't no rebel soldier," Thomas said. It wasn't a question, it was a statement. "I don't even get my title?" he asked Mr. Schaeffer, emotions building up in his throat.

Mr. Schaeffer still didn't look at Thomas. "I know, son."

Thomas sniffled without shedding a tear. He nodded, agreeing to unsaid words. "I'll get my own title back," he said, standing up in determination. "I get my own."

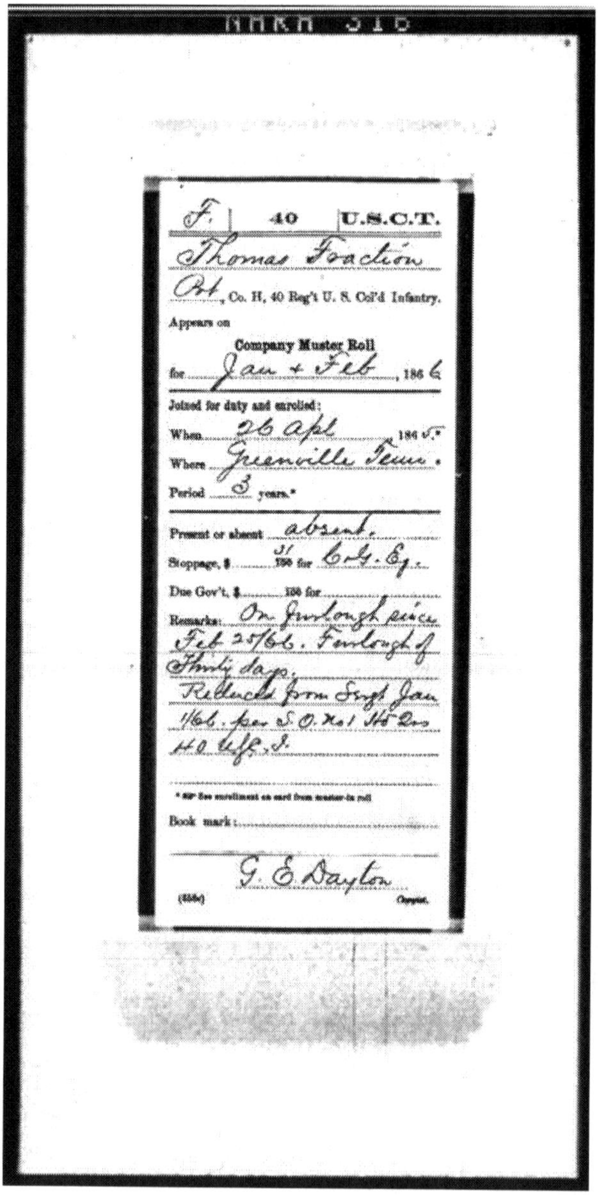

F. | 40 | U.S.C.T.

Thomas Fraction

Pvt, Co. H, 40 Reg't U. S. Col'd Infantry.

Appears on

Company Muster Roll

for Jan + Feb, 1866

Joined for duty and enrolled:

When 26 Apl 1865.*

Where Greenville Tenn.

Period 3 years.*

Present or absent absent.

Stoppage, $ 31/100 for C.G. Eq.

Due Gov't, $ 100 for

Remarks: On furlough since Feb 25/66. Furlough of thirty days.
Reduced from Sergt Jan 1/66. per S.O. No 1 Hd Qrs 40 USC.I.

* See enrollment on card from muster-in roll

Book mark:

G. E. Dayton

(358c) Copyist.

Thomas Fraction reduced from Sergeant to Private[13]

CHAPTER 14

DOUBLE JEOPARDY
REFUGEES

August 1867

Twenty-seven-year-old Thomas held up the end of a large log leveled up to his chest. He peered down the length of the log, which went in a downward slope, and met twenty-two-year old Othello's eyes. They were working on a cabin that Thomas was building for his growing family[1].

"Come on, Othello, last one, I promise. We just need to get it up on here," he nodded towards the log that the one they were holding was intended to be placed on top of. "And I promise that's it for the day." Thomas' own muscles twitched under the weight of the heavy log. He was tired too, but they needed to get the last one up before the mixture that would hold them all together dried. "Alright, on the count of three," he urged Othello. "One more lift, and then we slowly put the log up. Don't throw it. Don't do no good to catch either of our hands."

Othello grunted and nodded in agreement.

"Alright," Thomas said, sticking his tongue out to rest on his bottom lip. "One...two...three!"

On the count of three, Othello found one last burst of energy, brought the log up to his chest to level it out with Thomas' part of the log, and they slowly lifted the log and placed it on top of the other one. Othello leaned against the wall of the cabin that they were building. Thomas tapped the log like it was the side of a good horse and smiled at Othello.

"See, I knew you had it in you," he said.

Othello snapped his head towards Thomas and frowned. "I'm dying over here," he said.

Twenty-three-year old Isabella sat on a chair next to Mary. Mary, now twenty-eight-years old, sat next to her with her hands tucked between her thighs like she was trying to keep them warm. Mary looked over to Isabella, who was watching Thomas.

"He so strong," Isabella said in a wistful tone.

Mary looked at Thomas and then back at Isabella. "You can have 'em strong like that," she smiled. "I like to laugh. Everything else can get so terrible most times; I like that my husband makes me laugh when I'm with him."

Isabella looked over at Mary and smiled. "I'm happy too," she said.

Mary smiled back at Isabella, but then her smiled turned sad. "How's that belly doing?" she said, looking down at Isabella's stomach.

Isabella leaned back to show it to Mary. "Baby's good," she said, rubbing her protruding stomach and smiling at Mary.

"You got pregnant fast," Mary said, looking down at her hands. She was paranoid and apprehensive that perhaps she couldn't have children. She and Othello had been trying for a while now, and she still wasn't with child.

Isabella grabbed on to Mary's hand. "Don't worry. You'll have a baby. All in the good Lord's time," she said, squeezing Mary's hand before letting it go. "I may be having this baby," she said, looking at Thomas and Othello, who were standing in front of the unfinished cabin discussing their next move. "But ain't no house to put us in right yet." Mary and Isabella both started laughing.

Othello turned around. "Now, hold on. Laughing from my Mary that I ain't cause? I know Isabella ain't say nothing that funny."

Mary smiled at Othello. "Never," she said, exaggerating indignation. "Isabella just talking about ain't no house to put that baby in. At this rate, she going to have to have that baby in the bush," she continued.

Thomas turned around. He didn't find the subject humorous. "House'll be finished in time," he said, walking over to Isabella and grabbing her belly with both hands. He was so happy to have Isabella and even happier about this baby than he could have ever imagined. The only thing that he didn't anticipate was the fear that a baby brings. To have a baby with Isabella was wonderful, but to bring a baby into this world - he wasn't sure it was the best idea.

Isabella smiled up at Thomas. "I believe you'll have it ready. Look at it. You got up three walls already!"

Thomas looked up at Isabella and smiled. Since the day he met her, she always made him feel like a hero. He grabbed both of her hands and led her to stand.

"Come on now. I want to get you inside. Hop on up on that wagon. I'm a take you over to Pa's house."

Othello was picking up the chairs that the two women had sat in and put them behind the cabin as Thomas helped Isabella onto the wagon.

"I got it, Thomas. I'm with child, not a cripple. I still work as a chambermaid, don't I?" she said with a smile.

Thomas frowned. "You know I wish you wouldn't, though."

"I can do it 'til the baby's born," Isabella assured him. "After that, our care is all on you 'til I can work again."

Thomas leaned on the edge of the wagon, looking at Isabella as if she was speaking another language. "I can take care of us just fine."

"I know you can," Isabella said, patting his hand. "But no need to do it by yourself if you don't have to."

"You been taking care of me since the day I met you. I need to catch up now," Thomas said with a smile.

"Well, if she ain't claiming her debt, I'll take it," Othello said, helping Mary onto the wagon.

"Sorry, Othello, can't be given away," Thomas said as he climbed into the driver's seat of the wagon. Othello joined him upfront.

Othello looked back at Isabella. "Well, Isabella, if you ever need ideas, I got a list. You can do your brother-in-law some favors."

Thomas looked at Othello from the corner of his eyes. "No," he said again, snapping the horse's reins to urge the horse forward.

———

Once at John's house, the brothers led their wives inside and greeted their father. Virginia, who was in the corner folding laundry, slapped down a towel and scowled at him.

"Tell me you don't have that woman out there after I 'don told you that HER," she said, pointing an index finger in Isabella's face, "and THAT baby," she said, pointing at Isabella's stomach, "need to stay where it's safe." She waved her finger at Thomas and then placed her hands on her hips.

Thomas stopped. He was taken aback. He hadn't been scolded like that since his Ma was alive. "She wanted to go," he whispered to his sister, surprising himself with the feebleness that came out of his mouth.

John, now sixty-nine years old, laughed out loud.

"Haha! I ain't heard Thomas that meek since your Ma was around. You must be scaring him, Ginny," he said using the nickname that the Caperton and Preston family used for her. John could generally see the shape of his children and the colors around him. But at his age, his eyes had grayed over with cataracts and disease. He was not seeing much of anything these days, but he knew his children's voices.

"I'm sorry, Virginia," Isabella said. "I did really want to go. I like to see him work."

Virginia cut her eyes to Isabella and looked at her in a way that burned through her. "You got work of your own to do, Isabella. Making and having that baby is work," Virginia said. She lifted her index finger in warning. "I swear I better not hear of her being out in that cold like that again. You hear me, Thomas?" she said, her voice moving to a low baritone in warning of a pending reckoning.

"Yes, ma'am," Thomas agreed, still in a bit of shock.

Virginia turned her full attention to Isabella. "Now, let me check you out. When's the last time you ate?"

Isabella thought for a while, too long to satisfy Virginia. "Oh! That long ago?" she said, her voice going to a high pitch as she glared over at Thomas.

Thomas put his hands up in surrender. "I offered, and she said she ain't hungry."

Virginia looked back at Isabella. "What you mean you ain't hungry? You ain't hungry? Or you ain't have none of Ginny cooking?" Virginia walked over to a basket and pulled out some plates of food.

"Yes!" Othello said, walking over.

"Ah, no!" Virginia said to Othello as if scolding a misbehaving dog. "Food is for the ladies. You get that stew over in that pot."

Mary looked at Virginia with a shy expression on her face. "That ain't necessary, Virginia," she said with a sad smile. "I ain't having no baby. Isabella can get."

"Nonsense," Virginia said. "You ain't having no baby yet, but you will soon. We need to keep them hips ready for the carry." She said, grabbing Mary by her side, borderline violating Mary's personal space. "Take it from me-- hips mean babies."

"Yes…they…do…" Othello said, wagging his eyebrows at Mary.

"Oh god," Isabella said, hiding her face, embarrassed. Othello wasn't talking about her, but she felt like since she was the one with the pregnant belly, his comment brought back to everyone's attention exactly *how* she got the baby in the first place.

Virginia handed Isabella a plate. "Eat," she urged her. Isabella took the plate and started to eat. Virginia still was the best cook she ever tasted. She took out another plate. "Come on now," she said to Mary. "Have a seat so you can eat." Mary complied.

Thomas walked over to the pot and started to fill a bowl with stew. Othello walked up next to him, peering into the pot with disgust.

"Who made it?" he said, his face frowned like it was the most disgusting thing he had ever seen.

Thomas took a spoon full into his mouth and moaned. "Mmm," he said. "Whoever made it, it's good," he said, sitting down on the floor.

Othello picked up a bowl, filled it with the stew, got a spoon, and sat next to Thomas. Virginia swung one hip to the side and rested her hands on them.

"Of course I made it. You think Pa making that stew?"

"I could," John said with a shrug.

"Where's the spoon, Pa?" Virginia asked, making a point of John's bad eyesight.

"Bout to be upside yo' head if you don't watch who you talking to," John said.

Thomas took a slow, loud slurp of stew, smirking at Virginia. "Ohhhh," he said once he swallowed the stew in his mouth. "Somebody 'bout to get in trouble."

"You want to keep eatin' my stew?" Virginia asked Thomas with a warning. "I'd expect that from Othello," she said, faking hurt. "But you!? You, Thomas, are better than that!"

Othello choked on the spoon full of stew that he just put in his mouth. He coughed until his eyes started to water. "Oh god," he choked.

"Othello!" Mary said, putting down her plate and running over to him. When she reached him, she began rubbing his back. "You ok?" Mary asked him. She looked over at Thomas, who was sitting next to him. "Ain't you gonna do something? I think he choking!" she said as Thomas continuing to eat.

"He ain't choking," Thomas said nonchalantly, still eating.

"I think he is!" Mary said. She looked around at everyone in the room who appeared not to care that her husband was choking.

Thomas placed his spoon down in his stew, held his bowl in one hand, and with the other hand, gave one big slap on Othello's back. Othello gasped.

"See. Not choking," Thomas said as if he had just performed the most boring magic trick ever. Othello faked a faint.

———

August 18, 1867

Thomas stood at the counter of the local General Store. Othello was going to meet him at the cabin to continue building the home, but first, he had to get some supplies. It was a warm and dry day in August, and he was hoping to take advantage of the weather and get a lot of the foundation and structure of the house finished. Any extras inside of the cabin he could do later, as long as he could light a fire and get Isabella inside of it, was all that mattered right now. He took off his hat and looked around the store at all they had to offer. He often came to the store for Mr. Ballard to get odds and ends like ink for his pens, paper for his notes, and a few kitchen supplies for Virginia and the other cooks. He had been standing at the counter waiting to be serviced for quite some time, but as usual, since the proclamation, the clerk was ignoring him. Before, he was doing work for the Prestons, but now he was another Negro who didn't deserve anything.

A White man came into the store and approached the counter. He nodded at Thomas in acknowledgement. "Morning," the man said. Thomas nodded back.

The store clerk came over and looked straight at the man who had just entered. The clerk was a short man with hair that was balding in the most peculiar fashion. Thomas watched the clerk. He still had hair on the sides, but it was so thin you could see the blue veins in the man's head. *All the hair in the center of his head had already gone*, Thomas thought to himself. He stood on his toes for a better look, *looks like ages ago*. The clerk's mustache was gray with age, and it looked like it hadn't been cleaned in a while. Virginia used to always talk about the White folk and how they needed to keep their hair clean.

"When they get them bugs, them lice," she used to say. "It's nasty, and I have to pretend like I don't see it."

"Can I help you, sir?" the clerk said to the man.

The man pulled out a list. "I need a bag of flour, a bag of sugar, and some yeast."

The clerk took the list, grabbed the items, and promptly checked out the customer. The man grabbed his bag, nodded to Thomas again, and left. Thomas leaned on the counter and crossed his arms. The clerk left the counter again without servicing Thomas. He stood there for another half an hour, cleaning his nails and watching multiple White customers come and go quickly. When another White customer had come and left, the clerk placed his hands on the counter and took a deep sigh. "You just going to stand there all day, nigger?"

"Til I get what I came here for," Thomas said.

"You know there's another General Store about 10 miles down the road that don't mind serving niggers," the clerk said to Thomas as if offering him great advice.

"This store's closer," Thomas said. He turned towards the clerk. "Look. I don't want to give you my money as much as you don't want to take it. I just need a hammer, a can of nails, and some logging mix."

The clerk pierced his lips together, making his mustache twitch like a nerve. "We don't give store credit to niggers," he said, his mouth moving as if he was chewing invisible tobacco. "Even niggers whose Master was a Preston."

Thomas stared at the clerk. He didn't move or make a sound. He just glared at the clerk. Finally, he slowly blinked as he worked to stay calm. "I don't need store credit. You got what I need or not?" he asked.

The clerk blew air out of his nose in frustration. "You got money?"

Thomas just stared at the clerk again. "Didn't I say I don't need no store credit? That means I got money, right?" Thomas said.

The clerk sneered at Thomas. Finally, he went to the back room and returned with what Thomas wanted to buy. He placed the items on the counter, far from Thomas.

"Like I said, you got money?"

Thomas pulled money out of his pocket, counting the coins to what he knew the cost of the materials was. He extended his hand to the clerk, the coins in his palm.

The clerk looked down at his hand. "On the counter," he said, not wanting to touch Thomas. "Where you get that money? You robbing the good folks 'round here?"

Thomas slapped the money down on the counter. "I work the rails[2]," he answered the clerk.

"I got a nephew that been trying to work the rails. They pay good money. Figures niggers taking his job," the clerk said with no knowledge of Thomas' long history and skill working the rails both during and now after slavery. The clerk looked down at the money to count it. "You need another three cents," he said.

Thomas shook his head. "I been doing this work for a long time. You know I came in here buying supplies for Mr. Ballard. I know how much this stuff cost."

The clerk smiled, his rotting teeth hardly hidden under his mustache. "Since Lincoln's proclamation, we made some changes-- extra three cents is our new nigger tax. We sell to niggers...for a price."

Thomas went to grab the items when suddenly the clerk pulled out a shotgun from under the counter. He pulled back the hammer. "Without that three cents, you stealing nigger. I got the right to defend my store."

Thomas looked at the clerk. He placed up his hands in surrender. "I could take that gun from you and break your nose with it if I wanted to," he said to the clerk. The clerk looked to his left and right as if expecting someone there to back him up. "But you probably know that already, don't you, Jim?" Thomas said to the clerk as he took three steps back, showed the front and back of his hands to the clerk, and slowly reached into his pocket. He pulled out a handful of coins and offered the clerk three cents.

The clerk put down the gun. "Get your stuff and go on!" he said, frustrated by Thomas.

Thomas dropped the three cents on the counter, grabbed his supplies, and left.

———

When Thomas arrived back at the cabin, Othello was already at work sawing away at a log. He looked up as Thomas approached. "Oh, you got it? Jim give you problems?

Thomas put the can of nails down on the ground. "Of course he did," he said, rubbing his hands together.

Othello shook his head in disapproval. "How you hate people so much you don't even want their money?"

"Oh, he wants the money," Thomas said, moving to help Othello, "Jim charges a three-cent nigger tax now."

"Should I even ask what a nigger tax is? Or can I guess?" Othello said.

"I'm sure you can guess," Thomas replied.

"So he wants to charge an extra three cents for us to give him money?" Othello said.

Thomas nodded in agreement. He tapped Othello's arm, indicating for him to let the saw go and let him take over. Othello obliged. As Thomas kept sawing, Othello looked up at the sky.

"Looks like we get a nice day today," he said. "If we lucky, we can get this wall up and this roof on before the day's out. What you think?" he asked Thomas.

"I think so," Thomas agreed, sawing away. "We only got one more to put on that wall, then we finish the last one and can do the roof. Once we get all that, anything else on the inside I can do. I just want it so I can get Isabella in it."

Othello nodded in agreement. "Oh, I forgot. I borrowed a saw from the main house."

Thomas stopped sawing for a second and looked at Othello. "You ain't in no bondage no more. Just call it Smithfield like the White folks do."

Othello shrugged. "I don't get hung up on words."

"Well, you should," Thomas said, continuing to saw. "It's a good weapon."

Othello walked over to a corner of the outside of the cabin and picked up a saw off the ground. "It's nice and sharp," he declared, picking it up to look at it in the light of the day.

Thomas stopped sawing and walked over to Othello.

"Let me see it?" he said, taking the saw from Othello. Othello let the saw go and let Thomas take a good look at it. He looked at the saw for so long, Othello wasn't sure what he was looking for exactly.

"Probably the same sharpening from when you did it last," Othello said. Thomas kept looking at the saw. "Yeah, when I went up there, they look like they are struggling to..." Othello started to say.

Thomas cut him off, handing him back the saw. "It's good," he said as he walked back to the log he was sawing and continued to work.

"You know a lot of people going back to their plantations to work cause everybody having a hard time," Othello said.

"Everybody ain't going back cause it's what they want to do," Thomas said, thinking about the news Mr. Schaeffer told him about the Black Codes. Mr. Schaeffer and the Freedmen's Bureau were warning the Negros about the Black Codes in Virginia and the south. It was a new law that allowed the Negros to legally marry and own property, but it limited their rights. Negros could not access a lot of the court system, could not testify against a White person, serve on a jury, join the state military, and needed approval from their former owner to be employed by someone else[3].

"We're looking into all of this," Mr. Schaeffer had warned Thomas. "And we're watching the Prestons too. Waller's in a lot of trouble for terrorizing a few Negros[4], and Robert will likely get his pardon and take the loyalty oath in September. After that, I'm afraid he'll go back to his old ways," Mr. Schaeffer had told him.

Thomas had thanked Mr. Schaeffer for his warnings and promised him that he would stay in constant contact with him.

"Some people are leaving," Thomas continued answering Othello's point about Negros going back to their plantations. "Whole bunch of people going up north to Washington, Baltimore, New York, and Philadelphia. Everybody ain't go back to no plantation. And they can work plantations, just like you do. It don't have to be for their…" Thomas paused. He didn't want to call them Masters. "It don't have to be for their former owner," he said, continuing to saw at the log.

"Yeah, I know. Mary's father went to Baltimore. I'm just saying it look like they need some help adjusting, that's all," Othello said, trying to explain what he saw at Smithfield.

Thomas sawed harder and faster. "We all adjusting. My whole life is and was adjusting. Making sure the White folks happy. I can do it, they can do it." The end of the log broke and thumped to the ground. Thomas stood up straight and admired the cut. It was straight as an arrow. He smiled and looked up to meet Othello's eyes. His smile turned into a smirk. "You want to go back to Mister? To Solitude?"

Othello scuffed. "No! I ain't say nothing about Solitude. I said Smithfield."

"So you want to go back to Smithfield?" Thomas asked him.

"No," Othello said, although not as firmly. "I just feel sorry for em, that's all."

Thomas walked around the log, examining it. "I'm not cold-hearted," he said, looking at the log. "I feel sorry for em. I know they struggling, and I know they all ain't bad like Waller and Mister. I just think they can get through it. They the Prestons, after all, and there's more to my life than making sure they happy. I did that for the first half. This half is mines," he said, looking up at Othello, who nodded in agreement.

The next few hours, Thomas and Othello worked on the cabin until Thomas' conversation was interrupted by Othello's face going blank. First, they were working and talking, and then Othello looked up, his face dropped, and all expression was gone. Thomas lost his smile.

"What?" he said to Othello.

He turned around to see what Othello saw. When he did, there was Mister, coming down off his horse. Thomas looked around to see if there were any more men to make a group. He always expected a mob or reinforcements when it came to Mister. Thomas stood up straight and turned around to face Mister head-on. He didn't say anything, he just crossed his arms on his chest to wait for whatever it was that Mister had to say or do.

Robert Preston, now fifty-eight-years-old, walked around, examining the cabin. He did so as if it were a joint project or work that he had asked them to do. Thomas didn't say anything as he watched Mister's every move. After his walk around the cabin, Robert sucked his teeth and licked his lips. "That's good work,

Thomas, my boy. As usual. I expect nothing less from you." Thomas didn't respond, he just watched him. Robert looked around him to Othello. "Othello," he said, greeting him. "If I'm not mistaken, I think you've gotten a little bigger. You look like a man now. What work have you been doing since Lincoln's proclamation?" he said, moving to step around Thomas towards Othello. Thomas moved to stand in Robert's path, cutting off access to Othello. Robert cleared his throat. "You uh, you boys never came to thank me for not giving evidence in your case so that you couldn't be convicted."

"Seriously?" Thomas said, finally speaking, both his eyes brows rising in disbelief.

Robert chewed on the inside of his lip, making his mustache and beard move around like it was trying to move off his face. Thomas couldn't blame it.

"You working the rails?" he asked Thomas. "I hear that's where you at?"

"You checkin' on me?" Thomas asked, one eyebrow raised in the air.

Robert shook his head in disagreement. "No. I'm just wondering how you working the rails?"

"You know they know my work is good there. You had me up there all the time," Thomas answered.

Robert stroked his beard. "That's part of my problem. They know the Black Codes. I don't expect niggers to know the Black Codes, but I know they know the Black Codes. Law says I have a right to your labor first. I have to deny you employment 'fore you go working for someone else."

"What!?" Othello said in a pitch squeak.

Thomas turned his head slightly to make sure Othello could hear him.

"That's why you shouldn't feel sorry for them. They'll take care of themselves in some way." He looked back at Robert. "Mister, I know the Black Codes."

"So you know the law says you have to let me decide if I want to hire you 'fore someone else can hire you? I don't recall you asking me if I want to hire you."

"I didn't ask," Thomas said, a tick in his jaw clearly seen from any angle to his face.

"Well, you need to. I've decided I want you back on Solitude. I'm hiring you to get the plantation back to its lush condition," Robert said, still stroking his beard. "You and Othello. Both of you coming back."

"I am a Union soldier. I fought for my freedom, and I ain't working for no one but myself," Thomas answered as a matter of fact[5].

Robert stopped stroking his beard, a fire lit his eyes. He didn't like Thomas' answer at all. "You WILL return to Solitude!" he demanded.

"No," Thomas said pointedly.

Robert's face turned red. "I'll just go up to the rails and let them know by your employ they are breaking the law by violating the Black Codes."

Thomas sighed and bent down to pick up the hammer he was using. "Mister. You get your pardon yet from the Union?"

Robert looked around nervously. "What use does that information have to you?" he asked.

"I'm sure the Freedmen's Bureau would appreciate if we notify them that you looking to violate your pardon agreement[6] before the ink even dry. You suppose to respect my freedom," Thomas said, tired of dealing with Mister already.

"Virginia law's on my side," Robert pointed out.

"You lost the war, Mister. Mr. Schaeffer already said Washington looking at the Black Codes. They say it ain't legal."

"It's legal long as it's still law in Virginia," Robert answered.

"Well, we can let Mr. Schaeffer decide," Thomas said, walking away from him. "He already told me that you were told that your citizenship would not be restored if me or my family was harmed. You just need to find out if our working your plantation is worth your pardon."

Robert sneered at Thomas, turning even redder. He turned around and walked back to his horse, jumped on the back of the horse, tugged at the horse's reins to turn it around, and left. Othello watched Mister leave.

"You know that ain't the end of that," Othello said, still watching Mister's back.

"I know," Thomas said with a sigh.

———

August 1867

Thomas stood at the rear of the United Methodist Church that he, Othello, Isabella, and Mary had been attended Really, his whole family attended this church and had for quite a while now. It was just that some came more often than others. As Negros, they were kept separate from the Whites who congregated at the front of the church. Once service was about to begin, Thomas, Othello, Isabella, Mary and all the other Negros would enter here at the rear and sit in the balcony[7].

Right now, Thomas stood in the heat staring at an older woman who was frantically fanning herself with a hand fan while she went on and on about how she was coming along after Lincoln's proclamation. Thomas stared at the older woman as she continued to speak. He wondered when she would need to take a breath since there didn't seem to be an end in sight to her ranting. Unable to hold his cordial smile a moment longer, he started to bite his bottom lip and looked around, trying to find Isabella. He squinted from the bright sun and continued to scan the small crowd of Negros. *Wasn't it part of the wife's job to save her husband from situations like this*, he thought to himself.

Seeing that she no longer had his full attention, the older woman placed her hand on Thomas' bicep and proceeded to rub up and down his arm. She repeated the motion over and over again. Thomas looked down at the older woman's hand on his arm. Was she petting him now? He lifted one eyebrow and looked at the older woman, but her attention was on another woman who stood a few feet beyond them to their left. Unsure why the older woman was staring at the other woman, Thomas decided that he'd better pay attention to the woman's ranting to see what she was talking about. Apparently, she was pointing out to him how the woman she was looking at was from the house at the plantation where she worked and how the woman was struggling to adjust to farm work since it was harder than the work that she was used to. "Those house slaves ain't never know how to do real work," the older woman said to Thomas, shaking her head at the other woman across the crowd. Thomas looked behind the older woman to Othello, who was chewing on a piece of straw. Othello met Thomas' eyes, raised both eyebrows, and shrugged his shoulders, making it clear that he couldn't save him. Just then, Thomas felt a light touch on his other bicep.

"Thomas. We can go in now. Best be getting on to get a good seat," Isabella said, finally appearing to Thomas like the return of Jesus.

Thomas turned around and smiled at Isabella. "'Suppose you right," he said, taking Isabella's hand to lead her into the church. "You have a good day, Misses…" Thomas hesitated, realizing that he hadn't caught the woman's name.

"Freeman," the woman said. "I'm using Freeman since we free now," she said, smiling.

Thomas returned her smile. "Ms. Freeman," he said, lifting his hat in respect to acknowledge her.

Othello and Mary were already ahead, making their way inside of the church. Thomas moved quickly to catch up to ensure they all sat on the same pew. Church was a tradition for them, and for Thomas when the pastor started preaching, it was a moment of silence. Mostly, Thomas really enjoyed Negro pastors to stand at the pulpit and preach the Word. He found their delivery more entertaining.

As they entered the church, both he and Othello removed their hats from their heads, and they all filed into the first row of pews in the balcony. Isabella and Mary liked to sit close to the pulpit so that they could see the pastor. They both were adamant that if they couldn't see the pastor, they couldn't hear the preaching. "I don't think that's how hearing works," Thomas had said when Isabella made that observation, but all Isabella had to do was put her hands on her hips, and Thomas dropped the subject.

Once seated, Thomas closed his eyes and took a moment of solace as everyone around him talked to each other. It's not that he didn't want to talk to people, he just took every moment of peace that he could get. The best moments of peace he found were in the church. Right here, in the eyes of God. Regardless of how the pastors preached their sermons, he had seen the passages and read them. In Thomas' opinion, pastors liked to read the passages quickly when they were going to use them against the Negros, but he could read them, and he knew what God said. He knew that God said that he was a man, he was an equal, and he was loved and cherished by God. The Bible said that the first would be last, and the last would be first, and he definitely would be spending his days on earth as the last. Thomas imagined the peace of heaven. He sat there imagining an existence outside of having to fight all the time or please someone just because they were White.

"I bet God is a Negro," Othello said as if he was reading Thomas' mind.

"Why you say that?" Thomas asked, not opening his eyes.

"Cause pastor said the Bible say that we was made in God's image," he answered.

"Pastor read the Bible," Isabella answered. "They know how he look that's why they got the pictures hanging to show him," Isabella said, smiling proudly as she pointed out the pictures of Jesus throughout the church before adjusting her dress to limit the wrinkles that it would gain from her sitting down.

"Thomas read to us last week. Bible say skin like bronze and hair like wool. That's a Negro," Othello said, waving his hand to dismiss one of the pictures of a blond White Jesus hanging on the wall.

Thomas did not open his eyes, but he moaned in interest. "Could be a German that been out in the sun too long," he said with a small smile. "German's got bushy hair like wool."

"I ain't never seen no bronze German, red maybe, not bronze though," Othello said.

"Maybe you can't tell what he is. Like some of the mulattos running around here," Mary chimed in, referring to the Negros mixed with White, Native American, and everything else in between.

Thomas twisted his mouth in a way that indicated that he thought that might be true, and then he smiled. He was finished with the conversation, but Othello and Isabella continued to debate God's appearance. Thomas just sat there in the pew, waiting for the worship service to start. It didn't take long for him to find himself trying to stay awake. Something about the church made him fall asleep so easily.

Suddenly his peace was interrupted as his instinct went on alert when he felt a presence shadow over him. He clenched his jaw and abruptly opened both of his eyes as the conversation between Othello, Isabella, and Mary stopped. Mister stood there with his wife, who was also named Mary. He was dressed in his Sunday best, his jaw moving as if he were chewing on something. Thomas met Mister's eyes for a second before linking his fingers together, placing his hands in his lap, and looking beyond Mister to the pulpit as if the pastor was already there preaching. Robert just stood there looking down his nose at Thomas, his view partially obstructed by his large white beard laying on his round belly, ever still the Appalachian Santa Claus.

"You need to leave, boy," Robert said in a growl.

"With all due respect, Mister. I've been coming to this church longer than you and I…"

Robert cut him off. "I ain't worshiping in this church with this nigger," he said to his wife Mary as if she had asked him a question[8].

She smiled nervously. "I think our church is better. Let's go back there, Robert. I'm sure our pastor is…"

Robert cut her off. "My family is working with this church for the Olin Preston Institute[9]. We are supportin' the church, so we are worshiping here now," he said to Mary. He paused and looked at Thomas. "This here is *my* church now, so you need to leave."

By now, everyone around them was quiet and watching. Thomas twisted his hat in his hands but still stared at the pulpit ahead of him. He watched the side door to the pulpit that leads to the pastor's quarters open and saw the pastor coming out of the door. He had obviously come out early to help defuse the situation. Thomas watched the pastor disappear under the balcony, headed towards the stairs to ascend them, and come up to the Negro section to determine the issue.

Thomas wiped his lips with his fingers. "You came all the way up the Negros section to tell me to leave?" he asked Robert. "How'd you even know I was here?"

"I want to know who's in my church," Robert said, looking around at the group of Negros, all watching the situation. "Rest of ya'll all right; rest of ya'll niggers can stay. This one's got to go."

Just then, the pastor appeared in the small doorway to the balcony. "Is there a problem, Mr. Preston?" the pastor asked, his voice a soft tone that matched the peaceful type of man you would expect a pastor to be.

"Yes, pastor," Robert said, grabbing at the waist of his pants to hoist them up higher on his hips. "This nigger right here's got to leave," he said, pointing to Thomas.

"Well, Mr. Preston. All are welcome to worship in the house of the Lord," the pastor went on to explain. "As I'm sure you know, even before Lincoln's proclamation, we welcomed all Negros, slave and free to…"

Robert cut off the pastor. "All these other niggers are welcome. With our partnership for the Olin and Preston Institute, you asked me to worship at this church, and I ain't worshiping with this one," Robert said, jabbing his finger at Thomas.

The pastor cut his eyes at Thomas. Thomas, finally moving his gaze from the pulpit below, turned to look at the pastor, interested to see how this man of God was going to resolve this situation. Othello huffed out an un-amused laugh when it was obvious that the pastor was torn between his institute and Thomas' right to worship there.

"Thomas," the pastor said in a pleading voice. "You know half our Negro congregation is gone. They left to start the St. Paul AME church.[10]" The pastor rubbed one hand down his chest as if to wipe off the shame he should likely be feeling for himself right now. "I'm sure it's a fine church. Maybe you can try it for a few

Sundays? Come back, and I'm sure Mr. Preston here will have a change of heart. The Lord will reach out to him and help him find forgiveness."

"Forgiveness?" Thomas asked the pastor.

"Yes," the pastor said, still speaking in his soft, peaceful voice. "For whatever you did to him. I'm sure the Lord will help him forgive you."

From a few seats back in the balcony, Ms. Freeman, the woman that had been speaking to Thomas outside of the church, made a loud sound of disbelief. "Lord, child, this man just told him he needs to seek his former Master's forgiveness," she said, obviously speaking to every Negro on the balcony.

"I ain't got no Master," Thomas said out loud.

"I know, baby," Ms. Freeman said, giving herself one final blow of air from her hand fan before she stood up. "He been here long as I been here," she continued on talking to the pastor about Thomas. "I ain't never seen this White man, but you asking one of your members to leave?" She gave one loud laugh that indicated she found the situation genuinely funny and unbelievable. "Come on, ya'll," she said, waving her hand to everyone sitting on her pew. They looked at each other in confusion. They obviously had not come with Ms. Freeman, but she was an elder, so they'd listen. They stood up and started sliding out the pew behind her. "I don't know what kind of God they serving here, but it ain't the God we serve," Ms. Freeman said, continuing to wave her pew out of their seats and down the stairs to the outside of the church. Realizing that Thomas wasn't behind her, she stopped and pointed her hand fan at Thomas. "You too," she said like she was the woman that raised him. "Come on," she said again, waving her fan for him to follow.

Thomas stood up and stared at Robert until he towered over him, then he walked to leave behind Ms. Freeman. Othello, Isabella, and Mary followed. They all followed Ms. Freeman down the stairs and out of the church. Outside of the church, Ms. Freeman stood and opened her fan again to continue to provide herself with gusts of air.

"Oohh, it's hot," she said, frowning her face as if the heat was painful.

Thomas came up to Ms. Freeman. "Thank you, Ma'am, for..." he began to say, thanking her for stepping in for him.

She waved her fan dismissively. "I remember you. You fought in the war, right?" she asked him. Thomas nodded. "I'm spending my last days free 'cause of you," she said with a smile. " 'Least I can do is step in when they ain't doing you right. 'Specially a pastor. There's a reason God let ya'll win that war, and it wasn't for no church to cut no deal for no institute," she said, shaking her head in disgust. The strangers from Ms. Freeman's pew looked at her as if waiting for instructions. She reached out the hand that wasn't holding her fan and started to rub Thomas' bicep again. "Ok, baby. Which way is St. Paul?" she asked, referring to the African Methodist Episcopal church that half the Negro congregation had left to start[11].

"It's about a mile that way," one of the men from her pew said, pointing to the east. "And they ain't got no building yet, so church is out in the open while they build it."

The old woman's eyes went wide. "Oh, Jesus, be a breeze," she said in prayer. "I place it in your hands, Lord," she said. She stopped rubbing Thomas' arm and gave him one last squeeze before waving her fan at everyone to follow her. "Alright then. Come on, ya'll," she said as she waddled her way through the grass and down the road. Everyone followed her.

———

A week later, Thomas and Othello were cleaning up from working on the cabin. Both had gone back to work for their employers for a few days before returning to the task of the cabin. The sun was setting, and Thomas was satisfied with the progress that they had made for the day. They had just finished building Othello's cabin when Isabella announced that she was with child. Her announcement was great timing, and here they were able to start working on Thomas' cabin immediately. They were two brothers that had an unmistakable bond. If there was a word closer than brothers, it was them.

"We're pretty much finished," Othello said, looking at the cabin. "Just a few more details, and you're all ready to move in and start that family." He looked over at Thomas. "Ya'll pick out names yet. Boy and girl names for either case?" he asked Thomas.

Thomas nodded. "If it's a boy, imma name him after Pa. If a girl, after Virginia."

"So no little Othello?" Othello asked, teasing.

"You should save that for your own son. I'm sure the only other Othello that could ever exist would have to be your blood son," Thomas said.

Othello laughed. "Why not Thomas for your son?"

Thomas shrugged. "I'm not really interested in that. I want to honor Pa, and I want to give my son a name Mister didn't have to approve."

Othello nodded in understanding. "Virginia know you naming that baby after her?"

"I think Isabella told her. That's why she always fussing bout Isabella staying safe and fed," Thomas said with a smile. "She want that baby Virginia born just as uppity as she is," he laughed.

Suddenly, their conversation was interrupted by the sound of the Confederate war cry, what the rebel army called the "rebel yell"[12]. Thomas looked in the distance and saw three men on horses. They were carrying burning torches, and their heads were covered with white sheets. They rode quickly towards Thomas and Othello as they continued screaming the rebel yell. The ground shook from the efforts of their horses running forward. Both Thomas and Othello picked up a weapon- Othello a saw, and Thomas a hammer.

"These two the right niggers?" one of the men said, stopping his horse in front of the brothers. Thomas marked him, recognizing that he must be their leader.

"That's them," one of the other men said. "Bob said we'd find 'em here."

Thomas frowned at hearing Mister's Confederate nickname. Mister had sent these men here. He was sending others to do his dirty work. The man that had stopped in front of him got down off his horse. He adjusted his pants and looked Thomas up and down.

"He ain't that big," he said, looking back at the other men, his voice muffled by the sheet around his head. He looked back at Thomas. "What you doing, nigger? You make everything easier if you just go on and work for Bob? Why you gotta make things complicated?" the man said in almost a pleading tone.

"And steal good jobs from the White folks!" another man with a white sheet over his head yelled.

Thomas' eyes made a quick glance over to the other man who commented on the jobs. *Jim from the General Store*, he thought to himself.

The leader crossed his arms. "We are the knights of the Klu Klux Klan," the man announced, seemingly proud of his group. "We're an organization in its infancy, 'bout a year old, but we keep the niggers in order and in their place since the federals don't want to do it.[13]"

"What's with the sheet?" Thomas asked with no emotion in his voice.

"I don't answer your questions, nigger. You answer mines," the man said.

"No…I don't," Thomas answered.

The man looked back at his group as if asking what to do next. "I warned you about this nigger," Jim from the General Store said behind his hood. "He ain't big, but he ain't scared either."

The leader of the group turned back towards Thomas. "How 'bout your brother here? He a good nigger?"

Othello frowned and raised the saw as his body tightened to an even more defensive stand, making it clear that he would fight and defend him and his brother.

"He's the funny one," Thomas answered. "Don't he look like he think all this is funny?"

The leader hesitated before turning around and climbing back on his horse. He nodded at the third man that had arrived with them, and the man threw his torch against the side of the cabin, catching a log on fire. Othello lunged for the log, ripped off his shirt, and started to beat the flames so that they wouldn't grow larger and cause damage to the cabin. Jim from the General Store moved his horse towards Othello.

"Jim!" Thomas yelled in warning. "You know I'll kill you dead if you touch him."

Jim stopped his horse and looked at the other men in panic. "How he know my name!? How he know it's me. You said these sheets would work."

"Well, he might not have known it was you if you didn't admit it, Jim," the leader said.

"Stop saying my name!" Jim yelled.

"What's it matter!?" the leader yelled back.

Thomas could tell that Jim was pouting under the sheet. The man's whole demeanor had changed; he was disappointed that his secret was revealed.

"Look, nigger," the leader began. "Colonel Bob got his pardon. You niggers best either leave Montgomery County or go on and work Solitude. You're choice."

"I already gave *Colonel Bob* my answer," Thomas said with sarcasm at the name Colonel Bob. "I'm a Union soldier that fought for my freedom. I ain't working for nobody but myself[14],[15]" Thomas said.

"How about you, nigger?" the man said, yelling to Othello.

"No," Othello said, taking deep breaths, tired from the work of putting out the fire.

The man took a deep sigh. "Alright then. I tried to make it easy for you niggers. I know your little monkey brains can't think it through. If you just listen to the good White folks, you niggers would stay safe. Just follow the law, and you're safe. Why's that so hard?"

Neither Thomas nor Othello answered. The man gave out another rebel yell before striking his horse on the side and galloping away. The two men that came with him followed.

Thomas quickly walked over to where Othello was and examined the side of the cabin for damage.

"It's fine," Othello assured him. "I got it out 'fore anything bad happened."

Thomas grabbed his brother's shoulder in thanks. They were silent for a while, just staring at the log.

"What's a Ku Klux Klan?" Othello asked.

"They are," Thomas answered. He noticed the apprehension in Othello's eyes. "Just another group of White men trying to control things that ain't theirs to control. They ain't no different than the ones that rode around hanging Negros when they escaped their plantations, ok?" Thomas said, trying to reassure Othello that these men weren't any different than what they had been dealing with already. "They just rebels by a new name. You a soldier. You can handle a rebel."

Othello nodded.

———

September 1867

Othello walked down the dirt path that led to his cabin. Mary was likely inside getting supper ready. He slapped his hat on his thigh as he walked, creating a rhyme as he hummed a song. He liked to sometimes play around with music. It made him think of the story Pa had told them about their grandfather Jack and the time he sat everyone around a bonfire and told them a story about how he came from Yoruba to America. Othello would have loved to have been there to see the drumming, hear the songs, and see the dance. Pa had tried to show them once when he was younger, but even Pa said that it wasn't the same without the drums. They were all good at music; there just wasn't much time to get into it. None of them served as a musician for the Prestons. Mister, Mr. Ballard, and Mr. Preston all thought that their family, the Fractions, was the best at labor, farming, blacksmithing, maintaining houses, things like that. Even Virginia could sing. She would sing and cook all the time.

Othello stepped into his cabin and greeted Mary. "Hey, Mary," he said with a smile on his face. He walked over to where she was at the fireplace and kissed her on the cheek. She looked a little sad. "What's wrong?" he asked her.

"I got my monthly again," she said, meaning that she wasn't with child.

Othello placed his finger under her chin and lifted her face to meet his eyes. "Now don't you worry 'bout that, Mary. It'll happen in God's time. Either that, or it won't. I'd be fine either way."

Mary gave a sad smile. "But I *want* a baby."

"I know," he said, sitting down in a chair. "And I am willing to sacrifice myself and my time to keep trying," he said with a smirk.

Mary slapped Othello with a towel, but his joke broke through her sadness like it usually does. "Oh," she said, remembering something. "A messenger came a bit before you did. They say they need you at Smithfield."

Othello looked confused. "At Smithfield? Why?"

Mary shrugged. "They didn't say. Maybe they want your help with something?" she tried to guess.

Othello gave a deep sigh. "Okay. Well, let me go check on them now 'fore I get too tired. Keep supper warm for me?" Mary nodded and gave Othello a kiss. "Keep that sugar warm too," he said with a smile.

Othello left out the cabin. He didn't get ten feet away before a group of White men ran up, began punching him, grabbed him, and dragged him away[16]. Mary, hearing the scream of the men, peeked out of the window. She saw them grab her husband. She ran for the door but hesitated before opening it. Othello had told her to be smart about these things. She remembered when he once told her, "Don't sacrifice your backup plan running off of emotions." She looked around the cabin and thought about what she should do next. Suddenly, she threw her hands behind her back to untie her apron. "I'll go to the Sheriff. Somebody there will help. Then I'll get Thomas." She touched her face and found it wet. She hadn't even known that she was crying. A deep sob escaped her mouth. "Hold on, Othello. PLEASE," she said, pleading with Othello as if he could hear her. "Don't let 'em hang you. PLEASE, please, please, oh God, I can't live without you," she said, still sobbing. She rubbed her hand across her face trying to compose herself. She wiped her tears and nose and watched her hands shake from the adrenaline. She ran out the door towards the Sheriff's office, but little did she know that the Sheriff wasn't there.

In the thick of the trees, Othello found himself lying on the ground on his stomach, surrounded by men in white hoods. He went to his knees so that he could stand up, but one of the men punched him hard in the face, knocking him back down. He sprawled on the ground for a second as his mouth filled with the copper taste of blood. He grabbed his face and gave a small moan. Excited from the contact and the hit to Othello's face, the man bounced up and down on his toes like an excited child.

"See, you ain't tough without your brother, are you?" the man said.

Othello looked down at the ground, waiting for the stars in his eyes that came from the hit to clear away. Once his head was clear, he began to lift himself off the ground and went to stand.

"Well, if you let me get to my feet and fight me man to..." Othello began.

The man went to punch him again, but Othello blocked it. This infuriated the group, who all pounced on him, punching and kicking until Othello lost consciousness and was swallowed by the darkness.

———

Less than a mile away, Thomas stood in front of his cabin, a hammer in his hand. After his shift at the rails, he came to his cabin intending to take advantage of the last of the daylight and finish a few projects on the house. Now, he stood there, a hammer in his hand, surrounded by a few men and Mister who were obviously there for an attack[17]. The group comprised of eight White men in hooded white sheets and the Sheriff. The Sheriff's head was tilted so that his hat sat at the top of his forehead, ensuring he could have a clear view. Thomas looked over in the distance and saw Mister standing there leaning on a tree. Thomas ran his tongue across his front top teeth and looked at the situation around him. He was tired. He knew he was outnumbered, and his situation wasn't looking too good. Before he met Isabella, he wouldn't have cared to think of this day, this moment, as the day he would probably die. He always thought that as long as he went down fighting, he'd rather die than give in to any man who thought he was his Master, his owner, or his god. But now he had Isabella and a baby, and the stakes were higher.

The Sheriff smiled. "Ya'll feel better, boys?" he asked the group of men surrounding Thomas. "I told you if you separate the niggers ,they not as strong. I sent some boys for the brother. We get this one. The big scary one. Aint' that right, Jim?"

"God dang it!" a man in a white hood behind Thomas screamed. Again, it was Jim for the General Store.

The Sheriff nodded to Robert Preston in acknowledgement. "It's been reported to me," he continued to the group surrounding Thomas, "That there's been a case of illegal activity here."

Thomas looked at the Sheriff but didn't respond.

"What say you?" the Sheriff asked Thomas.

Thomas licked his lips. "I'm not sure how my building this here cabin is a crime. I've gotten permission to build on this land as it's reserved for freeman."

"You know what the case is here?" the Sheriff said to Thomas as if speaking to a confused child. Thomas just watched the Sheriff. "The Black Codes. You're violating the Black Codes. What did your Master tell you?"

"I ain't got no Master," Thomas said.

The Sheriff took an exaggerated deep breath. "Your former Master. What did your former Master tell you?"

"Why don't you ask him yourself. He's right over there," Thomas said.

The Sheriff looked around the area, his arms spread out in question. "I see no Robert Preston here. I assure you Mr. Preston takes his loyalty oath *very* seriously. He honors the emancipation of the slaves and the laws of the federal government."

Thomas looked at Mister in the distance and shook his head in disgust as Mister nodded in agreement.

"Now, what did your former Master tell you?" the Sheriff said, losing the humor in his voice.

Thomas frowned and swallowed. He was tired of this. "You're a man of the law, Sheriff. You at his beck and call?" Thomas said, nodding his head in Mister's direction.

The Sheriff took a deep breath. "He not listening. What should I do with him?" he screamed out loud.

He was obviously asking Mister but didn't want to acknowledge him directly so that he and his witnesses could continue to deny that Mister was there.

"Jail looking nice," Robert said, screaming across the distance.

The Sheriff lifted his fingers to his chin and tapped it there as if in deep thought. Thomas shifted as he felt the tension in the air thickened. This was it. He was going to die. He was convinced of it, but he wasn't going down without a fight and was taking someone with him.

"Boys. Let's leave Thomas here with a gift first," the Sheriff said.

Thomas held up his hammer as the eight men came down on him. He focused on one man and swung the hammer. The hammer hit the man on his shoulder even though Thomas was aiming for the man's face, but all the frenzy affected his aim. Another man grabbed Thomas around the waist, trying to pull him down to the ground while Thomas swung his fist, hitting another man across the face. The man's white sheet grew a red stain like a blooming flower. That was the last blow that Thomas landed before he went down.

A few moments later, Thomas found himself brutally beaten[18] and hanging from a tree by his wrist. His feet were barely touching the ground. He was bruised, and blood ran from too many places for him to count. He mentally checked himself. There was definitely a wound on his head, his nose was bleeding, and blood filled his mouth. He pushed the blood in his mouth down his chin to make sure that he wasn't swallowing it. His jaw was already swelling shut, and he ached everywhere. The men could have killed him. The only thing that stopped them was Mister screaming for them to stop.

"I don't want him dead," Robert said, rushing over. "I want him working for me. I want him home."

Instead of continuing the beating, the Sheriff tied Thomas' hands with a rope, threw the end of the rope over the branch of a tree, and had two men in the white hoods holster him up. The Sheriff stood in front of him talking to him, but Thomas could barely make out the words because his ears were ringing from the blows he took to the head. The Sheriff stopped talking and looked at Thomas like he was waiting for an answer. When Thomas didn't answer, the Sheriff waived one of the White men in the hoods forward.

"Burn the cabin, and let him watch," the Sheriff said. A man set fire to the cabin, and Thomas watched it burn until his eyes swelled completely shut. *That's good for me*, he thought as the darkness surrounded him. He didn't want the men to see him cry.

———

Thomas was limp as two men dragged him to the prison. They had been dragging him for quite some time now. It gave him a lot of time to think, and he decided that he couldn't determine if keeping him alive was the punishment or if killing him would be. It seemed like Mister couldn't decide either since he would try so hard and then change his mind in the last seconds of his attempts.

His eyes still swollen, he still couldn't see anything around him, but he heard Isabella's gasp when he entered the prison.

"Thomas!" she screamed, dropping whatever it was she was holding. Thomas couldn't see it, but he expected it was some type of chamber pot.

"Dang it, Isabella!" he heard someone scream. "Now you got piss all over the floor. Clean it up," Thomas heard a voice say.

"Nooo, my husband," he heard Isabella sob.

By now, his jaw was swollen, and he couldn't speak. Thomas heard a scuffle, and then he heard Isabella scream.

"Get off me!"

He had never heard her like that, demanding and unafraid. It made Thomas attempt to stand. He had to protect her. He couldn't quite get his feet to work, but he managed to get them under him so that he could stand. He struggled to his feet, with the two men still holding him under his arms, and stood as much as he could, his knees bent like a man that's had too much to drink.

"Jesus Christ," one of the men said. "Just stop it, nigger. Just STOP."

Thomas swayed, looking around, trying to find Isabella.

"Is...za," he tried to say through the swelling.

"I'm ok, Thomas," she ran over to him and touched his face. "I'm ok."

"Bab...?" he tried to ask her.

"Baby's just fine. You don't worry about that. You worry about you. Get you home to me, ok?" Isabella said, still crying.

The men grabbed him again and began to pull Thomas to walk forward. He may have been able to stand, but he definitely wasn't confident in his ability to walk. When he tried to take a step, he collapsed to his knees. The two men just adjusted their grasp on his arms and continued to drag him to a cell. Once there, they threw him on the floor, closed the door behind him, and left. When everything was silent, Thomas moved one leg and bumped into another solid figure. "Thomas?" someone said. He moved his face in the direction of the voice. It was Othello. He lay on the ground next to Thomas, his hands bound by rope. The whole right side of his face was bruised, he had a black eye and a large gash across his forehead above his left eye that left a huge trail of blood down his face. Othello moaned in pain as he tried to sit up to move his position to lay his face near Thomas' so that they could talk.

"I ain't have my weapon," Othello said to Thomas. "I left out without a weapon." Othello paused. "I'm sorry."

Thomas shook his head, trying to tell Othello that it was alright. That it wouldn't have mattered because he *did* have a weapon when they came for him.

"They tried to kill you?" Othello asked him.

Thomas didn't answer.

Othello pushed his brother. "Don't go to sleep. You gotta do something cause I can't tell if you sleep, ok?" he said to his brother. "Cause your eyes are..." Othello cut himself off.

Thomas lifted one finger in the air in an attempt to acknowledge that he was not asleep.

"We all good for something, right?" Othello asked Thomas. "I'll keep you up. It'll be my mouth that keeps you alive tonight." Thomas coughed a laugh.

———

A few hours later, Thomas and Othello heard arguing in the front of the prison and then feet approaching their cell.

"This is absolutely unacceptable!" one man screamed.

Othello looked up. "That sounds like Mr. Schaeffer," he announced. Thomas nodded slightly in agreement.

When Mr. Schaeffer entered the area where the cells were, he looked at Othello, who had sat up to hear the arguing in the distance, and sighed. Then he looked at Thomas. His eyes grew wide.

"Jesus Christ!" he said, exasperated. "Get him a doctor! Someone go find a doctor!"

The Sheriff, who had entered the room with Mr. Schaeffer, nodded to one of his officers to go and get the doctor.

"Open the cell, please! Now! Right now!" Mr. Schaeffer said to the Sheriff, completely frustrated and ready to bring the wrath of Washington down on this small-town prison. The Sheriff opened the cell, and Mr. Schaeffer walked in.

"I've been keeping him up," Othello announced. "He needs to stay awake."

Mr. Schaeffer nodded in agreement. "Thomas?" he said, trying to get Thomas' attention. "How you feeling?"

Thomas tried to lick his lips but could hardly get his lips to open from the swelling.

"Get him some water!" Mr. Schaeffer demanded from the Sheriff. Thomas shook his head. Mr. Schaeffer looked down at him. "What's wrong, son?"

Othello looked down at Thomas. "He don't trust them. Ain't no Negro in his right mind going drink nothing offered by them."

Mr. Schaeffer patted Thomas on the chest. "I'll get the water, son. Hold on." Mr. Schaeffer left out of the cell and returned shortly with water. He lifted it to Thomas' mouth. "Try to drink some."

Although it was difficult, Thomas did manage to drink some of the water.

"I sent Mary and Isabella to your sister on the Caperton estate," Mr. Schaeffer said, looking at Othello answering an unsaid question.

Othello sighed. "Good. Thank you, Mr. Schaeffer," Othello said.

"I'm just glad they came to get me. Soon as the doctor come and look you two over, we'll get you out of here so you can go home," Mr. Schaeffer said.

"They…bu…rn…ed…it," Thomas mumbled to Mr. Schaeffer.

"They burned your cabin?" Othello asked sadly. "Well, then you come to my house till we build another one," he said. "Us ox niggers gotta stick together," he said with a smile. Thomas coughed a laugh.

"I'm afraid those boys ain't going nowhere," The Sheriff announced.

Mr. Schaeffer watched Thomas before looking back at Othello. He met Othello's eyes for a bit and then looked back at the Sheriff. "Let's take care of this right now. Who's responsible for this, Sheriff?" Mr. Schaeffer already knew the answer, but without the Sheriff's testimony, or the testimony of a White man, he knew they had no cause as long as the Black Codes stayed in tack. Without the Sheriff or a White witness, the brothers could hardly take any case to court.

The Sheriff shrugged his shoulders. "I can't say, Mr. Schaeffer. The men were wearing sheets on their faces. No one knows who they were. I suppose not even the boys know who beat them like that. It's a hard case to solve; impossible, I think," he said.

Mr. Schaeffer shook his head. "No witnesses? Who brought them in?"

"Jim from the General Store and George brought in the Negro laying down," the Sheriff said. "Good thing they came along and found the young man hanging wrist only from a tree.

"And how did Othello get here?" Mr. Schaeffer asked.

"He was dumped on the doorstep unconscious," the Sheriff answered quickly.

"So these two men were found beaten, and the people that found them thought first to bring them to prison instead of to a doctor?" Mr. Schaeffer asked, disgusted that the Sheriff thought that he was that stupid.

The Sheriff shrugged. "I can't explain people."

Mr. Schaeffer lifted up Thomas' hands and saw the cuts and bruises on his knuckles. "Looks like he was fighting back," he said, looking back at the Sheriff.

"Don't matter," the Sheriff said. "They wanted men anyway."

"For what charge?" Mr. Schaeffer asked.

"For attempting the life of Mr. Robert Preston," the Sheriff said.

"That charge was dismissed months ago. You have no case or cause. These boys go home tonight," Mr. Schaeffer said.[19]

The Sheriff sneered at Mr. Schaeffer and left the room.

Finally, the doctor walked into the prison. He came over to the cell, took one look at the brothers. "Jesus," he mumbled under his breath as he rushed in and began to treat them both.

CHAPTER 15

SALEM

September 20, 1867

Thomas stood where his cabin used to be, his hat in his hands, and his feet covered in the ashes of what was once the home that he never had the opportunity to live in. He stood silent ,looking around at the damage and ashes, the only sound was the chirping of the birds in the distance. Thomas noted how carefree they sounded. He stuck his bottom lip into his mouth and lightly scraped the scar on his lip with his teeth. He was still healing from the brutal beating that Mister, the Sherriff, and their men had given him, but at least he was up and moving. The swelling had gone, but he was still bruised and the scars were scabbed over. He looked at the scars on his knuckles from fighting back and trying to block their blows. He was lucky they hadn't damaged his hands. When he had arrived at the rail for work a few days later, after he could fully open his eyes, his employer looked at him horrified and ensured Thomas that he should go home.

"No sir," Thomas had told him. "I'm ready to work," he had said, and that's what he did.

Thomas blinked and slowly turned in a circle, surveying all the damage before stopping and looking up to the sky. He closed his eyes to clear his mind for a moment before he had to stress about figuring out what to do next and how to start over. He looked down to the trees, up to the sky, and to the world around him, his eyes filled with sorrow and pleading for help. He was praying for something, anything supernatural, something God sent, something angelic to show up and give him all the answers that he needed. It was only moments like this when he was alone that Thomas was willing to show vulnerability, to show need, to hint to something out there that he needed help. He made a painful swallow as his throat began to burn with the first sign of tears. He took a deep breath to calm down his emotions. The system hadn't broken him yet, and he wasn't about to let them do it now. He ran his hands atop his thick hair, placed his hat on his head, and turned around to leave. He had only stopped by to see what Othello had described to him. He was actually on his way to see Mr. Schaeffer, who had asked that he and Othello come to see him.

At the office for the Freedmen's Bureau, Othello sat on a chair, leaning back so that the chair sat on the back two legs. He rocked it back and forth as he looked up at the ceiling, chewing on a piece of something in his hand. Mr. Schaeffer sat at a desk, frantically writing on a piece of paper.

"How long those reports be?" Othello asked him.

Mr. Schaeffer looked up. "Depends on the circumstances of the event. For obvious reasons, reports on you and Thomas 'tend to be longer than most."

"Washington tired of hearing our names yet?" Othello asked.

Mr. Schaeffer went back to writing. "That's part of the problem; it's why I called you and Thomas here."

Othello stopped looking at the ceiling and looked at Mr. Schaeffer while letting the chair fall to stand on all four legs again. He opened his mouth to ask Mr. Schaeffer what he meant, when Thomas walked in.

"Morning," he said, greeting everyone in the room as he removed his hat from his head.

"Right on time," Othello began. "'Parently Washington's tired of us."

"Why, what we do?" Thomas asked, looking from Othello to Mr. Schaeffer.

"It's the conflict between you and Mr. Preston," Mr. Schaeffer said.

"They think I assaulted some nice White men with my face or something?" Thomas asked.

Othello coughed out a laugh and quickly tried to cover it up. Thomas looked over at Othello impatiently.

"I'm sorry," Othello began. "I know it's not suppose to be funny, but I just saw in my mind you beating up some White men with hoods with your face and..." He waived his hand in the air dismissively. "Never the mind, it's not important. Serious business here."

Thomas looked back at Mr. Schaeffer. "What's the problem with Washington?" he asked

Mr. Schaeffer put down his pen again and ran his fingers down his cheeks as if trying to wipe away his fatigue. He sighed and looked at Thomas and Othello. "Can I?" he began in a question. "Can I have your ear for just a second?" he asked, looking for an opportunity to vent his own frustrations.

Thomas nodded in agreement.

"I just," Mr. Schaeffer began and then stopped again. "I took this job to help the Negro. I believe in the rights and the freedom of the Negro. And I took this job 'cause I thought Washington thought the same. And I think that was true for a while. At least it might have been true under Lincoln but," Mr. Schaeffer paused again, "my hands are tied." He plopped down in his chair defeated, and said nothing else.

Thomas took a deep breath and let it out slowly. He knew that something else was coming down the pike, more bad news, more trouble, something else that was their fault just for being Negros. Thomas heard his father's voice in his head.

"One thing I learned," John once said, "is they don't give a nigger nothing for free. We 'gon pay for our freedom one way or another, a lot of us with our lives."

Mr. Schaeffer went back to writing his report again. Thomas let the silence hang in the room.

"Am I the only one that don't know what's going on?" Othello asked, looking back and forth between Mr. Schaeffer and Thomas. "I'm certain Mr. Schaeffer didn't really say anything just now about why he called us here today."

Thomas looked over at Othello. "No, you right," he said. "Mr. Schaeffer hasn't really told us why his hands tied, and I ain't ask for him to explain it 'cause I'm not sure I want to know."

Mr. Schaeffer put down his pen again. "Washington says the Freedmen's Bureau has to pull back on intervening between you and Mr. Preston. They say your issue is using too much of our resources. You have a choice, stay here and wait for Mr. Preston to kill you, or leave the county.[1]"

Othello's eyes went wide as he looked at Thomas for his reaction. Thomas' jaw muscle flexed, and he ran his tongue across his top teeth.

"Leave?" Othello said.

"You leave or you die," Mr. Schaeffer said again.

"They should make Mister leave!" Othello said, standing from his chair. "He's the rebel soldier! He's the one that shot my brother! He's the one that threw us into jail and refused us trial! He's the one that had us beaten! He should leave!"

"He took an oath, and that means…" Mr. Schaeffer said before being cut off by Othello.

"Oath!" Othello screamed, peering at Mr. Schaeffer through squinted eyes like he couldn't believe what he was seeing. "When we were serving in the army," Othello began in a whisper, "we spent a lot of time fighting those Confederate guerillas. We'd arrest them and they'd all take that *oath,*" Othello said saying the word "oath" with sarcasm, "and you know what would happen?" he continued. "We'd be arresting them weeks later as they at it again breaking laws, and fighting against the rights of the Negro AND White folk in the nearby towns! And you know what?" Othello asked rhetorically to Mr. Schaeffer. "The Generals wasn't allowed to stop them then either. What are you even here for!? Who REALLY won the war!?" Othello screamed out, frustrated with everything: the terrorism, the Prestons, the whole state of Virginia.

Mr. Schaeffer stood up and slammed his hand on his desk. "Niggers only got rights in theory!!" he screamed. "The only thing you gained was the right to be paid to work! And they hardly do that! All the other cases I got, they fighting to get paid for the work they do. They fighting to stop whippings. They fighting to not be a slave any longer! And that's all the lead way I have Othello! They're pulling back everything else!" He said frustrated with Washington's directive. Mr. Schaeffer stopped talking and made an effort to calm himself down. He looked over to Thomas, who was silent through it all. "All I can do," he said in a pleading voice, "is make sure you don't go back to being a slave." He looked down at the desk again. "My hands," he took in a deep, shaky breath, "are tied."

Othello gave a short laugh of disgust and sat back down in the chair that he had been sitting in.

Mr. Schaeffer walked over to Thomas. "You need to leave to be safe. At least until Mr. Preston dies. He's an old man. You don't have to go far, just enough out of his reach." Mr. Schaeffer walked back to his desk and shuffled around until he found a specific piece of paper. "I got information. They're starting a Negro section in Salem with land from a former slave owner being sold to Negros to settle.²" Mr. Schaeffer reached out his arm to hand the paper to Thomas, but he didn't reach out to take the paper or answer. When it was obvious that Thomas wasn't going to take the paper, Mr. Schaeffer placed the paper back on his desk. He stretched his arms out in defeat and sat back down in his chair.

Thomas stood there looking around the room. Othello went back to rocking in the chair that he was sitting in. Thomas looked over at him and saw that Othello was angry. He thought about telling Othello that he was mad at the wrong person, Mr. Schaeffer can't do what Washington won't let him do. Thomas felt like Mr. Schaeffer was due some recognition for the work he did do until this moment. Thomas turned and looked out the window, then at his beaten hands, and then back out the window. He walked over to it and look at himself in the reflection that he could barely see. He took a long look at himself, the bruises, the cuts, his eyes, his round nose, his full lips, and his thick hair. He looked at the scar across his cheek that stretched from a little below his nose towards his ear to his across his cheekbone. He ran his finger across it and thought about his grandfather.

"My father Jack," John once said, "talked with his African accent until the day that he died. He had a broad chest and shoulders, and scars across his cheeks that looked like tiger stripes. They were the mark of his tribe. He said the mark of the tribe is how they all knew each other. A tribe was important. It was your family, your home, and your identity."

Thomas had one tiger strip now. He looked past his reflection in the window and looked at the Appalachian hills before turning around to look at Othello.

"If we can find work there," Thomas said, breaking the silence, "we'll go."

Othello's chair thumped to the ground again. He looked at Thomas with a frown.

"Why?" he said.

"Cause," Thomas said, walking over to his brother with a sigh. "We husbands now. We having children or going to have children. Is this county really that important to leave Mary as a widow?"

"Mister ain't going kill you or me," Othello said rolling his eyes at Thomas. "If he was, he'd have done it already. He just want us back there at Solitude and will threaten us 'til we come back."

"I know, but if you want to hurt Mister, leave him here old and alone," Thomas said walking back over to stand between Mr. Schaeffer's desk and Othello. "I'm starting to think that we all he got; that we the most interesting thing in his life. I'm leaving him to finish it out by himself. He needs to understand, we ain't never going back to Solitude."

Othello stared at Thomas for a while before standing up. "Fine," he said, seeming not to care either way. "IF we can find work." He said. "Both of us," he said waiving his finger between him and Thomas. "We can go."

Mr. Schaeffer let out a breath in relief. "You need the freeman land list? You need a plot?" he said to them.

Thomas didn't answer, but stretched his hand out to Mr. Schaeffer to get the list.

Mr. Schaeffer placed the list in Thomas' hand. "Now this list is just a lead, ain't no guarantee. You can imagine every Negro is trying to get a plot of land.

Thomas made a deep sigh because even *this* was going to be hard. Everything always had to be hard. He placed his hat back on his head to leave. "We'll make our way, Mr. Schaeffer."

The brothers left.

———

November 14, 1867

Thomas and Othello walked down the path towards the cabin that he and Othello were living in while they fully transitioned to living in Salem. Since visiting Mr. Schaeffer's office and deciding they'd consider leaving Montgomery County, they had found work in Salem and moved there. They were both still working on getting one of the freeman plots, so they both agreed to figure out how to make it on their own. Thomas spoke to his employer at the rails about being stationed in Salem since there was rail work there. Upon the request, his employer smiled.

"Turns out!" his employer said excitedly, "they need a brakeman[3] out there. Somebody strong and dependable. Perfect for you."

Othello, on the other hand, had inquired about work in the plantations and restaurants nearby. He found work, and they moved quickly in anticipation of Isabella giving birth soon. Today, as they were walking back to the cabin, as they came closer, they both could hear Isabella's screams. A large smile came across Othello's face as he looked at his brother. Thomas stood there in shock.

"That means exactly what you think that means," Othello said to Thomas, looking back at the cabin. "You 'bout to be a daddy."

Thomas suddenly began to run. He burst open the door and saw Mary there at the foot of the bed between Isabella's legs. Isabella was half propped up on a pillow. She was already covered in sweat. She looked over to the door as she took in deep breaths and met Thomas' eyes. He saw that she was terrified. She moved her hand up to her forehead, trying to move loose strands of hair that were plastered to her skin by her sweat. "I tried," she said, taking labored breaths. "I tried to wait," she said to Thomas, making a sad attempt at a smile under the circumstances.

Thomas shook his head and quickly walked over to Isabella. "It's alright. You don't have to wait for me. Just do good for you. How you feeling?" he said running his fingers through her hair.

Isabella nodded before going wide eyed and starting to scream again. Mary lifted her head from between Isabella's legs. She peeked just above Isabella's knee at Thomas.

"Well," she began. "Things going good down here," she nodded her head to between Isabella's legs. "Not much to do about the pain, but she's opening up right nice." Mary disappeared again between Isabella's legs.

The time seemed to go on forever as bursts of screams came from Isabella as she moved in and out of the excruciating pain of child-birth. Othello took on the task of ensuring that Mary kept hot water near her as she helped Isabella. Thomas sat at the head of the bed next to Isabella, just holding her hand. He looked at Othello.

"I don't like feeling helpless like this," he said.

"Any minute now," Mary said to no one in particular. She was really just updating everyone in the room. She was sure that, at this point, Isabella wasn't really aware of anything else that was going on in the room.

Isabella laid there, her head shaking back and forth like she couldn't believe that it hurt this much. "Somebody kill me," she whimpered to Thomas.

"Come on now, girl. Don't talk like that. You almost there. You doing good," he said wiping the sweat from her face.

Isabella made soft cries before her eyes went wide, and she began to scream again. It must have been a big contraction because she screamed, then took a deep breath and continued to scream. Othello stood in the middle of the room, looking anxious.

"I don't know what to do," he said smiling and shrugging his shoulders. Then his face lit up as if a light bulb went off, and he began to scream right along with Isabella. Mary peeped up just above Isabella's knee again and looked at Othello. He stopped screaming.

"No, no. That's helping," Mary said. "She's pushing more!" she said, beginning to scream right along with them. "Almost, almost! I see the head!" Mary said between screams.

Just then, a big foot pushed open the front door to the cabin. The doorway filled with a thirty-three-year-old man who was about five feet six inches tall.

"Looks like I made it just in time!" he said over top of the screams before beginning to scream right along with everyone.

Othello turned around, took one look at the man, and starting jumping up and down, and laughing while still screaming. "Ahhh-hhhhh..." he continued on before screaming and laughing, "OSCAR!" he said, continuing to scream along with Isabella and Mary.

Thomas looked up, saw his brother, looked down at Isabella and, with her next deep breath and new scream, screamed right along with everyone else. He started screaming, partly to help Isabella and part to greet his brother. Oscar began to jump around the room with Othello. Mary started laughing, and Isabella pushed out the new baby.

"It's a girl!" Mary panted to catch her breath.

The room was filled with the sounds of heavy breathing as everyone tried to catch their breath, before the room filled with the sounds of the baby's cry.

"Virginia," Isabella said in between deep breaths, her voice was scratchy from all the screaming. "It's Virginia," Isabella said laughing.

Thomas hugged her and kissed the crown of her head. Mary wrapped the baby in a blanket before handing her to Isabella. Thomas pulled back the blanket to get a better look at his baby girl.

"Would you look at that?" he said smiling at Isabella.

———

The next afternoon, Thomas sat on a chair beside Isabella's bedside. He had one leg bent in a sitting position and the other stretch out before him. He was holding baby Virginia and bouncing her a bit to sooth the baby. The baby wasn't crying; it was just instinct that told Thomas that this is something that babies liked. Othello had left the cabin early that morning at dawn with his horse and wagon to announce to Pa and Virginia that baby Virginia had been born, and to gather them up and bring them to the cabin to see the baby.

"And!?" Oscar had said that morning when Othello announced his plans and did not mention that Pa and Virginia would also want to see him since he had come into town for a visit.

"Well, sure they want to see you too. But come on! It's a baby, and her name is Virginia. Do you KNOW what Ginny has been putting us through taking care of Isabella waiting for this baby to be born!? And Pa! All that fussing they did 'cause that baby was either going to be named John or Virginia. And I don't have to tell you how Thomas and Isabella was going to choose," Othello had explained to Oscar.

"A baby girl name John would be different," Oscar said with a smile.

A few hours later, Thomas, Isabella, Oscar, and Mary were in the cabin waiting for Othello to return with Pa and Virginia. On the other side of the room near the fireplace, Oscar sat on the ground, one leg propped up so that he rested his arm on it, and the other stretch out before him. He watched his younger brother and noted that they were almost sitting in the same position. That observation made him smile to see the similarities between him and his siblings. It had been so long since he had visited Montgomery County, Virginia, and his family. Even though he had decided to settle in Kent, Ohio, he missed his family very much. Right now, Oscar was looking for more work, and decided to take the opportunity to come and visit his family; to stay awhile really[4]. Oscar looked down and fiddled with his hat that was sitting next to him on the ground.

"So let me get this straight," he said looking back up at Thomas. "Mister was a rebel soldier, a Colonel none the less, and upon your visit, he shot you, threw you and Othello in the jail, made sure you didn't get a trial, afterwards, told you that you need to come back and work for him, when you said no, he sent the Sheriff and some men that you say call themselves the Klu Kluck Band?" he said with a question.

"No, the Klu Klux Klan," Thomas clarified, still bouncing the baby in his arms.

"Ah yes, that makes more sense. The Klu Kluck Band would just be silly," he said sarcastically. "Anyway," Oscar continued. "So the men beat up Othello 'til he's lights out. Beat you almost to death. And the Freedmen's Bureau say it's you two that need to move?"

"Yup," Thomas acknowledged.

Oscar went quiet, not really from disbelief, as this was Virginia after all, but more in disgust. "Ya'll should come to Ohio. It's pretty nice up there. Lots of work you can find. They got the B & O for you." Oscar said referring to the Baltimore and Ohio railroad for Thomas' line of work.

Thomas shook his head. "I ain't going that far. I'm staying in Appalachia."

"Suit yourself," Oscar said, intending not to belabor the point.

Isabella stretched out her arms. "Imma try feeding again," she said.

Thomas stood up and shifted baby Virginia in his arms like she was a fragile glass trinket. Isabella smiled, took the baby, and proceeded to urge baby Virginia to latch onto her breast for feeding. The baby did and immediately began to feed. Thomas sat back down in his chair and looked at Oscar.

"How long you planning on visiting?" Thomas asked him.

"Probably awhile. I'm in between work. I decided instead of looking for more in Ohio, I'd take the time to visit my family. Maybe find a few months of work down here before I make my way back up there," Oscar answered.

"Lonely?" Thomas asked him with a smile.

Oscar smiled. "There's people I know up there."

"Ain't like family, though. You should think about coming back down here," Thomas said.

Oscar shook his head. "Think about how much more trouble that would have been if Mister had me, you, and Othello to focus on. I'm not offering myself as no target for him."

Before Thomas could respond, the sound of Othello's wagon could be heard outside. Oscar immediately stood up, eager and ready to greet his family. He went to reach for the door and was almost knocked down by Virginia storming into the cabin.

"Where's my baby?!" she said.

Oscar stretched his arms out for a hug. Virginia looked over at him with impatience. "You my baby and I love you, Oscar, but

I'm talking about the *baby* baby. Baby Virginia, honey!" she said with a hearty laugh moving over to Isabella to see the baby.

Oscar exaggerated his deflated disappointment that Virginia wasn't as happy to see him as she was about the baby. He stuck out his bottom lip, attempting to complete with the cuteness of the new baby. John finally made his way up the two stairs into the cabin, his cane hitting the ground hard.

"I'll take that hug. Oh, look at my boy!" John said in a voice so excited that he began to cough.

"Take it easy, Pa. Take it easy," Oscar said with a laugh, hugging his father.

"I'm happy all three of my sons made it out that war. All three!" John said.

He and Oscar patted each other on the back before releasing their hug. John pushed Oscar back to stand arms length away from him. "Let me get a good look at you," he said looking his son up and down. "You looking good. What they feeding you up in Ohio? You ain't got no woman yet?"

Oscar laughed. "I got my eye on a...."

"Whoa, whoa ,whoa," Othello interrupted as he entered the cabin.

Once he fully entered, he placed down the bags and basket that Virginia made him carry and stood straight.

"Alright, go on now. I'm here. You got your eye on who?" Othello said urging Oscar on.

"Well, I arrived into town, and walking down Main I saw a woman. She caught my eye and all I could think was 'there goes my wife'," Oscar explained.

"You just said you still going back to Ohio. How you going back to Ohio and you think you just met your wife?" Thomas asked Oscar.

"Imma take her with me," Oscar answered.

"Don't she gotta want to go to Ohio? She just going to up and leave her family to go with you to Ohio?" Mary asked.

"Once she see that we're in love. She'll come," Oscar said.

The room went quiet. No one wanted to ruin the romantic view that Oscar still had of love. After all, the rest of them had found love in the middle of a horror story, Othello in slavery and Thomas in prison.

"So, um," Othello attempted to break the awkward silence. "What's her name?"

"I don't know," Oscar said, just realizing that he in fact did not know the woman's name.

Thomas placed his fingers to lightly squeeze the bridge of his nose in impatience.

"Ok," he said to his older brother. "Your first task tomorrow is to go back to where she work, and find out her name."

Oscar looked at Thomas with a blank stare, as if he was a hare frozen in place in the bush so that the fox would go ahead and walk by.

"What?" Thomas asked him.

"I don't think I can talk to her," Oscar said, looking over at Thomas with an expression on his face like he had realized an epiphany of biblical proportions.

"Ah. Well everything will be fine," Othello said to both of them. "We in Salem now. We starting over new. Everything will be alright now. Ain't that right Thomas?" Othello looked over at Thomas with a smile, waiting for confirmation.

Thomas' smile slowly disappeared from his face. He didn't have the answer to that question. He crossed his arms over his chest and looked down at his shoes to think about it for a second. He looked up and met the eyes of everyone in the room. Isabella there feeding Virginia, Mary walking over to hold Othello's hand, John in the corner smiling proud of all his children, and Oscar there newly love struck. Thomas looked out the window, sucked his bottom lip into his mouth and lightly bit it.

"We'll try to make it," he said turning back around to his family with a small smile on his face.

NOTES

1. First Generation

1. Virginia Archives. State Probate Court Documents. Susanna Preston. January 2, 1826.
2. Smithfield Plantation Tours; Moxley, T. 2002. "Slave Life Tour Unveiled At Smithfield Plantation". http://appvoices.org/2002/03/01/2921/. Retrieved on August 12, 2016.
3. Research suggests that the Fraction family was held in high regard relative to other enslaved at the Smithfield Plantation. Seventeenth century narratives from slave traders suggest that traders regarded higher class Africans as more valuable in the slave trade, and more intelligent in terms of assigning task within slavery-they were often assigned to be enslaved in the "house" or as foreman. See Piersen, William D. "African-American Culture." *Encyclopedia of the North American Colonies*, edited by Jacob Ernest Cooke, vol. 2, Charles Scribner's Sons, 1993. *U.S. History in Context*, montgomerycollege.idm.oclc.org/login?url=http://link.galegroup.com/apps/doc/BT2350022001/UHIC?u=rock-77357&xid=cf6a1a4d. Accessed 19 May 2017.
4. Wisconsin. State Historical Society. Library; Draper, Lyman Copeland, 1815-1891; Weaks, Mabel Clare, 1883-. (1915). Madison. Retrieved from https://archive.org/stream/prestonvirginiap00wiscuoft#page/n13/mode/2up. July 12, 2016.
5. Brown, Ellen A. (2012). "What Really Happened at Drapers Meadows? The Evolution of a Frontier Legend" (PDF). Virginia History Exchange. Retrieved October 15, 2016
6. DNA testing of the descendants of John Fraction placed them in region of modern day Nigeria in West Africa; specifically Benin, Togo. Historically this would have been Yoruba.
7. Seybert, Tony. 2004, August 4. "Slavery and Native Americans in British North America and the United States: 1600 to 1865". Slavery in America.
8. Patrick Minges (2003), Slavery in the Cherokee Nation: the Keetoowah Society and the defining of a people, 1855–1867. Psychology Press, p. 27, ISBN 978-0-415-94586-8
9. Virginia Tech Magazine. James Patton Preston. 2015. Photograph. Virginia Tech Magazine: Family Tree, Campus cemeteries reveal our past. http://www.vtmag.vt.edu/fall15/family-tree.html. May 3, 2016.

2. Patriarch

1. Wolfe, B., & McCartney, M. Indentured Servants in Colonial Virginia. (2015, October 28). In Encyclopedia Virginia. Retrieved from http://www.EncyclopediaVirginia.org/Indentured_Servants_in_Colonial_Virginia. May 20, 2016.

2. Preston-Smithfield Foundation. Smithfield Plantation. 2016. Photograph. Smithfield Plantation. http://www.smithfieldplantation.org/. October 3, 2016.

3. Merriment

1. Smithfield Plantation (2017). "Merry Oak". Historic Smithfield. Retrieved from https://historicsmithfield.wordpress.com/2017/02/28/merry-oak/ . May 22, 2017.
2. Emory University (2013). Slave Voyages Database. Retrieved from http://slavevoyages.org/ . February 3, 2016.
3. Wise, C., Wheat D., (February, 2014). African Laborers for a New Empire: Iberia, Slavery, and the Atlantic World. Lowcountry Digital History Initiative. Retrieved from http://ldhi.library.cofc.edu/exhibits/show/african_laborers_-for_a_new_emp. January 12, 2016.

4. Legacy

1. Virginia Tech Special Collections. John Preston Estate Inventory. Document. Virginia Tech Special Collections. April 4, 2016
2. Root, E. S. The Virginia Slavery Debate of 1831–1832. (2015, September 23). In Encyclopedia Virginia. Retrieved from http://www.EncyclopediaVirgini-a.org/Virginia_Slavery_Debate_of_1831-1832_The. January 18, 2016.
3. National Historical Publications and Records Commission. "To George Washington from John Preston, 6 November 1784". National Archives, Founders Online. Retrieved from https://founders.archives.gov/documents/Washington/04-02-02-0106. May 3, 2016.

5. Rambunctious

1. "Virginia, Freedmen's Bureau Field Office Records, 1865-1872," database with images, FamilySearch (https://familysearch.org/ark:/61903/3:1:S3HT-XC39-XR5?cc=1596147&wc=9LML-JW5%3A1078512402%2C1078513602 : 25 June 2014), Christianburg (Montgomery County, assistant superintendent) > image 51 of 123; citing NARA microfilm publication M1913 (College Park, Maryland: National Archives and Records Administration, n.d.).
2. Ancestry.com (2009). 1870 United States Federal Census. Year: 1870; Census Place: Blacksburg, Montgomery, Virginia; Roll: M593_1664; Page: 81B; Image: 167; Family History Library Film: 553163Ancestry.com Operations, Inc. Provo,UT, USA.
3. Virginia Tech. (n.d). Virginia Tech Buildings. Retrieved from http://www.vt.e-du/about/buildings/Solitude.html. May 12, 2016.
4. Preston, Robert Taylor, 1809-1880, "Certificate, by Governor John Letches regarding the commission to Colonel for Robert Preston, Va, May 5, 1861 (Ms1992-003)," VT Special Collections Online, accessed May 19, 2017, http://digitalsc.lib.vt.edu/Ms1992-003/Ms1992_003_PrestonRobert-T_B1F2_Commission__1861_0505.

5. Anna Whitehead Kenney Papers, Ms1991-022, Special Collections, Virginia Tech, Blacksburg, Va. "Letter of J.P.P. to F.P. Jan (24) 1832.
6. Gabel, Christopher. R. Railroad Generalship: Foundations of Civil War Strategy. U.S. Army Command and General Staff College. Combat Studies Institute. Retrieved at http://usacac.army.mil/cac2/cgsc/carl/download/csipubs/gabel4.pdf. May 22, 2016.
7. "Virginia, Freedmen's Bureau Field Office Records, 1865-1872" citing NARA microfilm publication M1913 (College Park, Maryland: National Archives and Records Administration, n.d.).
8. Virginia Tech Magazine. William Ballard Preston. 2015. Photograph. Virginia Tech Magazine: Family Tree, Campus cemeteries reveal our past. http://www.vtmag.vt.edu/fall15/family-tree.html. May 3, 2016
9. Virginia Tech Magazine. Robert Taylor Preston. 2015. Photograph. Virginia Tech Magazine: Family Tree, Campus cemeteries reveal our past. http://www.vtmag.vt.edu/fall15/family-tree.html. May 3, 2016
10. Ancestry.com. 1860 U.S. Federal Census-Slave Schedules. Photograph. Ancestry.com Operations Inc. 2010. Provo, UT, USA.

6. Virginia

1. Historic Smithfield Plantation. "Visit." Retrieved from http://www.smithfield-plantation.org/visit-1.html. December 10, 2015.
2. Virginia Archives. Montgomery County Death Records.

7. The Planned and Unplanned

1. Luebke, P. C. John B. Floyd (1806–1863). (2014, May 27). In Encyclopedia Virginia. Retrieved from http://www.EncyclopediaVirginia.org/Floyd_John_B_1806-1863. Retrieved April 22, 2016.
2. To Colored Men!; ca. 1861 - 1865; Records of the Adjutant General's Office, Record Group 94. [Online Version, https://www.docsteach.org/documents/document/to-colored-men, May 19, 2017]
3. Ancestry.com. U.S., Colored Troops Military Service Records, 1863-1865. The National Archives at Washington, D.C.; Washington, D.C.; Compiled Military Service Records of Volunteer Union Soldiers Who Served with the United States Colored Troops, Infantry Organizations; Microfilm Serial: M1822; Microfilm Roll: 22. 2007.

8. The Route

1. "Virginia, Freedmen's Bureau Field Office Records, 1865-1872," database with images, FamilySearch (https://familysearch.org/ark:/61903/3:1:S3HT-XC39-XR5?cc=1596147&wc=9LML-JW5%3A1078512402%2C1078513602 : 25 June 2014), Christianburg (Montgomery County, assistant superintendent) > image 51 of 123; citing NARA microfilm publication M1913 (College Park, Maryland: National Archives and Records Administration, n.d.).

2. Wise, John Sergeant. (1899) "The End of An Era: Electronic Edition". UNC-CH project, Documenting the American South, Beginnings to 1920. Davis Library, UNC-CH. Call number E605.W8 1899. This work is the property of the University of North Carolina at Chapel Hill. It may be used freely by individuals for research, teaching and personal. Retrieved from http://www.docsouth.unc.edu/fpn/wise/wise.html. March 5, 2016.
3. Sons of The South. Coltons-slave-map-1862-550. unknown. Photograph. Sons of the South. http://www.sonofthesouth.net/slavery/slave-maps/coltons-slave-map-1862-550.jpg . May 3, 2016
4. The National Archives at Washington, D.C.; Washington, D.C.; *Compiled Military Service Records of Volunteer Union Soldiers Who Served with the United States Colored Troops: Infantry Organizations, 36th through 40th*; Microfilm Serial: *M1993*; Microfilm Roll: *105*
5. The National Archives at Washington, D.C.; Washington, D.C.; *Compiled Military Service Records of Volunteer Union Soldiers Who Served with the United States Colored Troops: Infantry Organizations, 36th through 40th*; Microfilm Serial: *M1993*; Microfilm Roll: *105*
6. The National Archives at Washington, D.C.; Washington, D.C.; *Compiled Military Service Records of Volunteer Union Soldiers Who Served with the United States Colored Troops: Infantry Organizations, 36th through 40th*; Microfilm Serial: *M1993*; Microfilm Roll: *105*
7. The National Archives at Washington, D.C.; Washington, D.C.; *Compiled Military Service Records of Volunteer Union Soldiers Who Served with the United States Colored Troops: Infantry Organizations, 36th through 40th*; Microfilm Serial: *M1993*; Microfilm Roll: *105*
8. The National Archives at Washington, D.C.; Washington, D.C.; *Compiled Military Service Records of Volunteer Union Soldiers Who Served with the United States Colored Troops: Infantry Organizations, 36th through 40th*; Microfilm Serial: *M1993*; Microfilm Roll: *105*
9. The National Archives at Washington, D.C.; Washington, D.C.; *Compiled Military Service Records of Volunteer Union Soldiers Who Served with the United States Colored Troops: Infantry Organizations, 36th through 40th*; Microfilm Serial: *M1993*; Microfilm Roll: *105*
10. The National Archives at Washington, D.C.; Washington, D.C.; *Compiled Military Service Records of Volunteer Union Soldiers Who Served with the United States Colored Troops: Infantry Organizations, 36th through 40th*; Microfilm Serial: *M1993*; Microfilm Roll: *105*
11. The National Archives at Washington, D.C.; Washington, D.C.; *Compiled Military Service Records of Volunteer Union Soldiers Who Served with the United States Colored Troops: Infantry Organizations, 36th through 40th*; Microfilm Serial: *M1993*; Microfilm Roll: *105*

9. Welcome to Tennessee, Boys

1. Morgan, Edmund S. American Slavery, American Freedom: The Ordeal of Colonial Virginia. New York: W. W. Norton and Company, 1995.
2. Elliott, S. D.(2010). Isham G. Harris of Tennessee: Confederate Governor and United States Senator. Baton Rouge: Louisiana State University Press.

Retrieved May 25, 2017, from Project MUSE database. http://muse.jhu.e-du/book/17275. May 3, 2016.

3. The National Archives at Washington, D.C.; Washington, D.C.; *Compiled Military Service Records of Volunteer Union Soldiers Who Served with the United States Colored Troops: Infantry Organizations, 36th through 40th*; Microfilm Serial: *M1993*; Microfilm Roll: *105*

4. McRae, B. (nd). Lest We Forget: African American Military History by Historian, Author, and Veteran Bennie McRae, Jr. "40th Regiment, United States Colored Infantry. Hampton University. Retrieved from http://lestweforget.hamptonu.edu/page.cfm?uuid=9FEC3BE5-BA17-2861-0540FC5033C83828. June 3, 2016.

5. Freeman, Elsie, Wynell Burroughs Schamel, and Jean West. "The Fight for Equal Rights: A Recruiting Poster for Black Soldiers in the Civil War." Social Education 56, 2 (February 1992): 118-120. [Revised and updated in 1999 by Budge Weidman.]

6. Wigginton, R. (2009, December 25). "Louisville and Nashville Railroad". The Tennessee Encyclopedia of History and Culture [Last Updated January 1, 2010]. Retrieved from https://tennesseeencyclopedia.net/entry.php?rec=1099. June 2, 2016.

7. Baugess, J. S. (2008). Confederate Guerrilla: The Civil War Memoir of Joseph Bailey (review). Southwestern Historical Quarterly 112(1), 97-98. Texas State Historical Association. Retrieved May 25, 2017, from Project MUSE database.

8. Curry, Richard O., and F. Gerald Ham. "The Bushwhackers' War: Insurgency and Counter-Insurgency in West Virginia." *Civil War History* 10, no. 4 (Dec. 1964): 416-433.

9. Tennessee Civil War Sourcebook (n.d). "May 1865: May 12, 1865-Denying amnesty to guerrillas near Tullahoma". Republish of OR, SER. I, Vol. 49, pt II, p. 737. Retrieved from http://www.artcirclelibrary.info/Reference/civilwar/1865-05.pdf. June 15, 2016.

10. Tennessee Civil War Sourcebook (n.d). "March - May 1865". Republish of OR, SER. I, Vol. 49, pt II, p. 737. Retrieved from http://www.artcirclelibrary.info/Reference/civilwar/1865-05.pdf. June 15, 2016.

11. Allyn, J. (n.d). "Minnesota Regiments at Nashville, Part 2: The 11th Minnesota Infantry." Battle of Nashville Preservation Society, Inc. Retrieved from http://www.bonps.org/features/minnesota-regiments-at-nashville/. June 22, 2016.

12. Wise, John Sergeant. (1899) "The End of An Era: Electronic Edition". UNC-CH project, Documenting the American South, Beginnings to 1920. Davis Library, UNC-CH. Call number E605.W8 1899. This work is the property of the University of North Carolina at Chapel Hill. It may be used freely by individuals for research, teaching and personal. Retrieved from http://www.docsouth.unc.edu/fpn/wise/wise.html. March 5, 2016.

13. B.H. Polk to Assistant Adjutant-General, Gattalin, Tennessee, October 10, 1864; War of the Rebellion: Serial 079 Page 0200 KY., SW. VA., TENN., MISS., ALA., AND N. G. A. Chapter LI. Original Records of the Civil War; National Archives Building, Washington, DC.

14. War of the Rebellion: Serial 079 Page 0200 KY., SW. VA., TENN., MISS., ALA., AND N. G. A. Chapter LI. Original Records of the Civil War; National Archives Building, Washington, DC.

15. Tennessee Civil War Sourcebook (n.d). "March - July 1865". Republish of OR, SER. I, Vol. 49, pt II, p. 737. Retrieved from http://www.artcirclelibrary.info/Reference/civilwar/1865-07.pdf. June 15, 2016.
16. Tennessee Civil War Sourcebook (n.d). "March - July 1865". Republish of OR, SER. I, Vol. 49, pt II, p. 737. Retrieved from http://www.artcirclelibrary.info/Reference/civilwar/1865-07.pdf. June 15, 2016.
17. Tennessee Civil War Sourcebook (n.d). "March - July 1865". Republish of OR, SER. I, Vol. 49, pt II, p. 737. Retrieved from http://www.artcirclelibrary.info/Reference/civilwar/1865-07.pdf. June 15, 2016.
18. Tennessee Civil War Sourcebook (n.d). "March - July 1865". Republish of OR, SER. I, Vol. 49, pt II, p. 737. Retrieved from http://www.artcirclelibrary.info/Reference/civilwar/1865-07.pdf. June 15, 2016.

10. Furlough

1. Finkleman, P. "Black Codes".Encyclopedia of African-American Culture and History. v.1. New York: Macmillan Library Reference, USA, 1996.
2. Staunton Spectator, September 26, 1865 NOTE 1 . NOTE 1: As cited in: http://valley.vcdh.virginia.edu. ; Tennessee Civil War Sourcebook (n.d). "March - July 1865". Republish of OR, SER. I, Vol. 49, pt II, p. 737. Retrieved from http://www.artcirclelibrary.info/Reference/civilwar/1865-09.pdf. June 15, 2016.
3. Litwack, Leon F., North of Slavery. The Negro in the Free States, 1790-1860. Chicago: University of Chicago Press, 1961.
4. Johnson, R. W., (1886). A Soldier's Reminiscences in Peace and War. J.R. Lippincotti Company. Retrieved at https://books.google.com/books?id=X9F-BAAAAIAAJ&pg=PP11&source=gbs_selected_-pages&cad=2#v=onepage&q&f=false. May 20, 2016.
5. Ancestry.com. (2007) "U.S., Colored Troops Military Service Records, 1863-1865. Ancestry.com Operations Inc. Provo, UT, USA. The National Archives at Washington, D.C.; Washington, D.C.; Compiled Military Service Records of Volunteer Union Soldiers Who Served with the United States Colored Troops: Infantry Organizations, 36th through 40th; Microfilm Serial: M1993; Microfilm Roll:
6. "Virginia, Freedmen's Bureau Field Office Records, 1865-1872," database with images, FamilySearch (https://familysearch.org/ark:/61903/3:1:S3HT-XC39-XR5?cc=1596147&wc=9LML-JW5%3A1078512402%2C1078513602 : 25 June 2014), Christianburg (Montgomery County, assistant superintendent) > image 51 of 123; citing NARA microfilm publication M1913 (College Park, Maryland: National Archives and Records Administration, n.d.).
7. "Virginia, Freedmen's Bureau Field Office Records, 1865-1872," database with images, FamilySearch (https://familysearch.org/ark:/61903/3:1:S3HT-XC39-XR5?cc=1596147&wc=9LML-JW5%3A1078512402%2C1078513602 : 25 June 2014), Christianburg (Montgomery County, assistant superintendent) > image 51 of 123; citing NARA microfilm publication M1913 (College Park, Maryland: National Archives and Records Administration, n.d.).
8. Ancestry.com. (2007) "U.S., Colored Troops Military Service Records, 1863-1865. Ancestry.com Operations Inc. Provo, UT, USA. The National Archives at Washington, D.C.; Washington, D.C.; Compiled Military Service Records of

Volunteer Union Soldiers Who Served with the United States Colored Troops: Infantry Organizations, 36th through 40th; Microfilm Serial: M1993; Microfilm Roll:

11. Isabella

1. Compiled service record, Thomas Fraction, Pvt. Infantry. Pension Record, Can number 17134, Bundle #38. Military Record #18611865. National Archives. Washington, DC.
2. National Archives. "Freedmen's Bureau Filed Office Records". National Archives Trust Fund Board. Retrieved from https://www.archives.gov/files/research/african-americans/freedmens-bureau/brochure.pdf. May 15, 2016.
3. Compiled service record, Thomas Fraction, Pvt. Infantry. Pension Record, Can number 17134, Bundle #38. Military Record #18611865. National Archives. Washington, DC.
4. Compiled service record, Thomas Fraction, Pvt. Infantry. Pension Record, Can number 17134, Bundle #38. Military Record #18611865. National Archives. Washington, DC
5. Compiled service record, Thomas Fraction, Pvt. Infantry. Pension Record, Can number 17134, Bundle #38. Military Record #18611865. National Archives. Washington, DC
6. Compiled service record, Thomas Fraction, Pvt. Infantry. Pension Record, Can number 17134, Bundle #38. Military Record #18611865. National Archives. Washington, DC

12. Home

1. Adams, M. "Family Tree: Campus cemeteries reveal our past". Virginia Tech Magazine. Fall 2015. Retrieved from http://www.vtmag.vt.edu/fall15/family-tree.html. September 15, 2015.
2. Virginia Tech Special Collections. Caperton Family Papers.
3. Ancestry.com. Virginia, Select Marriages, 1785-1940 [database on-line]. Provo, UT, USA: Ancestry.com Operations, Inc, 2014.
4. Montgomery County (VA.) Register of Colored Persons Cohabiting, 1866. Cohabitation Registers Digital Collection. Library of Virginia. Richmond, Virginia, 23219. Retrieved from http://digitool1.lva.lib.va.us:8881/R/7DHM-DRAXPXC1V76X9SH38RGII3YVUA2NVM2NNLRRGTHM88I86K-07233?func=collections-result&collection_id=1522&pds_handle=GUEST. May 2, 2016.
5. "Virginia, Freedmen's Bureau Field Office Records, 1865-1872," database with images, FamilySearch (https://familysearch.org/ark:/61903/3:1:S3HT-XC39-XR5?cc=1596147&wc=9LML-JW5%3A1078512402%2C1078513602 : 25 June 2014), Christianburg (Montgomery County, assistant superintendent) > image 51 of 123; citing NARA microfilm publication M1913 (College Park, Maryland: National Archives and Records Administration, n.d.).
6. "Virginia, Freedmen's Bureau Field Office Records, 1865-1872," database with images, FamilySearch (https://familysearch.org/ark:/61903/3:1:S3HT-XC39-XR5?cc=1596147&wc=9LML-JW5%3A1078512402%2C1078513602 : 25

June 2014), Christianburg (Montgomery County, assistant superintendent) > image 51 of 123; citing NARA microfilm publication M1913 (College Park, Maryland: National Archives and Records Administration, n.d.).

13. Handcuffs

1. "Virginia, Freedmen's Bureau Field Office Records, 1865-1872," database with images, FamilySearch (https://familysearch.org/ark:/61903/3:1:S3HT-XC39-XR5?cc=1596147&wc=9LML-JW5%3A1078512402%2C1078513602 : 25 June 2014), Christianburg (Montgomery County, assistant superintendent) > image 51 of 123; citing NARA microfilm publication M1913 (College Park, Maryland: National Archives and Records Administration, n.d.).
2. "Virginia, Freedmen's Bureau Field Office Records, 1865-1872," database with images, FamilySearch (https://familysearch.org/ark:/61903/3:1:S3HT-XC39-XR5?cc=1596147&wc=9LML-JW5%3A1078512402%2C1078513602 : 25 June 2014), Christianburg (Montgomery County, assistant superintendent) > image 51 of 123; citing NARA microfilm publication M1913 (College Park, Maryland: National Archives and Records Administration, n.d.).
3. "Virginia, Freedmen's Bureau Field Office Records, 1865-1872," database with images, FamilySearch (https://familysearch.org/ark:/61903/3:1:S3HT-XC39-XR5?cc=1596147&wc=9LML-JW5%3A1078512402%2C1078513602 : 25 June 2014), Christianburg (Montgomery County, assistant superintendent) > image 51 of 123; citing NARA microfilm publication M1913 (College Park, Maryland: National Archives and Records Administration, n.d.).
4. "Virginia, Freedmen's Bureau Field Office Records, 1865-1872," database with images, FamilySearch (https://familysearch.org/ark:/61903/3:1:S3HT-XC39-XR5?cc=1596147&wc=9LML-JW5%3A1078512402%2C1078513602 : 25 June 2014), Christianburg (Montgomery County, assistant superintendent) > image 51 of 123; citing NARA microfilm publication M1913 (College Park, Maryland: National Archives and Records Administration, n.d.).
5.
6. Compiled service record, Thomas Fraction, Pvt. Infantry. Pension Record, Can number 17134, Bundle #38. Military Record #18611865. National Archives. Washington, DC
7. "Virginia, Freedmen's Bureau Field Office Records, 1865-1872," database with images, FamilySearch (https://familysearch.org/ark:/61903/3:1:S3HT-XC39-XR5?cc=1596147&wc=9LML-JW5%3A1078512402%2C1078513602 : 25 June 2014), Christianburg (Montgomery County, assistant superintendent) >; citing NARA microfilm publication M1913 (College Park, Maryland: National Archives and Records Administration, n.d.).
8. "Virginia, Freedmen's Bureau Field Office Records, 1865-1872," database with images, FamilySearch (https://familysearch.org/ark:/61903/3:1:S3HT-XC39-XR5?cc=1596147&wc=9LML-JW5%3A1078512402%2C1078513602 : 25 June 2014), Christianburg (Montgomery County, assistant superintendent) >; citing NARA microfilm publication M1913 (College Park, Maryland: National Archives and Records Administration, n.d.).
9. "Virginia, Freedmen's Bureau Field Office Records, 1865-1872," database with images, FamilySearch (https://familysearch.org/ark:/61903/3:1:S3HT-XC39-XR5?cc=1596147&wc=9LML-JW5%3A1078512402%2C1078513602 : 25

June 2014), Christianburg (Montgomery County, assistant superintendent) >; citing NARA microfilm publication M1913 (College Park, Maryland: National Archives and Records Administration, n.d.).

10. "Virginia, Freedmen's Bureau Field Office Records, 1865-1872," database with images, FamilySearch (https://familysearch.org/ark:/61903/3:1:S3HT-XC39-XR5?cc=1596147&wc=9LML-JW5%3A1078512402%2C1078513602 : 25 June 2014), Christianburg (Montgomery County, assistant superintendent) >; citing NARA microfilm publication M1913 (College Park, Maryland: National Archives and Records Administration, n.d.).

11. "Virginia, Freedmen's Bureau Field Office Records, 1865-1872," database with images, FamilySearch (https://familysearch.org/ark:/61903/3:1:S3HT-XC39-XR5?cc=1596147&wc=9LML-JW5%3A1078512402%2C1078513602 : 25 June 2014), Christianburg (Montgomery County, assistant superintendent) >; citing NARA microfilm publication M1913 (College Park, Maryland: National Archives and Records Administration, n.d.).

12. "Virginia, Freedmen's Bureau Field Office Records, 1865-1872," database with images, FamilySearch (https://familysearch.org/ark:/61903/3:1:S3HT-XC39-XR5?cc=1596147&wc=9LML-JW5%3A1078512402%2C1078513602 : 25 June 2014), Christianburg (Montgomery County, assistant superintendent) >; citing NARA microfilm publication M1913 (College Park, Maryland: National Archives and Records Administration, n.d.).

13. The National Archives at Washington, D.C.; Washington, D.C.; Compiled Military Service Records of Volunteer Union Soldiers Who Served with the United States Colored Troops: Infantry Organizations, 36th through 40th; Microfilm Serial: M1993; Microfilm Roll

14. Double Jeopardy Refugees

1. "Virginia, Freedmen's Bureau Field Office Records, 1865-1872," database with images, FamilySearch (https://familysearch.org/ark:/61903/3:1:S3HT-XC39-XR5?cc=1596147&wc=9LML-JW5%3A1078512402%2C1078513602 : 25 June 2014), Christianburg (Montgomery County, assistant superintendent) >; citing NARA microfilm publication M1913 (College Park, Maryland: National Archives and Records Administration, n.d.).

2. Compiled service record, Thomas Fraction, Pvt. Infantry. Pension Record, Can number 17134, Bundle #38. Military Record #18611865. National Archives. Washington, DC

3. Hart, Gary. (2003). "Virginia's Black Codes: Uncovering the Evolution of Legal Slavery". OAH Magazine of History, v17 n3 p35-36. April 2003. ERIC Database. ERIC Number EJ673810. ISSN: ISSN-0882-228X.

4. "Virginia, Freedmen's Bureau Field Office Records, 1865-1872," database with images, FamilySearch (https://familysearch.org/ark:/61903/3:1:S3HT-XC39-XR5?cc=1596147&wc=9LML-JW5%3A1078512402%2C1078513602 : 25 June 2014), Christianburg (Montgomery County, assistant superintendent) >; citing NARA microfilm publication M1913 (College Park, Maryland: National Archives and Records Administration, n.d.).

5. "Virginia, Freedmen's Bureau Field Office Records, 1865-1872," database with images, FamilySearch (https://familysearch.org/ark:/61903/3:1:S3HT-XC39-XR5?cc=1596147&wc=9LML-JW5%3A1078512402%2C1078513602 : 25

June 2014), Christianburg (Montgomery County, assistant superintendent) >; citing NARA microfilm publication M1913 (College Park, Maryland: National Archives and Records Administration, n.d.).

6. Virginia Tech Special Collections. Robert Taylor Preston Pardon Certificate. Photograph. Virginia Tech Special Collections. https://vtspecialcollections.-wordpress.com/2014/07/24/rtp-pardon-1865/#jp-carousel-1844. May 4, 2016.

7. Donald, C.R., Tilman, Rev. Dr. G. (2005, April 16). "Blacksburg Methodist Churches: Blacksburg Methodist Episcopal Church, South and the Beginnings of St. Paul African Methodist Episcopal Church". Lectures for Blacksburg UMC and St. Paul AMEC at the Whisner building, Blacksburg UMC, Blacksburg, VA. Retrieved from http://www.joepayne.org/MethodisminBlacksburg.pdf. October 12, 2016.

8. "Virginia, Freedmen's Bureau Field Office Records, 1865-1872," database with images, FamilySearch (https://familysearch.org/ark:/61903/3:1:S3HT-XC39-XR5?cc=1596147&wc=9LML-JW5%3A1078512402%2C1078513602 : 25 June 2014), Christianburg (Montgomery County, assistant superintendent) >; citing NARA microfilm publication M1913 (College Park, Maryland: National Archives and Records Administration, n.d.).

9. Blacksburg Museum and Cultural Foundation. (n.d). "Blacksburg United Methodist Church". Retrieved at http://blacksburgmuseum.org/about/historic-churches/blacksburg-united-methodist-church/. September 13, 2016. Donald, Christopher, "Growth and Independence of Methodist Congregations in Blacksburg; A Virginia Town," Smithfield Review, Volume X. 2006; Harrison, Charles H., The Story of a Consecrated Life, Commemorative of Rev. Charles S. Schaeffer, Brevet-Captain U. S. V., J. B. Lippincott Company, Philadelphia. 1900. Retrieved from http://archive.org/details/storyofconsecrat00harr; Raboteau, Albert J., Slave Religion, Oxford University Press, New York. 1978.

10. Donald, C.R., Tilman, Rev. Dr. G. (2005, April 16). "Blacksburg Methodist Churches: Blacksburg Methodist Episcopal Church, South and the Beginnings of St. Paul African Methodist Episcopal Church". Lectures for Blacksburg UMC and St. Paul AMEC at the Whisner building, Blacksburg UMC, Blacksburg, VA. Retrieved from http://www.joepayne.org/MethodisminBlacksburg.pdf. October 12, 2016

11. Blacksburg Museum and Cultural Foundation. (n.d). "Blacksburg United Methodist Church". Retrieved at http://blacksburgmuseum.org/about/historic-churches/blacksburg-united-methodist-church/. September 13, 2016. Donald, Christopher, "Growth and Independence of Methodist Congregations in Blacksburg; A Virginia Town," Smithfield Review, Volume X. 2006; Harrison, Charles H., The Story of a Consecrated Life, Commemorative of Rev. Charles S. Schaeffer, Brevet-Captain U. S. V., J. B. Lippincott Company, Philadelphia. 1900. Retrieved from http://archive.org/details/storyofconsecrat00harr; Raboteau, Albert J., Slave Religion, Oxford University Press, New York. 1978.

12. Smithsonian Magazine. "What Did the Rebel Yell Sound Like?".Library of Congress, Motion Picture, Broadcasting and Recorded Sound Division. (n.d). Retrieved from http://www.smithsonianmag.com/videos/category/3play_1/what-did-the-rebel-yell-sound-like/. June 20, 2016.

13. Southern Poverty Law Center. (2011). Ku Klux Klan: A History of Racism and Violence. The Southern Poverty Law Center, Klanwatch Project, 6th Edition.

Retrieved from https://www.splcenter.org/sites/default/files/Ku-Klux-Klan-A-History-of-Racism.pdf. November 15, 2016.

14.

15. "Virginia, Freedmen's Bureau Field Office Records, 1865-1872," database with images, FamilySearch (https://familysearch.org/ark:/61903/3:1:S3HT-XC39-XR5?cc=1596147&wc=9LML-JW5%3A1078512402%2C1078513602 : 25 June 2014), Christianburg (Montgomery County, assistant superintendent) >; citing NARA microfilm publication M1913 (College Park, Maryland: National Archives and Records Administration, n.d.).

16. "Virginia, Freedmen's Bureau Field Office Records, 1865-1872," database with images, FamilySearch (https://familysearch.org/ark:/61903/3:1:S3HT-XC39-XR5?cc=1596147&wc=9LML-JW5%3A1078512402%2C1078513602 : 25 June 2014), Christianburg (Montgomery County, assistant superintendent) >; citing NARA microfilm publication M1913 (College Park, Maryland: National Archives and Records Administration, n.d.).

17. "Virginia, Freedmen's Bureau Field Office Records, 1865-1872," database with images, FamilySearch (https://familysearch.org/ark:/61903/3:1:S3HT-XC39-XR5?cc=1596147&wc=9LML-JW5%3A1078512402%2C1078513602 : 25 June 2014), Christianburg (Montgomery County, assistant superintendent) >; citing NARA microfilm publication M1913 (College Park, Maryland: National Archives and Records Administration, n.d.).

18. "Virginia, Freedmen's Bureau Field Office Records, 1865-1872," database with images, FamilySearch (https://familysearch.org/ark:/61903/3:1:S3HT-XC39-XR5?cc=1596147&wc=9LML-JW5%3A1078512402%2C1078513602 : 25 June 2014), Christianburg (Montgomery County, assistant superintendent) >; citing NARA microfilm publication M1913 (College Park, Maryland: National Archives and Records Administration, n.d.).

19. "Virginia, Freedmen's Bureau Field Office Records, 1865-1872," database with images, FamilySearch (https://familysearch.org/ark:/61903/3:1:S3HT-XC39-XR5?cc=1596147&wc=9LML-JW5%3A1078512402%2C1078513602 : 25 June 2014), Christianburg (Montgomery County, assistant superintendent) >; citing NARA microfilm publication M1913 (College Park, Maryland: National Archives and Records Administration, n.d.).

15. Salem

1. "Virginia, Freedmen's Bureau Field Office Records, 1865-1872," database with images, FamilySearch (https://familysearch.org/ark:/61903/3:1:S3HT-XC39-XR5?cc=1596147&wc=9LML-JW5%3A1078512402%2C1078513602 : 25 June 2014), Christianburg (Montgomery County, assistant superintendent) >; citing NARA microfilm publication M1913 (College Park, Maryland: National Archives and Records Administration, n.d.).

2. Long, J.D., Pezzoni J.D. (2001). "South of Main: a history of the Water Street Community of Salem, Virginia". Salem Museum and Historical Society. 2001. Salem, VA.

3. Compiled service record, Thomas Fraction, Pvt. Infantry. Pension Record, Can number 17134, Bundle #38. Military Record #18611865. National Archives. Washington, DC

4. Virginia Court Records. Blacksburg, Virginia Court Records: Marriage and Divorce Records. Case of Lovely vs. Lovely.

ABOUT THE AUTHOR

Dr. Kerri Moseley-Hobbs is the 3rd great-granddaughter of Thomas Fraction. Her passion for education and history has and continues to lead her on ventures to uncover hidden stories and forgotten legacies. After discovering that the Smithfield Plantation was still in existence, and was being managed as a museum house in Blacksburg, Virginia, Dr. Moseley-Hobbs immediately took a trip to see the place where much of Thomas' story occurred. After her trip to visit the grounds in 2015, she was asked to join the board for the Smithfield-Preston Foundation who currently owns and manages the Smithfield Plantation. As a member of the board Dr. Moseley-Hobbs was tasked with assisting to change the narrative and presentation of the enslaved and indentured servant community throughout the history of Smithfield, as it relates to the Preston family.

At the publication of this book, Dr. Moseley-Hobbs was continuing a more than 15 year career in higher education administration and teaching. She holds a bachelor's degree in Criminal Justice, a master's degree in Interdisciplinary Management, a Master's in Business Administration (MBA), and a Doctorate in Education. Dr. Moseley-Hobbs lives in Baltimore, Maryland with her son, Anthony Michael Hobbs (the 4th great-grandson of Thomas Fraction), who by twelve-years-old was already an award-winning actor and filmmaker.

Made in the USA
Columbia, SC
10 August 2024

39683980R00161